LECTURES ON

THE
PRINCIPLES
OF
POLITICAL
OBLIGATION

by
Thomas Hill Green

Introduction by Lord Lindsay of Birker

Ann Arbor Paperbacks
The University of Michigan Press

PREFACE

THE present volume consists of the late Professor Green's lectures on the 'Principles of Political Obligation,' together with a chapter on the different senses of the term 'Freedom,' taken from a course directly connected with the former. The work thus re-issued is a reprint of pp. 307–553 of Vol. II. of Professor Green's Philosophical Works, with the addition of a brief supplement (p. 248) furnished by the present writer, consisting of English renderings for some quotations which appear in the text (pp. 49–59).

The reason for this re-issue is as follows. The course of lectures in question has long been known to teachers as a most valuable text-book for students of political theory. But as a portion of a large and expensive volume, which is itself part of a set of collected works, it naturally was not accessible to members of popular audiences. In discussing the selection of a text-book for a projected course of instruction on political theory, to be given in London, it was suggested that a separate volume containing the 'Principles of Political Obligation' would be the best conceivable book for the purpose. No other recent writer, it was felt, has the classical strength and sanity of Professor Green, who was never more thorough and more at home than when dealing with those questions affecting citizenship in and for which, it may be said, he lived. Many of the troubles of to-day reflect the distraction of minds to which a sane and balanced view of society has never been adequately presented; and the importance of the service which might be rendered to general education by the re-issue of these lectures in a convenient form appeared to justify an application to those who had the power of carrying out the suggestion which had been made.

The friends of genuine political philosophy will have good cause, it is hoped, to be grateful to Mrs. T. H. Green for her cordial assent to the proposed republication, as also to Messrs. Longman for their promptitude in agreeing to undertake it. The elaborate table of contents, reprinted from the Philosophical Works, was compiled by their editor, the late Mr. Lewis Nettleship. It adds very greatly to the value of the book.

BERNARD BOSANQUET

THE Introduction contributed by LORD LINDSAY, formerly Master of Balliol College, is reprinted with slight modifications from *The Social and Political Ideas of Some Representative Thinkers of the Victorian Age*, edited by F. J. C. HEARNSHAW, M.A., LL.D., by kind permission of Lord LINDSAY, and Messrs. GEORGE HARRAP & Co. LTD.

INTRODUCTION

By A. D. LINDSAY

Lectures on the Principles of Political Obligation were first delivered by T. H. Green in 1879 and not published until after his death in 1882. They represent the most important contribution to political theory of the school of thought sometimes known as the Oxford Idealists, though Bosanquet's *Philosophical Theory of the State* published in 1899 is of almost equal importance. The other member of the school who wrote much on political theory was D. G. Ritchie, who was born in 1853, became a Fellow of Jesus in 1878, and died in 1893. His writings on political theory, *Darwinism and Politics, Principles of State Interference, Darwin and Hegel,* and *Natural Rights,* were published between 1889 and 1895.

Edward Caird, Master of Balliol from 1893 to 1907, and William Wallace, who succeeded Green as Whyte's Professor of Moral Philosophy in 1882, were also members of this school. With them should perhaps be numbered Arnold Toynbee, who was a Fellow of Balliol from 1878 until his death in 1883.

Green and his fellow-idealists represent the renewed liberalism of the last quarter of the nineteenth century. They are all of them, for all their Platonism and Hegelianism, in the succession of the Utilitarians. They were all fundamentally individualists and democrats. But they were convinced that Utilitarianism had become barren as a political creed because of the inadequate philosophy upon which it was based, and that no further progress could be made in an understanding of politics till a new philosophic basis was found for liberalism. Utilitarianism had equated human purposes with happiness. That had meant not simply that the State should take men as it found them—a doctrine for which much is to be said—but that men should take themselves as they found themselves—a very different doctrine, and one for which there is almost nothing to be said. The individual in Benthamite philosophy was reduced to a bundle of pleasures or desires, and the State to a collection of independent atoms. When the progress of the Industrial Revolution disappointed the facile optimism of the earlier Utilitarians their individualistic creed, which had in the early part of the century been a doctrine of reform and liberty, became largely a bulwark of reaction and privilege.

It demanded reform in the early days on the ground that if unwise State restrictions and interference were removed the natural harmony of economic interests would ensure that all would be well. When these restrictions had been removed and *laissez-faire* largely realised the doctrine was used to oppose any attempt to deal with the disharmonies of economic interests. Utilitarianism had done all that it could, but democracy was more alive than ever and faced with any number of new and unexpected problems. If democracy was to grapple with these new problems with any success some way had to be found of reconciling a true individualism with the new functions which were being thrust upon the State.

Green and his fellow-idealists had been profoundly influenced by Carlyle and his bitter criticism of the creed of ' each for himself and the devil take the hindmost.' They were far removed from either the facile optimism of the early Utilitarians or the rather cynical pessimism which succeeded it. They were concerned for the sufferings of the poor, and were abundantly conscious of the inequalities of the existing economic system. But, unlike Carlyle and Ruskin, they remained convinced democrats, and thought of social reform as the task of the new democratic State. They did not share Carlyle's contempt for the ordinary man nor his leanings towards aristocracy. For they had got from Kant what Kant got from Rousseau, a profound belief in the worth and dignity of the ordinary man. They were political democrats because they were first of all spiritual democrats. They were convinced that the theoretical basis of democracy laid down by the Utilitarians was fundamentally unsound. Its foundations were not nearly deep enough ; its conception of human nature too shallow. They felt that a new start had to be made and a proper conception of human nature and action acquired before an adequate political theory could be constructed. That is why none of them were concerned only with political theory. Their politics were to be the outcome of a view of human nature and of the world—of moral philosophy and of metaphysics.

In making their new start they went back beyond the

French writers, who had, on the whole, inspired the Utilitarians—back to the real founders of modern democracy, the seventeenth-century Puritans, whose ideas the French writers of the eighteenth century had clarified, popularised, and cheapened. A recent writer on democracy, Mr. Leonard Woolf, has argued that democracy and Christianity are incompatible. Green and his school would have argued that such a judgment is profoundly mistaken, that democracy was, and must be, based on religion, that the doctrine of human equality is a religious doctrine or it is nothing. The fate of Utilitarianism, they would have said, shows how entirely insufficient, because how shallow, is a theory of democracy which seeks to-day to minimise the importance of religion. The Utilitarian doctrine of man, because it was essentially irreligious, had proved far too narrow to stand the strains and stresses of social and political life.

They were growing up when the reigning philosophy in the universities was that of John Stuart Mill. His fine and noble character had struggled in vain with the creed he had inherited, and his philosophy was really an eclecticism which had inspiring elements in it, but was incapable of producing fruitful social or political principles. A comprehensive philosophical system had to be put in its place. Utilitarianism or Associationism or Empiricism had to be fought all along the line. And so these liberals went for their philosophical inspiration to some very undemocratic sources, to Plato and to Hegel, as well as to Kant and the seventeenth-century Puritans ; but their purpose in so doing was to carry out better and more thoroughly what the Utilitarians had begun.

We may perhaps elucidate the relation between the Utilitarians and the idealists by asking ourselves how, if the Utilitarian view of human nature is as fundamentally erroneous as the idealists maintained it to be, the Utilitarians accomplished as much as they did. Utilitarian psychology and Utilitarian ethics are really indefensible. A very little examination must show that it is just not the case that all men seek happiness in the sense in which the Utilitarians define happiness, and that the famous Utilitarian passage from each seeking his own pleasure to each seeking the greatest happiness of the greatest number is an obvious fallacy, and that the psychological Hedonism which the Utilitarians taught with such confidence is incompatible with the principles of justice which they so nobly defended in practice. ' Each to count as one and none to count as more than one,' so far from being derived from Hedonism, is flatly incompatible with it. There can seldom have been a doctrine which accomplished so much, and that on the basis of being scientific and systematic, which would so little bear criticism. If Utilitarianism was so fundamentally unsound, how did it accomplish such great things ?

The answer may be partly that the practical success of a doctrine is no witness to its intellectual consistency : witness the extraordinary power of the Marxian theory of value. But it is also that the Utilitarians looked at politics from the point of view of the legislator, and they were largely concerned with saying what the State ought not to do. When Bentham said that pushpin was as good as poetry, what he meant practically by that absurd statement was not that it was as good for a man to like pushpin as to like poetry, but that the State should not use its power to encourage people to find pleasure in poetry rather than in pushpin. For the purpose of the State was to promote liberty, to take for granted man's free activities and use its power to promote and not to hinder freedom—a view which found eloquent and noble expression in John Stuart Mill's *Liberty*. The Utilitarians had found prevailing a view that it was the State's business to make men moral—a view which they rightly repudiated. They were convinced that the compulsory activities of the State must have strict limitations, because they believed in the beneficent effect of the men's voluntary non-political activities. These voluntary activities the State must take for granted. At the most they admitted that there might arise from such activities disharmonies and inequalities which the State, with due precautions taken, might correct. Its purpose in such action should always be to promote more harmoniously men's voluntary activities.

Now in this matter up to a point both Utilitarians and idealists are in agreement. For while the Utilitarians hold that you cannot by compulsion make men happy, but only, by removing hindrances, give men scope to find their own happiness, the idealists hold that you cannot by compulsion make men moral, but only, by removing hindrances, give men scope to live the good life. And up to a point the liberty which each school seeks to attain is the same, or rather, perhaps, certain kinds of State interference are equally condemned by both doctrines. Green says :

Any direct enforcement of the outward conduct, which ought to flow from social interests, by means of threatened penalties—and a law requiring such conduct necessarily implies penalties for disobedience to it—does interfere with the spontaneous action of those interests, and consequently checks the growth of the capacity which is the condition of the beneficial exercise of rights.

Here Green is saying something the practical implication of which is the same as Utilitarian doctrine, at least up to a point. So long, therefore, as the Utilitarians were concerned with attacking State interference which was directed towards making men moral, it did not matter that they misconceived the way in which men make themselves moral. The work of freeing the individual from wrong kinds of State-compulsion had to be done in any case. There is a sense in which legislation has to take the individual and his possibilities for granted. It is the aim of legislation to set free the possibilities of the individual, and some setting free can be done regardless of what these possibilities are.

But sooner or later the limits of such action were bound to be reached, and a consideration of what the State should or should not do had to take account of what could and what could not be expected of individuals. Thus the inadequacy of Utilitarian psychology proved fatal. For Utilitarianism had taken the individual for granted, not in the sense that when the State has done all that it can the success of all social and political effort depends on individual effort and faith and vigour, but too much in the sense that individuals left to themselves work in natural harmony. Each seeking unhindered his individual happiness will produce the happiness of all. The Utilitarians had approached the problems of democracy as superior persons, calculating, from the calm height of the scientific legislator, like Bentham, or of the civil servant at the India House, like James Mill, the efforts of the masses whom their wisdom was to guide. They wanted to make politics as much as possible an exact science ; and the scientist, when he approaches social questions, is always apt to regard human nature other than his own as being atomistic and homogeneous. The more it is so the more is it ready for the impress of his experimenting genius. The idealists, on the other hand, were real democrats. They approached the problem of democracy from the standpoint of the ordinary citizen. T. H. Green, though a college tutor and a university professor, was intensely interested in the affairs of his own city of

Oxford. He was a member of the Oxford School Board and a hard-working member of the Oxford City Council. It was characteristic of him that he was not appointed to the City Council as one of the University members, but stood in the ordinary way as a candidate for the north ward of the city. He did his share in the dull, day-to-day committee work of party organisation. He both served on the School Board and was the chief agent in founding the City of Oxford School for Boys. He took an active part in the agitation for temperance reform, and characteristically at the same time set up a coffee tavern in St. Clement's. He saw more than most people what an amount of steady, disinterested devotion from ordinary men and women it takes to run a modern democracy. He understood that because he had taken part in the running of politics himself. He knew what being an active citizen meant. Something of the same could be said of Edward Caird's life in Glasgow and Bosanquet's in London. Their understanding of the State came from their serving it as ordinary citizens.

Such a standpoint was bound to make all the difference to their democratic philosophy. They knew well how much democracy asks of the ordinary man, and therefore how entirely inadequate Hedonism is as a foundation of democratic theory. They knew, as all do who take an active part in the citizens' side of politics, the active and inspiring work done in that kind of political effort by those who get their inspiration from religion. They started with an active participation in social life and social work, and then asked what could the State and the State's activities do to help them in their problems. The only way in which democracy can be understood is by being one of the ordinary people who have to work it. It cannot be understood from the top, from the standpoint of the professional legislator or the professional civil servant. In talking of these men as idealists we are apt to imply that idealists are remote from practical affairs, men speculating abstractly in the State without knowing anything of the ordinary difficulties of politics. But it is only men and women who have taken part in the dull spadework of politics and social effort, grappling along with other ordinary men with difficulties arising from incompetence and complacence and fatalism, who know what an unusual amount of idealism goes to the running of a practical democracy. T. H. Green and his school were idealists, but they were under no illusions about human nature—no illusions either way. Their idealism consisted in regarding the State from the point of view of what could be made out of it. They had learned from Plato that the nature of any social institution which has had an historical development is best understood by looking at it from its highest realisation downward rather than from its rudimentary beginnings upward. The justification of the State, and, indeed, of any institution, depended for them on the opportunities which it awarded men for their good use of it. Such an attitude is entirely compatible with recognising how far institutions fall short of what they might be, or what perverted use men may make of them. There is a great chapter in Green's *Principles of Political Obligation* entitled ' Will, not Force, is the Basis of the State.' The very title is taken by some critics to show a hopelessly idealistic outlook. But how sane is the temper of this paragraph !

The idea of a common good which the State fulfils has never been the sole influence actuating those who have been agents in the historical process by which States have come to be formed ; and even so far as it has actuated them, it has been only as conceived in some very imperfect form that it has done so. This is equally true of those who contribute to the formation and maintenance of States rather as agents, and of those who do so rather as patients. No one could pretend that even the most thoughtful and dispassionate publicist is capable of the idea of the good served by the State to which he belongs, in its fulness. He apprehends it only in some of its bearings ; but it is as a common good that he apprehends it, *i.e.*, not as a good for himself or for this man or that more than for another, but for all members equally, in virtue of their relation to each other and their common nature. The idea which the ordinary citizen has of the common good served by the State is much more limited in content. Very likely he does not think of it at all in connection with anything which the State represents to him. But he has a clear understanding of certain interests and rights common to himself with his neighbours, if only such as consist in getting his wages paid at the end of the week, in getting his money's worth at the shop, in the inviolability of his own person and that of his wife. Habitually and instinctively, *i.e.*, without asking the reason why, he regards the claim which in these respects he makes for himself as conditional upon his recognising a like claim in others, and thus as in the proper sense a right—a claim of which the essence lies in its being common to himself with others. Without this instinctive recognition he is one of the ' dangerous classes,' virtually outlawed by himself. With it, though he have no reverence for the State under that name, no sense of an interest shared by others in maintaining it, he has the needful elementary conception of a common good maintained by law. It is the fault of the State if this conception fails to make him a loyal subject, if not an intelligent patriot. It is a sign that the State is not a true State, that it is not fulfilling its primary function of maintaining law equally in the interest of all, but is being administered in the interest of classes ; whence it follows that the obedience which, if not rendered willingly, the State compels the citizen to render is not one that he feels any spontaneous interest in rendering, because it does not present itself to him as the condition of the maintenance of those rights and interests, common to himself with his neighbours, which he understands.[1]

T. H. Green and his school are also idealists in that they are concerned with the moral questions involved in politics. They are not simply trying to describe what the State actually is or does, but to deal with the principle of political obligation. That is regarded by them first and foremost from the point of view of the individual—' Why should I obey the State ? ' but the answer to that question depends for them on what the State contributes or is capable of contributing towards the moral life. In the first paragraph of his lectures Green says :

My purpose is to consider the moral function or object served by law or by the system of rights and obligations which the State enforces, and in so doing to discover the true ground or justification for obedience to law. My plan will be (1) to state in outline what I consider the true function of law to be, this being at the same time the true ground of our moral duty to obey the law, and throughout I distinguish moral duty from legal obligation ; (2) to examine the chief doctrines of political obligation that have been current in modern Europe and by criticising them to bring out more clearly the main points of a truer doctrine ; (3) to consider in detail the chief rights and obligations enforced in civilised States, inquiring what is their justification, and what is the ground for respecting them on the principle stated.[2]

Green then argues that

the value of the institutions of civil life lies in their operation as giving reality to the capacities of will and reason, and enabling them to be freely exercised. In their general effect, apart from particular aberrations, they render it possible for a man to be freely determined by the idea of a possible satisfaction of himself instead of being driven this way and that by external forces, and thus they give reality to the capacity called will ; and they enable him to realise his reason ; i.e., his idea of self-perfection, by

[1] *Principles of Political Obligation*, § 121.   [2] *Op. cit.*, § 1.

acting as a member of a social organisation in which each contributes to the better being of all the rest.[1]

This is the moral justification of social institutions in general. But law and the State need a special justification in that, as distinguished from the other institutions of social life, they imply force, and the relation of force to the moral life is a peculiar one.

The *jus naturæ* is distinguished from the sphere of moral duty because admitting of enforcement by law. Moral duties do not admit of being so enforced. The question sometimes put, whether moral duties should be enforced by law, is really an unmeaning one ; for they simply cannot be enforced. Nay, the enforcement of an outward act, the moral character of which depends on a certain motive and disposition, may often contribute to render that motive and disposition impossible ; and from this arises a limitation to the proper province of law in enforcing acts. . . . Thus the *jus naturæ*, the system of rights and obligations, as it should become no less than as it actually is maintained, is distinct from morality in the proper sense. But it is related to it. . . .[2]

Thus we begin the ethical criticism of law with two principles : (1) that nothing but external acts can be matter of ' obligation ' (in the restricted sense) ; and (2) that, in regard to that which can be made matter of obligation, the question of what should be made matter of obligation—the question of how far rights and obligations as actually established by law correspond to the true *jus naturæ*—must be considered with reference to the moral end, as serving which alone law and the obligations imposed by law have their value. In a later paragraph he says :

The business of law is to maintain certain conditions of life—to see that certain actions are done which are necessary to the maintenance of those conditions, others omitted which would interfere with them.[3]

This is, then, Green's fundamental position as regards the moral function of law—that compulsory morality is a contradiction in terms, and yet that law serves a moral end because it helps to maintain certain conditions of life. Because its relation to morality is ancillary, not creative, the State on this view must be distinguished from society. It acts as a framework within which social institutions, which have a real life of their own, may flourish. ' A State presupposes other forms of community, with the rights that arise out of

[1] *Op. cit.*, § 7.   [2] *Op. cit.*, § 10.   [3] *Op. cit.*, §§ 10 and 11.

them, and only exists as sustaining, securing, and completing them.' From this general position there follows Green's account of the nature of rights and the new and significant meaning he gives to ' natural rights.'

The end of the State is

to render it possible for a man to be freely determined, and therefore rights—the separate purpose of the State—are aids to liberty or liberties. But liberties are of no use or have no meaning except in relation to a good for which they are to be used. ' Should be ' implies on the part of whoever is capable of it the conception of an ideal, unattained condition of himself, as an absolute end. Without this conception the recognition of a power as a right would be impossible. A power on the part of anyone is so recognised by others, as one which should be exercised, when these others regard it as in some way a means to that ideal good of themselves which they alike conceive ; and the possessor of the power comes to regard it as a right through consciousness of its being thus recognised as contributory to a good in which he too is interested. No one, therefore, can have a right except (1) as a member of a society ; and (2) of a society in which some common good is recognised by the members of the society as their own ideal good, as that which should be for each of them.[1]

Granted, then, that in any given society there is some kind of recognition of a common good, there are certain powers of action which ought to be safeguarded and recognised, because they contribute to the maintenance and furtherance of that common good. It does not follow that they will be so recognised, and therefore a distinction must be made between rights which are actually recognised, legal rights, and rights which ought to be recognised. This obviously corresponds to the old distinction of positive and natural law ; but natural law is given an entirely new nature by Green. It remains an ideal to which actual law ought to conform, but it is not an immutable ideal, the same at all times and places. It is itself dependent on the moral conditions of society at any given time. The rights which ought to be recognised depend on the common good actually recognised by that society at that time. In that sense politics must always take ethics for granted.

When we, therefore, as active citizens, are considering how far we should call on the resources of the State to maintain a certain system of rights and obligations, not only are we to remember that any system of rights and obliga-

[1] *Op. cit.*, § 25.

tions can only maintain favourable circumstances for the exercise of the good life, not create the good life, but we are also to remember that our conception of what is the good life which is to be furthered and assisted by law must depend not on an abstract good, not on our own conception of good, but on what we believe members of society in general will recognise to be for the common good. When we appeal from the law as it is to the law as it ought to be our appeal is to be based on a reasoned faith in the capacities and decencies of the ordinary man of our own time and society. Our appeal is to be from the State as it is to the State as it reasonably might be, considering what its citizens are.

This has none of the definite and decisive character of the old appeals to natural and inalienable rights. It assumes a democracy which has got beyond slogans and formulæ and is able to consider political questions on their merits. But there is no question that it does presuppose that the State is being asked continually to justify itself before its citizens. The doctrine that the justification of the State's force depends on the services which that force renders ought to imply that when these services are not rendered the State's force is not justified, and political obligation disappears. It is one of the merits of Green that he both recognised that the State should and might render immense services to morality, and was also perfectly clear that it did not always render that service,—might, indeed, do the opposite ; that the citizen had therefore rights against the State. If the State normally merits the citizen's obedience there are times when it is the citizen's duty to disobey the State.

If we regard the State as the sustainer and harmoniser of social relations it would follow that the individual can have no right against the State ; that its law must be to him of absolute authority. But in fact, as actual States at best fulfil but partially their ideal function, we cannot apply this rule to practice. The general principle that the citizen must never act otherwise than as a citizen does not carry with it an obligation under all conditions to conform to the law of his State, since those laws may be inconsistent with the true end of the State as the sustainer and harmoniser of social relations. . . . Thus to the question : Has the individual no rights against enactments founded on imperfect views of social well-being ? we may answer : He has no rights against those founded on any right to do as he likes. Whatever counter-rights he has must be founded on a relation to the social well-being and that a relation of which his fellow citizens are aware. He must be able to point to some public interest, generally recognised as such, which is involved in the exercise of the power claimed by him as a right ; to show that it is not the general well-being, even as conceived by his fellow-citizens, but some special interest of a class that is concerned in promoting the exercise of the power claimed.[1]

But though Green is careful to state all the conditions which must exist before a citizen can have rights against the State, he does yet agree that

there may be cases in which the public interest—not merely according to some remote philosopher's view of it, but according to conceptions which the people are able to assimilate—is best served by a violation of some actual law.

We get from Green, therefore, a far higher conception of the State's function than we do from the Utilitarians. The good life is the end of all social activity. It cannot exist without freedom. The State can only further it indirectly, and may, by mistaking its sphere and capacities, do harm. But the State's compulsions are not the only hindrances to liberty, and the good citizen will consider what in social and economic conditions are harming the conditions necessary to the living of the good life, and ask whether the State's compulsion may not be so used in the removal of these harmful conditions as to produce an addition of real liberty. So the social legislation of the last half of the nineteenth century could be defended on the principle that such State action, by hindering economic or social inequality or lack of freedom, increased men's freedom. This is the line, for example, taken by Ritchie in his *Principles of State Interference*. This political theory is in practice far more empirical than was Utilitarianism. For it implies that when we ask what the State ought or ought not to do we have to consider the capacities of the social institutions of the time and of the citizens, and our answer will probably only be that the balance of advantages are in one direction or another. This idealism does not pretend to relieve men of their responsibilities as citizens, of studying the facts as thoroughly and carefully as they can, and thus acting on what is a reasoned faith. To those, therefore, who think that a political theory should give definite and clear-cut answers to practical political questions, and explain just what the State ought and just what it ought not to do, or exactly

---

[1] *Op. cit.*, §§ 143 and 144.

when the citizen is justified in disobeying the law, Green's teaching may seem indefinite and inconclusive.

In such a state of things, the citizen has no rule of ' right ' (in the strict sense of the word) to guide him. . . . Was there then nothing to direct him either way ?   Simply, I should answer, the general rule of looking to the moral good of mankind, to which a necessary means is the organisation of the State, which again requires unity of .control in the common interest, over the outward actions of men. . . . It must be admitted that without more knowledge and foresight than the individual can be expected to possess, this rule, if he had recognised it, could have afforded him no sure guidance ; but this is only to say that there are times of political difficulty in which the line of conduct adopted may have the most important effect, but in which it is very hard to know what is the proper line to take.[1]

There are, no doubt, times when to be told that circumstances alter cases and principles need knowledge and judgment for their application may only paralyse men's actions, when the clear-cut if erroneous pronouncements of dogmatic schools are actually more effective.   Green's principles imply for their proper application an educated democracy.

Yet they have writ no rule
nor rubric whereby conduct can in lesser affairs
accommodate these principles, when they conflict
in upright personalities, nor square their use
with the intricate contingencies that knit our lives,
and the interaction of unrelated sequences.
In that uncharted jungle a good man will do right,
while an ill-disposition will miss and go wrong.[2]

[1] *Op. cit.*, § 106.   [2] Robert Bridges, *The Testament of Beauty.*

CONTENTS

LECTURES ON THE PRINCIPLES OF POLITICAL OBLIGATION.

A. *The grounds of political obligation.*

PAGE

H. *Has the citizen rights against the state?*

I. *Private rights. The right to life and liberty.*

K. *The right of the state over the individual in war.*

O. *The right of the state in regard to the family.*

ON THE DIFFERENT SENSES OF 'FREEDOM' AS APPLIED TO WILL AND TO THE MORAL PROGRESS OF MAN.

ON THE DIFFERENT SENSES OF 'FREEDOM' AS APPLIED TO WILL AND TO THE MORAL PROGRESS OF MAN

1. SINCE in all willing a man is his own object, the will is always free. Or, more properly, a man in willing is necessarily free, since willing constitutes freedom,[1] and 'free will' is the pleonasm 'free freedom.' But while it is important to insist upon this, it is also to be remembered that the nature of the freedom really differs—the freedom means quite different things—according to the nature of the object which the man makes his own, or with which he identifies himself. It is one thing when the object in which self-satisfaction is sought is such as to prevent that self-satisfaction being found, because interfering with the realisation of the seeker's possibilities or his progress towards perfection : it is another thing when it contributes to this end. In the former case the man is a free agent in the act, because through his identification of himself with a certain desired object—through his adoption of it as his good—he makes the motive which determines the act, and is accordingly conscious of himself as its author. But in another sense he is not free, because the objects to which his actions are directed are objects in which, according to the law of his being, satisfaction of himself is not to be found. His will to arrive at self-satisfaction not being adjusted to the law which determines where this self-satisfaction is to be found, he may be considered in the condition of a bondsman who is carrying out the will of another, not his own. From this bondage he emerges into real freedom, not by overcoming the law of his being, not

---

[1] In that sense in which 'freedom' expresses a state of the soul, as distinct from a civil relation.

by getting the better of its necessity,—every fancied effort
to do so is but a new exhibition of its necessity,—but by
making its fulfilment the object of his will; by seeking the
satisfaction of himself in objects in which he believes it
should be found, and seeking it in them *because* he believes
it should be found in them. For the objects so sought,
however various otherwise, have the common characteristic
that, because they are sought in such a spirit, in them self-
satisfaction is to be found; not the satisfaction of this or
that desire, or of each particular desire, but that satisfaction,
otherwise called peace or blessedness, which consists in the
whole man having found his object; which indeed we never
experience in its fulness, which we only approach to fall
away from it again, but of which we know enough to be
sure that we only fail to attain it because we fail to seek it
in the fulfilment of the law of our being, because we have
not brought ourselves to 'gladly do and suffer what we must.'

To the above statement several objections may be made.
They will chiefly turn on two points; (*a*) the use made of the
term 'freedom'; (*b*) the view that a man is subject to a
law of his being, in virtue of which he at once seeks self-
satisfaction, and is prevented from finding it in the objects
which he actually desires, and in which he ordinarily seeks it.

2. As to the sense given to 'freedom,' it must of course be
admitted that every usage of the term to express anything but
a social and political relation of one man to others involves
a metaphor. Even in the original application its sense is by
no means fixed. It always implies indeed some exemption
from compulsion by others, but the extent and conditions
of this exemption, as enjoyed by the 'freeman' in different
states of society, are very various. As soon as the term
'freedom' comes to be applied to anything else than an established relation between a man and other men, its sense
fluctuates much more. Reflecting on their consciousness, on
their 'inner life' (i.e. their life as viewed from within), men
apply to it the terms with which they are familiar as
expressing their relations to each other. In virtue of that
power of self-distinction and self-objectification, which he
expresses whenever he says 'I,' a man can set over against
himself his whole nature or any of its elements, and apply to
the relation thus established in thought a term borrowed
from relations of outward life. Hence, as in Plato, the terms

'freedom' and 'bondage' may be used to express a relation between the man on the one side, as distinguishing himself from all impulses that do not tend to his true good, and those impulses on the other. He is a 'slave' when they are masters of him, 'free' when master of them. The metaphor in this form was made further use of by the Stoics, and carried on into the doctrines of the Christian Church. Since there is no kind of impulse or interest which a man cannot so distinguish from himself as to present it as an alien power, of which the influence on him is bondage, the particular application of the metaphor is quite arbitrary. It may come to be thought that the only freedom is to be found in a life of absolute detachment from all interests; a life in which the pure ego converses solely with itself or with a God, who is the same abstraction under another name. This is a view into which both saints and philosophers have been apt to fall. It means practically, so far as it means anything, absorption in some one interest with which the man identifies himself in exclusion of all other interests, which he sets over against himself as an influence to be kept aloof.

With St. Paul the application of the metaphor has a special character of its own. With him 'freedom' is specially freedom from the law, from ordinances, from the fear which these inspire,—a freedom which is attained through the communication of what he calls the 'spirit of adoption' or 'sonship.' The law, merely as law or as an external command, is a source of bondage in a double sense. Presenting to man a command which yet it does not give him power to obey, it destroys the freedom of the life in which he does what he likes without recognising any reason why he should not (the state of which St. Paul says 'I was alive without the law once') ; it thus puts him in bondage to fear, and at the same time, exciting a wish for obedience to itself which other desires (φρόνημα σαρκός) prevent from being accomplished, it makes the man feel the bondage of the flesh. 'What I will, that I do not'; there is a power, the flesh, of which I am the slave, and which prevents me from performing my will to obey the law. Freedom (also called 'peace,' and 'reconciliation') comes when the spirit expressed in the law (for the law is itself 'spiritual' according to St. Paul; the 'flesh' through which it is weak is mine, not the law's) becomes the principle of action in the man. To the man thus delivered, as St. Paul conceives him, we might almost apply phraseology like Kant's. 'He is free because conscious of himself as the author of the law which he obeys.' He is no longer a servant, but a son. He is conscious of union with God, whose will as an external law he before sought in vain to obey, but whose 'righteousness is fulfilled' in him now that he 'walks after the spirit.' What was before 'a law of sin and death' is now a 'law of the spirit of life.' (See *Epistle to the Romans,* viii.)

3. But though there is a point of connection between St. Paul's conception of freedom and bondage and that of Kant, which renders the above phrase applicable in a certain sense to the 'spiritual man' of St. Paul, yet the two conceptions are very different. Moral bondage with Kant, as with Plato and the Stoics, is bondage to the flesh. The heteronomy of the will is its submission to the impulse of pleasure-seeking, as that of which man is not in respect of his reason the author, but which belongs to him as a merely natural being. A state of bondage to law, as such, he does not contemplate. It might even be urged that Kant's 'freedom' or 'autonomy' of the will, in the only sense in which he supposed it attainable by man, is very much like the state described by St. Paul as that from which the communication of the spirit brings deliverance,—the state in which 'I delight in the law of God after the inward man, but find another law in my members warring with the law of my reason and bringing me into captivity to the law of sin in my members.' For Kant seems to hold that the will is actually 'autonomous,' i.e. determined by pure consciousness of what should be, only in rare acts of the best man. He argues rather for our being conscious of the possibility of such determination, as evidence of an ideal of what the good will is, than for the fact that anyone is actually so determined. And every determination of the will that does not proceed from pure consciousness of what should be he ascribes to the pleasure-seeking which belongs to man merely as a 'Natur-wesen,' or as St. Paul might say 'to the law of sin in his members.' What, it may be asked, is such 'freedom,' or rather such consciousness of the possibility of freedom, worth? May we not apply to it St. Paul's words, 'By the law is the knowledge of sin'? The practical result to the individual of that consciousness of the possibility of freedom which is all that the autonomy of will, as really attainable by

man, according to Kant's view, amounts to, is to make him aware of the heteronomy of his will, of its bondage to motives of which reason is not the author.

4. This is an objection which many of Kant's statements of his doctrine, at any rate, fairly challenge. It was chiefly because he seemed to make freedom [1] an unrealised and unrealisable state, that his moral doctrine was found unsatisfactory by Hegel. Hegel holds that freedom, as the condition in which the will is determined by an object adequate to itself, or by an object which itself as reason constitutes, is realised in the state. He thinks of the state in a way not familiar to Englishmen, a way not unlike that in which Greek philosophers thought of the πόλις, as a society governed by laws and institutions and established customs which secure the common good of the members of the society —enable them to make the best of themselves—and are recognised as doing so. Such a state is 'objective freedom'; freedom is realised in it because in it the reason, the self-determining principle operating in man as his will, has found a perfect expression for itself (as an artist may be considered to express himself in a perfect work of art); and the man who is determined by the objects which the well-ordered state presents to him is determined by that which is the perfect expression of his reason, and is thus free.

5. There is, no doubt, truth in this view. I have already tried to show [2] how the self-distinguishing and self-seeking consciousness of man, acting in and upon those human wants and ties and affections which in their proper human character have as little reality apart from it as it apart from them, gives rise to a system of social relations, with laws, customs, and institutions corresponding; and how in this system the individual's consciousness of the absolutely desirable, of something that should be, of an ideal to be realised in his life, finds a content or object which has been constituted or brought into being by that consciousness itself as working through generations of men; how interests are thus supplied to the man of a more concrete kind than

[1] In the sense of ' autonomy of rational will,' or determination by an object which reason constitutes, as distinct from determination by an object which the man makes his own; this latter determination Kant would have recognised as characteristic of every human act, properly so called.

[2] [In a previous course of lectures. See *Prolegomena to Ethics*, III. iii.]

the interest in fulfilment of a universally binding law because universally binding, but which yet are the product of reason, and in satisfying which he is conscious of attaining a true good, a good contributory to the perfection of himself and his kind. There is thus something in all forms of society that tends to the freedom [1] at least of some favoured individuals, because it tends to actualise in them the possibility of that determination by objects conceived as desirable in distinction from objects momentarily desired, which is determination by reason. [2] To put it otherwise, the effect of his social relations on a man thus favoured is that, whereas in all willing the individual seeks to satisfy himself, this man seeks to satisfy himself, not as one who feels this or that desire, but as one who conceives, whose nature demands, a permanent good. So far as it is thus in respect of his rational nature that he makes himself an object to himself, his will is autonomous. This was the good which the ideal πόλις, as conceived by the Greek philosophers, secured for the true πολίτης, the man who, entering into the idea of the πόλις, was equally qualified ἄρχειν καὶ ἄρχεσθαι. No doubt in the actual Greek πόλις there was some tendency in this direction, some tendency to rationalise and moralise the citizen. Without the real tendency the ideal possibility would not have suggested itself. And in more primitive forms of society, so far as they were based on family or tribal relations, we can see that the same tendency must have been at work, just as in modern life the consciousness of his position as member or head of a family, wherever it exists, necessarily does something to moralise a man. In modern Christendom, with the extension of citizenship, the security of family life to all men (so far as law and police can secure it), the establishment in various forms of Christian fellowship of which the moralising functions grow as those of the magistrate diminish, the number of individuals whom society awakens to interests in objects contributory to human perfection tends to increase. So far the modern state, in that full sense in which Hegel uses the term (as including all the agencies for common good of a law-abiding people), does contribute to the realisation of freedom, if by freedom we understand the autonomy of the will or its determination by

---

[1] In the sense of 'autonomy of will.'
[2] [This last clause is queried in the MS.]

rational objects, objects which help to satisfy the demand of reason, the effort after self-perfection.

6. On the other hand, it would seem that we cannot significantly speak of freedom except with reference to individual persons; that only in them can freedom be realised; that therefore the realisation of freedom in the state can only mean the attainment of freedom by individuals through influences which the state (in the wide sense spoken of) supplies,—'freedom' here, as before, meaning not the mere self-determination which renders us responsible, but determination by reason, 'autonomy of the will'; and that under the best conditions of any society that has ever been such realisation of freedom is most imperfect. To an Athenian slave, who might be used to gratify a master's lust, it would have been a mockery to speak of the state as a realisation of freedom; and perhaps it would not be much less so to speak of it as such to an untaught and under-fed denizen of a London yard with gin-shops on the right hand and on the left. What Hegel says of the state in this respect seems as hard to square with facts as what St. Paul says of the Christian whom the manifestation of Christ has transferred from bondage into 'the glorious liberty of the sons of God.' In both cases the difference between the ideal and the actual seems to be ignored, and tendencies seem to be spoken of as if they were accomplished facts. It is noticeable that by uncritical readers of St. Paul the account of himself as under the law (in *Romans* vii.), with the 'law of sin in his members warring against the law of his reason,' is taken as applicable to the regenerate Christian, though evidently St. Paul meant it as a description of the state from which the Gospel, the 'manifestation of the Son of God in the likeness of sinful flesh,' set him free. They are driven to this interpretation because, though they can understand St. Paul's account of his deliverance as an account of a deliverance achieved for them but not in them, or as an assurance of what is to be, they cannot adjust it to the actual experience of the Christian life. In the same way Hegel's account of freedom as realised in the state does not seem to correspond to the facts of society as it is, or even as, under the unalterable conditions of human nature, it ever could be; though undoubtedly there is a work of moral liberation, which

society, through its various agencies, is constantly carrying on for the individual.

7. Meanwhile it must be borne in mind that in all these different views as to the manner and degree in which freedom is to be attained, ' freedom' does not mean that the man or will is undetermined, nor yet does it mean mere self-determination, which (unless denied altogether, as by those who take the strictly naturalistic view of human action) must be ascribed equally to the man whose will is heteronomous or vicious, and to him whose will is autonomous; equally to the man who recognises the authority of law in what St. Paul would count the condition of a bondman, and to him who fulfils the righteousness of the law in the spirit of adoption. It means a particular kind of self-determination; the state of the man who lives indeed for himself, but for the fulfilment of himself as a 'giver of law universal' (Kant); who lives for himself, but only according to the true idea of himself, according to the law of his being, 'according to nature' (the Stoics) ; who is so taken up into God, to whom God so gives the spirit, that there is no constraint in his obedience to the divine will (St. Paul) ; whose interests, as a loyal citizen, are those of a well-ordered state in which practical reason expresses itself (Hegel). Now none of these modes of self-determination is at all implied in ' freedom' according to the primary meaning of the term, as expressing that relation between one man and others in which he is secured from compulsion. All that is so implied is that a man should have power to do what he wills or prefers. No reference is made to the nature of the will or preference, of the object willed or preferred; whereas according to the usage of ' freedom' in the doctrines we have just been considering, it is not constituted by the mere fact of acting upon preference, but depends wholly on the nature of the preference, upon the kind of object willed or preferred.

8. If it were ever reasonable to wish that the usage of words had been other than it has been (any more than that the processes of nature were other than they are), one might be inclined to wish that the term 'freedom' had been confined to the juristic sense of the power to ' do what one wills ': for the extension of its meaning seems to have caused much controversy and confusion. But, after all, this extension

does but represent various stages of reflection upon the
self-distinguishing, self-seeking, self-asserting principle, of
which the establishment of freedom, as a relation between
man and man, is the expression. The reflecting man is not
content with the first announcement which analysis makes
as to the inward condition of the free man, viz. that he can
do what he likes, that he has the power of acting according
to his will or preference. In virtue of the same principle
which has led him to assert himself against others, and thus
to cause there to be such a thing as (outward) freedom, he
distinguishes himself from his preference, and asks how he is
related to it, whether he determines it or how it is determined. Is he free to will, as he is free to act; or, as the
act is determined by the preference, is the preference determined by something else? Thus Locke (*Essay*, II. 21) begins
with deciding that freedom means power to do or forbear
from doing any particular act upon preference, and that,
since the will is merely the power of preference, the question
whether the will is free is an unmeaning one (equivalent to
the question whether one power has another power); that
thus the only proper question is whether a man (not his will)
is free, which must be answered affirmatively so far as he
has the power to do or forbear, as above. But he recognises
the propriety of the question whether a man is free to will
as well as to act. He cannot refuse to carry back the
analysis of what is involved in a man's action beyond the
preference of one possible action to another, and to inquire
what is implied in the preference. It is when this latter
question is raised, that language which is appropriate enough
in a definition of outward or juristic freedom becomes misleading. It having been decided that the man civilly free
has power over his actions, to do or forbear according to
preference, it is asked whether he has also power to prefer.

9. But while it is proper to ask whether in any particular
case a man has power over his actions, because his nerves and
limbs and muscles may be acted upon by another person or
a force which is not he or his, there is no appropriateness in
asking the question in regard to a preference or will, because
this cannot be so acted on. If so acted on, it would not be
a will or preference. There is no such thing as a will which
a man is not conscious of as belonging to himself, no such
thing as an act of will which he is not conscious of as

issuing from himself. To ask whether he has power over it, or whether some other power than he determines it, is like asking whether he is other than himself. Thus the question whether a man, having power to act according to his will, or being free to act, has also power over his will, or is free to will, has just the same impropriety that Locke points out in the question whether the will is free. The latter question, on the supposition that there is power to enact the will,—a supposition which is necessarily made by those who raise the ulterior question whether there is power over the will,—is equivalent, as Locke sees, to a question whether freedom is free. For a will which there is power of enacting constitutes freedom, and therefore to ask whether it is free is like asking (to use Locke's instance) whether riches are rich ('rich' being a denomination from the possession of riches, just as 'free' is a denomination from the possession of freedom, in the sense of a will which there is power to enact). But if there is this impropriety in the question whether the will is free, there is an equal one in the question which Locke entertains, viz. whether man is free to will, or has power over his will. It amounts to asking whether a certain power is also a power over itself: or, more precisely, whether a man possessing a certain power—that which we call freedom—has also the same power over that power.

10. It may be said perhaps that we are here pressing words too closely ; that it is of course understood, when it is asked whether a man has power over his will, that 'power' is used in a different sense from that which it bears when it is asked whether he has power to enact his will : that 'freedom,' in like manner, is understood to express a different kind of power or relation when we ask whether a man is free to will, and when we ask whether he is free to act. But granting that all this has been understood, the misleading effects of the question in the form under consideration ('Is a man free to will as well as to act? ' 'Has he power over his will? ') remain written in the history of the 'free-will controversy.' It has mainly to answer for two wrong ways of thinking on the subject; (a) for the way of thinking of the determining motive of an act of will, the object willed, as something apart from the will or the man willing, so that in being determined by it the man is supposed not to be self-determined, but to be determined as one natural event by

another, or at best as a natural organism by the forces
acting on it: (b), for the view that the only way of escaping
this conclusion is to regard the will as independent of
motives, as a power of deciding between motives without
any motive to determine the decision, which must mean
without reference to any object willed. A man, having (in
virtue of his power of self-distinction and self-objectification)
presented his will to himself as something to be thought
about, and being asked whether he has power over it,
whether he is free in regard to it as he is free against other
persons and free to use his limbs and, through them,
material things, this way or that, must very soon decide that
he is not. His will is himself. His character necessarily
shows itself in his will. We have already, in a previous
lecture,[1] noticed the practical fallacy involved in a man's
saying that he cannot help being what he is, as if he were
controlled by external power; but he being what he is, and
the circumstances being what they are at any particular con-
juncture, the determination of the will is already given, just
as an effect is given in the sum of its conditions. The determination of the will might be different, but only through the
man's being different. But to ask whether a man has power
over determinations of his will, or is free to will as he is to
act, as the question is commonly understood and as Locke
understood it, is to ask whether, the man being what at any
time he is, it is still uncertain (1) whether he will choose or
forbear choosing between certain possible courses of action,
and (2) supposing him to choose one or other of them, which
he will choose.

11. Now we must admit that there is really no such
uncertainty. The appearance of it is due to our ignorance
of the man and the circumstances. If, however, because this
is so, we answer the question whether a man has power over
his will, or is free to will, in the negative,[2] we at once
suggest the conclusion that something else has power over
it, viz. the strongest motive. We ignore the truth that in
being determined by a strongest motive, in the only sense
in which he is really so determined, the man (as previously

---

[1] [*Prolegomena to Ethics*, §§ 107, ff.]
[2] Instead of saying (as we should)
that it is one of those inappropriate
questions to which there is no answer;
since a man's will is himself, and
'freedom' and 'power' express relations between a man and something
other than himself.

explained)[1] is determined by himself, by an object of his own making, and we come to think of the will as determined like any natural phænomenon by causes external to it. All this is the consequence of asking questions about the relation between a man and his will in terms only appropriate to the relation between the man and other men, or to that between the man and his bodily members or the materials on which he acts through them.

12. On the other side the consciousness of self-determination resists this conclusion; but so long as we start from the question whether a man has power over his will, or is free to will as well as to act, it seems as if the objectionable conclusion could only be avoided by answering this question in the affirmative. But to say that a man has power over determinations of his will is naturally taken to mean that he can change his will while he himself remains the same; that given his character, motives, and circumstances as these at any time are, there is still something else required for the determination of his will; that behind and beyond the will as determined by some motive there is a will, itself undetermined by any motive, that determines what the determining motive shall be,—that ' has power over ' his preference or choice, as this has over the motion of his bodily members. But an unmotived will is a will without an object, which is nothing. The power or possibility, beyond any actual determination of the will, of determining what that determination shall be is a mere negation of the actual determination. It is that determination as it becomes after an abstraction of the motive or object willed, which in fact leaves nothing at all. If those moral interests, which are undoubtedly involved in the recognition of the distinction between man and any natural phænomenon, are to be made dependent on belief in such a power or abstract possibility, the case is hopeless.

13. The right way out of the difficulty lies in the discernment that the question whether a man is free to will, or has power over the determinations of his will, is a question to which there is no answer, because it is asked in inappropriate terms; in terms that imply some agency beyond the will which determines what the will shall be (as the will itself is an agency beyond the motions of the muscles which determines what those motions shall be), and that as to this

[1] [See *Prolegomena to Ethics*, § 105.]

agency it may be asked whether it does or does not lie in the
man himself.   In truth there is no such agency beyond the
will and determining how the will shall be determined ; not
in the man, for the will *is* the self-conscious man ; not elsewhere than in the man, not outside him, for the self-conscious
man has no outside.   He is not a body in space with other
bodies elsewhere in space acting upon it and determining
its motions.   The self-conscious man is determined by
objects, which in order to be objects must already be in consciousness, and in order to be *his* objects, the objects which
determine him, must already have been made his own.   To
say that they have power over him or his will, and that he
or his will has power over them, is equally misleading.
Such language is only applicable to the relation between an
agent and patient, when the agent and the patient (or at any
rate the agent) can exist separately.   But self-consciousness
and its object, will and its object, form a single individual
unity.   Without the constitutive action of man or his will
the objects do not exist; apart from determination by some
object neither he nor his will would be more than an unreal
abstraction.

14. If, however, the question is persisted in, 'Has a man
power over the determinations of his will?' we must
answer both 'yes' and 'no.'   'No,' in the sense that he is
not other than his will, with ability to direct it as the will
directs the muscles.   'Yes,' in the sense that nothing external to him or his will or self-consciousness has power over
them.   'No,' again, in the sense that, given the man and
his object as he and it at any time are, there is no possibility
of the will being determined except in one way, for the will
is already determined, being nothing else than the man as
directed to some object.   'Yes,' in the sense that the determining object is determined by the man or will just as much
as the man or will by the object.   The fact that the state of
the man, on which the nature of his object at any time
depends, is a result of previous states, does not affect the
validity of this last assertion, since (as we have seen[1]) all
these states are states of a self-consciousness from which all
alien determination, all determination except through the
medium of self-consciousness, is excluded.

15. In the above we have not supposed any account to be

[1] [*Prolegomena to Ethics*, § 102.]

taken of the character of the objects willed in the application
to the will itself of the question 'free or not free,' which is
properly applied only to an action (motion of the bodily
members) or to a relation between one man and other men.
Those who unwisely consent to entertain the question whether
a man is free to will or has power over determinations of his
will, and answer it affirmatively or negatively, consider their
answer, whether 'yes' or 'no,' to be equally applicable whatever the nature of the objects willed.   If they decide that a
man is 'free to will,' they mean that he is so in all cases of
willing, whether the object willed be a satisfaction of animal
appetite or an act of heroic self-sacrifice; and conversely, if
they decide that he is not free to will, they mean that he is not
so even in cases when the action is done upon cool calculation or
upon a principle of duty, as much as when it is done on impulse or in passion.   Throughout the controversy as to free
will that has been carried on among English psychologists
this is the way in which the question has been commonly dealt
with.   The freedom, claimed or denied for the will, has been
claimed or denied for it irrespectively of those objects willed,
on the nature of which the goodness or badness of the will
depends.

16. On the other hand, with the Stoics, St. Paul, Kant,
and Hegel, as we have seen, the attainment of freedom (at
any rate of the reality of freedom, as distinct from some
mere possibility of it which constitutes the distinctive human
nature) depends on the character of the objects willed.   In
all these ways of thinking, however variously the proper object
of will is conceived, it is only as directed to this object, and
thus (in Hegelian language) corresponding to its idea, that
the will is supposed to be free.   The good will is free, not
the bad will.   Such a view of course implies some element
of identity between good will and bad will, between will as
not yet corresponding to its idea and will as so corresponding.   St. Paul indeed, not being a systematic thinker and
being absorbed in the idea of divine grace, is apt to speak as
if there were nothing in common between the carnal or natural
man (the will as in bondage to the flesh) and the spiritual
man (the will as set free); just as Plato commonly ignores
the unity of principle in all a man's actions, and represents virtuous actions as coming from the God in man,
vicious actions from the beast.   Kant and Hegel, however,—

though they do not consider the will as it is in every man, good and bad, to be free; though Kant in his later ethical writings, and Hegel (I think) always, confine the term 'Wille' to the will as having attained freedom or come to correspond to its idea, and apply the term 'Willkür' to that self-determining principle of action which belongs to every man and is in their view the mere possibility, not actuality, of freedom,—yet quite recognise what has been above insisted on as the common characteristic of all willing, the fact that it is not a determination from without, like the determination of any natural event or agent, but the realisation of an object which the agent presents to himself or makes his own, the determination by an object of a subject which itself consciously determines that object; and they see that it is only for a subject free in this sense ('an sich' but not 'für sich,' $\delta\upsilon\nu\acute{a}\mu\epsilon\iota$ but not $\grave{\epsilon}\nu\epsilon\rho\gamma\epsilon\acute{\iota}\alpha$) that the reality of freedom can exist.

17. Now the propriety or impropriety of the use of 'freedom' to express the state of the will, not as directed to any and every object, but only to those to which, according to the law of nature or the will of God or its 'idea,' it should be directed, is a matter of secondary importance. This usage of the term is, at any rate, no more a departure from the primary or juristic sense than is its application to the will as distinct from action in any sense whatever. And certainly the unsophisticated man, as soon as the usage of 'freedom' to express exemption from control by other men and ability to do as he likes is departed from, can much more readily assimilate the notion of states of the inner man described as bondage to evil passions, to terrors of the law, or on the other hand as freedom from sin and law, freedom in the consciousness of union with God, or of harmony with the true law of one's being, freedom of true loyalty, freedom in devotion to self-imposed duties, than he can assimilate the notion of freedom as freedom to will anything and everything, or as exemption from determination by motives, or the constitution by himself of the motives which determine his will. And there is so far less to justify the extension of the usage of the term in these latter ways than in the former. It would seem indeed that there is a real community of meaning between 'freedom' as expressing the condition of a citizen of a civilised state, and 'freedom' as expressing the condition of a man who is inwardly 'master of himself.'

That is to say, the practical conception by a man ('practical' in the sense of having a tendency to realise itself) of a self-satisfaction to be attained in his becoming what he should be, what he has it in him to be, in fulfilment of the law of his being,—or, to vary the words but not the meaning, in attainment of the righteousness of God, or in perfect obedience to self-imposed law,—this practical conception is the outcome of the same self-seeking principle which appears in a man's assertion of himself against other men and against nature ('against other men,' as claiming their recognition of him as being what they are; 'against nature,' as able to use it). This assertion of himself is the demand for freedom, freedom in the primary or juristic sense of power to act according to choice or preference. So far as such freedom is established for any man, this assertion of himself is made good; and such freedom is precious to him because it is an achievement of the self-seeking principle. It is a first satisfaction of its claims, which is the condition of all other satisfaction of them. The consciousness of it is the first form of self-enjoyment, of the joy of the self-conscious spirit in itself as in the one object of absolute value.

18. This form of self-enjoyment, however, is one which consists essentially in the feeling by the subject of a possibility rather than a reality, of what it has it in itself to become, not of what it actually is. To a captive on first winning his liberty, as to a child in the early experience of power over his limbs and through them over material things, this feeling of a boundless possibility of becoming may give real joy; but gradually the sense of what it is not, of the very little that it amounts to, must predominate over the sense of actual good as attained in it. Thus to the grown man, bred to civil liberty in a society which has learnt to make nature its instrument, there is no self-enjoyment in the mere consciousness of freedom as exemption from external control, no sense of an object in which he can satisfy himself having been obtained.

Still, just as the demand for and attainment of freedom from external control is the expression of that same self-seeking principle from which the quest for such an object proceeds, so 'freedom' is the natural term by which the man describes such an object to himself,—describes to himself the state in which he shall have realised his ideal of

himself, shall be at one with the law which he recognises as
that which he ought to obey, shall have become all that he
has it in him to be, and so fulfil the law of his being or 'live
according to nature.' Just as the consciousness of an
unattainable ideal, of a law recognised as having authority
but with which one's will conflicts, of wants and impulses
which interfere with the fulfilment of one's possibilities, is a
consciousness of impeded energy, a consciousness of oneself
as for ever thwarted and held back, so the forecast of
deliverance from these conditions is as naturally said to be
a forecast of 'freedom' as of 'peace' or 'blessedness.' Nor
is it merely to a select few, and as an expression for a
deliverance really (as it would seem) unattainable under the
conditions of any life that we know, but regarded by saints
as secured for them in another world, and by philosophers
as the completion of a process which is eternally complete
in God, that 'freedom' commends itself. To any popular
audience interested in any work of self-improvement (e.g.
to a temperance-meeting seeking to break the bondage to
liquor), it is as an effort to attain freedom that such work
can be most effectively presented. It is easy to tell such
people that the term is being misapplied; that they are
quite 'free' as it is, because every one can do as he likes
so long as he does not prevent another from doing so;
that in any sense in which there is such a thing as 'free
will,' to get drunk is as much an act of free will as anything else. Still the feeling of oppression, which always
goes along with the consciousness of unfulfilled possibilities, will always give meaning to the representation of the
effort after any kind of self-improvement as a demand for
'freedom.'

19. The variation in the meaning of 'freedom' having
been thus recognised and accounted for, we come back to the
more essential question as to the truth of the view which
underlies all theories implying that freedom is in some sense
the goal of moral endeavour; the view, namely, that there
is some will in a man with which many or most of his voluntary actions do not accord, a higher self that is not satisfied
by the objects which yet he deliberately pursues. Some
such notion is common to those different theories about freedom which in the rough we have ascribed severally to the
Stoics, St. Paul, Kant, and Hegel. It is the same notion

which was previously[1] put in the form, 'that a man is subject to a law of his being, in virtue of which he at once seeks
self-satisfaction, and is prevented from finding it in the
objects which he actually desires, and in which he ordinarily
seeks it.' 'What can this mean?' it may be asked. 'Of
course we know that there are weak people who never succeed in getting what they want, either in the sense that they
have not ability answering to their will, or that they are
always wishing for something which yet they do not will.
But it would not be very appropriate to apply the above
formula to such people, for the man's will to attain certain
objects cannot be ascribed to the same law of his being as
the lack of ability to attain them, nor his wish for certain
objects to the same law of his being as those stronger desires
which determine his will in a contrary direction. At any
rate, if the proposition is remotely applicable to the man
who is at once selfish and unsuccessful, how can it be true
in any sense either of the man who is at once selfish and
succeeds, who gets what he wants (as is unquestionably the
case with many people who live for what *a priori* moralists
count unworthy objects), or of the man who 'never thinks
about himself at all'? So far as the proposition means anything, it would seem to represent Kant's notion, long ago
found unthinkable and impossible, the notion of there being
two wills or selves in a man, the 'pure' will or ego and the
'empirical' will or ego, the pure will being independent of a
man's actual desires and directed to the fulfilment of a universal law of which it is itself the giver, the empirical will
being determined by the strongest desire and directed to this
or that pleasure. In this proposition the 'objects which the
man actually desires and in which he ordinarily seeks satisfaction' are presumably objects of what Kant called the
'empirical will,' while the 'law of his being' corresponds to
Kant's 'pure ego.' But just as Kant must be supposed to
have believed in some identity between the pure and empirical will, as implied in the one term 'will,' though he
does not explain in what this identity consists, so the proposition before us apparently ascribes man's quest for self-
satisfaction as directed to certain objects, to the same law of
his being which prevents it from finding it there. Is not
this nonsense?'

[1] [Above, section 1.]

20. To such questions we answer as follows. The proposition before us, like all the theories of moral freedom
which we have noticed, undoubtedly implies that the will
of every man is a form of one consciously self-realising
principle, which at the same time is not truly or fully expressed in any man's will. As a form of this self-realising
principle it may be called, if we like, a 'pure ego' or 'the
pure ego' of the particular person; as directed to this or that
object in such a way that it does not truly express the self-
realising principle of which it is a form, it may be called the
'empirical ego' of that person. But if we use such language,
it must be borne in mind that the pure and empirical egos
are still not two egos but one ego; the pure ego being the
self-realising principle considered with reference either to its
idea, its possibility, what it has in itself to become, the law
of its being, or to some ultimate actualisation of this possibility;
the empirical ego being the same principle as it appears in
this or that state of character, which results from its action,
but does not represent that which it has in itself to become,
does not correspond to its idea or the law of its being. By
a consciously self-realising principle is meant a principle
that is determined to action by the conception of its own
perfection, or by the idea of giving reality to possibilities
which are involved in it and of which it is conscious as so
involved; or, more precisely, a principle which at each stage
of its existence is conscious of a more perfect form of existence as possible for itself, and is moved to action by that
consciousness. We must now explain a little more fully how
we understand the relation of the principle in question to
what we call our wills and our reason,—the will and reason
of this man and that,—and how we suppose its action to constitute the progress of morality.

21. By 'practical reason' we mean a consciousness of a
possibility of perfection to be realised in and by the subject
of the consciousness. By 'will' we mean the effort of a self-
conscious subject to satisfy itself. In God, so far as we can
ascribe reason and will to Him, we must suppose them to
be absolutely united. In Him there can be no distinction
between possibility and realisation, between the idea of
perfection and the activity determined by it. But in men
the self-realising principle, which is the manifestation of
God in the world of becoming, in the form which it takes

as will at best only *tends* to reconciliation with itself in the form which it takes as reason. Self-satisfaction, the pursuit of which is will, is sought elsewhere than in the realisation of that consciousness of possible perfection, which is reason. In this sense the object of will does not coincide with the object of reason. On the other hand, just because it is self-satisfaction that is sought in all willing, and because by a self-conscious and self-realising subject it is only in the attainment of its own perfection that such satisfaction can be found, the object of will is intrinsically or potentially, and tends to become actually, the same as that of reason. It is this that we express by saying that man is subject to a law of his being which prevents him from finding satisfaction in the objects in which under the pressure of his desires it is his natural impulse to seek it. This 'natural impulse' (not strictly 'natural') is itself the result of the operation of the self-realising principle upon what would otherwise be an animal system, and is modified, no doubt, with endless complexity in the case of any individual by the result of such operation through the ages of human history. But though the natural impulses of the will are thus the work of the self-realising principle in us, it is not in their gratification that this principle can find the satisfaction which is only to be found in the consciousness of becoming perfect, of realising what it has it in itself to be. In order to any approach to this satisfaction of itself the self-realising principle must carry its work farther. It must overcome the 'natural impulses,' not in the sense of either extinguishing them or denying them an object, but in the sense of fusing them with those higher interests, which have human perfection in some of its forms for their object. Some approach to this fusion we may notice in all good men; not merely in those in whom all natural passions, love, anger, pride, ambition, are enlisted in the service of some great public cause, but in those with whom such passions are all governed by some such commonplace idea as that of educating a family.

22. So far as this state is reached, the man may be said to be reconciled to 'the law of his being' which (as was said above) prevents him from finding satisfaction in the objects in which he ordinarily seeks it, or anywhere but in the realisation in himself of an idea of perfection. Since the

law is, in fact, the action of that self-realising subject which
is his self, and which exists in God as eternally self-realised,
he may be said in this reconciliation to be at peace at once
with himself and with God.

Again, he is 'free,' (1) in the sense that he is the author
of the law which he obeys (for this law is the expression of
that which is his self), and that he obeys it because
conscious of himself as its author; in other words, obeys it
from that impulse after self-perfection which is the source
of the law or rather constitutes it.   He is 'free' (2) in the
sense that he not merely 'delights in the law after the
inward man' (to use St. Paul's phrase), while his natural
impulses are at once thwarted by it and thwart him in his
effort to conform to it, but that these very impulses have
been drawn into its service, so that he is in bondage neither
to it nor to the flesh.

From the same point of view we may say that his will is
'autonomous,' conforms to the law which the will itself constitutes, because the law (which prevents him from finding satisfaction anywhere but in the realisation in himself of an idea
of perfection) represents the action in him of that self-
realising principle of which his will is itself a form.   There
is an appearance of equivocation, however, in this way of
speaking, because the 'will' which is liable not to be autonomous, and which we suppose gradually to approach autonomy
in the sense of conforming to the law above described, is
not this self-realising principle in the form in which this
principle involves or gives the law.   On the contrary, it
is the self-realising principle as constituting that effort
after self-satisfaction in each of us which is liable to be and
commonly is directed to objects which are not contributory
to the realisation of the idea of perfection,—objects which
the self-realising principle accordingly, in the fulfilment of
its work, has to set aside.   The equivocation is pointed out by
saying, that the good will is 'autonomous' in the sense of
conforming to a law which the will itself, as reason, constitutes ;
which is, in fact, a condensed way of saying, that the good
will is the will of which the object coincides with that of
practical reason ; that will has its source in the same self-
realising principle which yields that consciousness of a
possible self-perfection which we call reason, and that it can
only correspond to its idea, or become what it has the possi-

bility of becoming, in being directed to the realisation of that consciousness.

23. According to the view here taken, then, reason and will, even as they exist in men, are one in the sense that they are alike expressions of one self-realising principle. In God, or rather in the ideal human person as he really exists in God, they are actually one; i.e. self-satisfaction is for ever sought and found in the realisation of a completely articulated or thoroughly filled idea of the perfection of the human person. In the historical man—in the men that have been and are coming to be—they *tend* to unite. In the experience of mankind, and again in the experience of the individual as determined by the experience of mankind, both the idea of a possible perfection of man, the idea of which reason is the faculty, and the impulse after self-satisfaction which belongs to the will, undergo modifications which render their reconciliation in the individual (and it is only in individuals that they can be reconciled, because it is only in them that they exist) more attainable. These modifications may be stated summarily as (1) an increasing concreteness in the idea of human perfection; its gradual development from the vague inarticulate feeling that there is such a thing into a conception of a complex organisation of life, with laws and institutions, with relationships, courtesies, and charities, with arts and graces through which the perfection is to be attained; and (2) a corresponding discipline, through inheritance and education, of those impulses which may be called ' natural ' in the sense of being independent of any conscious direction to the fulfilment of an idea of perfection. Such discipline does not amount to the reconciliation of will and reason; it is not even, properly speaking, the beginning of it; for the reconciliation only begins with the direction of the impulse after self-satisfaction to the realisation of an idea of what should be, as such (*because* it should be); and no discipline through inheritance or education, just because it is only impulses that are natural (in the sense defined) which it can affect, can bring about this direction, which, in theological language, must be not of nature, but of grace. On the contrary, the most refined impulses may be selfishly indulged; i.e. their gratification may be made an object in place of that object which consists in the realisation of the idea of perfection. But unless a discipline and refinement of the natural

impulses, through the operation of social institutions and arts, went on *pari passu* with the expression of the idea of perfection in such institutions and arts, the direction of the impulses of the individual by this idea, when in some form or other it has been consciously awakened in him, would be practically impossible. The moral progress of mankind has no reality except as resulting in the formation of more perfect individual characters; but on the other hand every progress towards perfection on the part of the individual character presupposes some embodiment or expression of itself by the self-realising principle in what may be called (to speak most generally) the organisation of life. It is in turn, however, only through the action of individuals that this organisation of life is achieved.

24. Thus the process of reconciliation between will and reason,—the process through which each alike comes actually to be or to do what it is and does in possibility, or according to its idea, or according to the law of its being,—so far as it comes within our experience may be described as follows. A certain action of the self-realising principle, of which individuals susceptible in various forms to the desire to better themselves have been the media, has resulted in conventional morality; in a system of recognised rules (whether in the shape of law or custom) as to what the good of society requires, which no people seem to be wholly without. The moral progress of the individual, born and bred under such a system of conventional morality, consists (1) in the adjustment of the self-seeking principle in him to the requirements of conventional morality, so that the modes in which he seeks self-satisfaction are regulated by the sense of what is expected of him. This adjustment (which it is the business of education to effect) is so far a determination of the will as in the individual by objects which the universal or national human will, of which the will of the individual is a partial expression, has brought into existence, and is thus a determination of the will by itself. It consists (2) in a process of reflection, by which this feeling in the individual of what is expected of him becomes a conception (under whatever name) of something that universally should be, of something absolutely desirable, of a single end or object of life. The content of this conception may be no more than what was already involved in the individual's feeling of what

is expected of him; that is to say, if called upon to state in detail what it is that has to be done for the attainment of the absolute moral end or in obedience to the law of what universally should be, he might only be able to specify con-duct which, apart from any such explicit conception, he felt was expected of him. For all that there is a great difference between feeling that a certain line of conduct is expected of me and conceiving it as a form of a universal duty. So long as the requirements of established morality are felt in the former way, they present themselves to the man as imposed from without. Hence, though they are an expression of practical reason, as operating in previous generations of men, yet, unless the individual conceives them as relative to an absolute end common to him with all men, they become antagonistic to the practical reason which operates in him, and which in him is the source at once of the demand for self-satisfaction and of the effort to find himself in, to carry his own unity into, all things presented to him. Unless the actions required of him by 'the divine law, the civil law, and the law of opinion or reputation' (to use Locke's classifica-tion) tend to realise his own idea of what should be or is good on the whole, they do not form an object which, as contem-plated, he can harmonise with the other objects which he seeks to understand, nor, as a practical object, do they form one in the attainment of which he can satisfy himself. Hence before the completion of the process through which the in-dividual comes to conceive the performance of the actions expected of him under the general form of a duty which in the freedom of his own reason he recognises as binding, there is apt to occur a revolt against conventional morality. The issue of this may either be an apparent suspension of the moral growth of the individual, or a clearer apprehension of the spirit underlying the letter of the obligations laid on him by society, which makes his rational recognition of duty, when arrived at, a much more valuable influence in promot-ing the moral growth of society.

25. Process (2), which may be called a reconciliation of reason with itself, because it is the appropriation by reason as a personal principle in the individual of the work which reason, acting through the media of other persons, has already achieved in the establishment of conventional morality, is the condition of the third stage in which the moral progress of

the individual consists; viz. the growth of a personal interest in the realisation of an idea of what should be, in doing what is believed to contribute to the absolutely desirable, or to human perfection, because it is believed to do so.   Just so far as this interest is formed, the reconciliation of the two modes in which the practical reason operates in the individual is effected.   The demand for self-satisfaction (practical reason as the will of the individual) is directed to the realisation of an ideal object, the conceived 'should be,' which practical reason as our reason constitutes.   The 'autonomy of the will' is thus attained in a higher sense than it is in the 'adjustment' described under (1), because the objects to which it is directed are not merely determined by customs and institutions which are due to the operation of practical reason in previous ages, but are embodiments or expressions of the conception of what absolutely should be as formed by the man who seeks to satisfy himself in their realisation.   Indeed, unless in the stage of conformity to conventional morality the principle of obedience is some feeling (though not a clear conception) of what should be, of the desirable as distinct from the desired,—if it is merely fear of pain or hope of pleasure,—there is no approach to autonomy of the will or moral freedom in the conformity.   We must not allow the doctrine that such freedom consists in a determination of the will by reason, and the recognition of the truth that the requirements of conventional morality are a product of reason as operating in individuals of the past, to mislead us into supposing that there is any moral freedom, or anything of intrinsic value, in the life of conventional morality as governed by 'interested motives,' by the desire, directly or indirectly, to obtain pleasure.   There can be no real deter- mination of the will by reason unless both reason and will are operating in one and the same person.   A will is not really anything except as the will of a person, and, as we have seen, a will is not really determinable by anything foreign to itself: it is only determinable by an object which the person willing makes his own.   As little is reason really anything apart from a self-conscious subject, or as other than an idea of per- fection to be realised in and by such a subject.   The de- termination of will by reason, then, which constitutes moral freedom or autonomy, must mean its determination by an object which a person willing, in virtue of his reason, presents to himself, that object consisting in the realisation of an idea of perfection in and by himself. Kant's view that the action which is merely 'pflichtmässig,' not done 'aus Pflicht,' is of no moral value in itself, whatever may be its possible value as a means to the production of the will which does act 'aus Pflicht,' is once for all true, though he may have taken too narrow a view of the conditions of actions done 'aus Pflicht,' especially in supposing (as he seems to do) that it is necessary to them to be done painfully. There is no determination of will by reason, no moral freedom, in conformity of action to rules of which the establishment is due to the operation of reason or the idea of perfection in men, unless the principle of conformity in the persons conforming is that idea itself in some form or other.

LECTURES ON THE PRINCIPLES OF POLITICAL OBLIGATION

———◆◆◆———

Note of the Editor.

These lectures, which are partly critical and partly expository, treat of the moral grounds upon which the state is based and upon which obedience to the law of the state is justified. They were delivered in 1879–80, following upon the course from which the discussion of Kant's moral theory in this volume is taken. The two courses are directly connected, civil institutions being throughout regarded as the external expression of the moral progress of mankind, and as supplying the material through which the idea of perfection must be realised.

As is implied in section 5, the inquiry into the nature of political obligation forms part of a wider inquiry into the concrete forms of morality in general, 'the detail of goodness.' The lecturer had intended to complete the course by a consideration of 'social virtues' and 'moral sentiments'; but this intention was not carried out. (See section 251.)

LECTURES ON THE PRINCIPLES OF POLITICAL OBLIGATION

A. *THE GROUNDS OF POLITICAL OBLIGATION.*

1. THE subject of this course of lectures is the principles of political obligation; and that term is intended to include the obligation of the subject towards the sovereign, the obligation of the citizen towards the state, and the obligation of individuals to each other as enforced by a political superior. My purpose is to consider the moral function or object served by law, or by the system of rights and obligations which the state enforces, and in so doing to discover the true ground or justification for obedience to law. My plan will be (1) to state in outline what I consider the true function of law to be, this being at the same time the true ground of our moral duty to obey the law; and throughout I distinguish moral duty from legal obligation; (2) to examine the chief doctrines of political obligation that have been current in modern Europe, and by criticising them to bring out more clearly the main points of a truer doctrine; (3) to consider in detail the chief rights and obligations enforced in civilised states, inquiring what is their justification, and what is the ground for respecting them on the principle stated.

2. In previous lectures I have explained what I understand moral goodness to be, and how it is possible that there should be such a thing; in other words, what are the conditions on the part of reason and will which are implied in our being able to conceive moral goodness as an object to be aimed at, and to give some partial reality to the conception. Our results on this question may be briefly stated as follows.

The highest moral goodness we found was an attribute of character, in so far as it issued in acts done for the sake

of their goodness, not for the sake of any pleasure or any
satisfaction of desire which they bring to the agent. But
it is impossible that an action should be done for the sake
of its goodness, unless it has been previously contemplated
as good for some other reason than that which consists in
its being done for the sake of its goodness. It must have
been done, or conceived as possible to be done, and have
been accounted good, irrespectively of the being done from
this which we ultimately come to regard as the highest
motive. In other words, a prior morality, founded upon
interests which are other than the pure interest in being
good, and governed by rules of conduct relative to a standard
of goodness other than that which makes it depend on this
interest, is the condition of there coming to be a character
governed by interest in an ideal of goodness. Otherwise
this ideal would be an empty one ; it would be impossible to
say what the good actions were, that were to be done for
the sake of their goodness ; and the interest in this ideal
would be impossible, since it would be an interest without
an object.

3. When, however, morality of the latter kind has come
to be recognised as the highest or the only true morality,
the prior morality needs to be criticised from the point of
view thus gained. Those interests, other than the interest
in being good, which form the motives on the part of the
individual on which it rests, will not indeed be rejected as
of no moral value ; for no one can suppose that without
them, or except as regulating them, the pure interest in
being good could determine conduct at all. But they will
be estimated according to their value as leading up to, or
as capable of becoming elements in, a character in which
this interest is the governing principle. Again, those rules
of conduct, according to which the terms right and wrong,
good and bad, are commonly applied, and which, as was just
now said, are relative to a standard certainly not founded on
the conception of the good as consisting in the character
described, are not indeed to be rejected ; for without them
there would be nothing to define the duties which the highest
character is prepared to do for their own sake. But they
have to be revised according to a method which inquires
into their rationale or justification, as conditions of approximation to the highest character.

4. Such a criticism of moral interests—of the general motives which determine moral conduct and regulate such moral approbation or disapprobation as is not based on a strict theory of moral good—may be called by the name of 'a theory of moral sentiments.' The criticism of recognised rules of conduct will fall under two heads, according as these rules are embodied in positive law (law of which the observance is enforced on the individual by a political superior), or only form part of the 'law of opinion' (part of what the individual feels to be expected of him by some person or persons to whose expectations he ought to conform).

5. Moral interests are so greatly dependent on generally recognised rules of conduct that the criticism of the latter should come first. The law of opinion, again, in so many ways presupposes a social fabric supported by 'positive' law, that we can only fairly take account of it when we have considered the moral value and justifiability of the fabric so supported. I propose therefore to begin our inquiry into the detail of goodness—into the particular kinds of conduct which the man wishing to do good for the sake of its goodness is entitled to count good—by considering what is of permanent moral value in the institutions of civil life, as established in Europe; in what way they have contributed and contribute to the possibility of morality in the higher sense of the term, and are justified, or have a moral claim upon our loyal conformity, in consequence.

6. The condition of a moral life is the possession of will and reason. Will is the capacity in a man of being determined to action by the idea of a possible satisfaction of himself. An act of will is an action so determined. A state of will is the capacity as determined by the particular objects in which the man seeks self-satisfaction; and it becomes a character in so far as the self-satisfaction is habitually sought in objects of a particular kind. Practical reason is the capacity in a man of conceiving the perfection of his nature as an object to be attained by action. All moral ideas have their origin in reason, i.e. in the idea of a possible self-perfection to be attained by the moral agent. This does not mean that the moral agent in every stage of his progress could state this idea to himself in an abstract form, any more than in every stage in the acquisition of

knowledge about nature a man can state to himself in an abstract form the conception of the unity of nature, which yet throughout conditions the acquisition of his knowledge. Ideas do not first come into existence, or begin to operate, upon the formation of an abstract expression for them. This expression is only arrived at upon analysis of a concrete experience, which they have rendered possible. Thus we only learn to express the idea of self-perfection in that abstract form upon an analysis of an experience of self-improvement which we have ourselves gone through, and which must have been gone through by those with whom we are connected by the possession of language and an organisation of life, however elementary : but the same analysis shows that the same idea must have been at work to make such experience possible. In this idea all particular moral ideas—all ideas of particular forms of conduct as estimable—originate, though an abstract expression for the latter is arrived at much sooner than such an expression for the idea in which they originate. They arise, as the individual's conception of the society on the well-being of which his own depends, and of the constituents of that well-being, becomes wider and fuller ; and they are embodied in the laws, institutions, and social expectation, which make conventional morality. This embodiment, again, constitutes the moral progress of mankind. This progress, however, is only a *moral* progress in so far as it tends to bring about the harmony of will and reason, in the only form in which it can really exist, viz. in the characters of persons. And this result is actually achieved, in so far as upon habits disciplined by conformity to conventional morality there supervenes an intelligent interest in some of the objects contributory to human perfection, which that conventional morality subserves, and in so far as that interest becomes the dominant interest of the character.

7. The value then of the institutions of civil life lies in their operation as giving reality to these capacities of will and reason, and enabling them to be really exercised. In their general effect, apart from particular aberrations, they render it possible for a man to be freely determined by the idea of a possible satisfaction of himself, instead of being driven this way and that by external forces, and thus they give reality to the capacity called will: and they enable

him to realise his reason, i.e. his idea of self-perfection, by acting as a member of a social organisation in which each contributes to the better-being of all the rest. So far as they do in fact thus operate they are morally justified, and may be said to correspond to the 'law of nature,' the *jus naturæ*, according to the only sense in which that phrase can be intelligibly used.

8. There has been much controversy as to what the *jus naturæ* (' Naturrecht') really is, or whether there is such a thing at all. And the controversy, when it comes to be dealt with in English, is further embarrassed by the fact that we have no one term to represent the full meaning of 'jus' or 'Recht,' as a system of correlative rights and obligations, actually enforced or that should be enforced by law. But the essential questions are : (1) whether we are entitled to distinguish the rights and obligations which are anywhere actually enforced by law from rights and obligations which really exist though not enforced; and (2), if we are entitled to do so, what is to be our criterion of rights and obligations which are really valid, in distinction from those that are actually enforced.

9. No one would seriously maintain that the system of rights and obligations, as it is anywhere enforced by law, —the 'jus' or 'Recht' of any nation—is all that it ought to be. Even Hobbes holds that a law, though it cannot be unjust, may be pernicious. But there has been much objection to the admission of *natural* rights and obligations. At any rate the phrase is liable to misinterpretation. It may be taken to imply that rights and obligations can exist in a 'state of nature'—a state in which every individual is free to do as he likes—; that legal rights and obligations derive their authority from a voluntary act by which individuals contracted themselves out of this state; and that the individual retains from the state of nature certain rights with which no legal obligations ought to conflict. Such a doctrine is generally admitted to be untenable; but it does not follow from this that there is not a true and important sense in which natural rights and obligations exist,—the same sense as that in which duties may be said to exist though unfulfilled. There is a system of rights and obligations which *should be* maintained by law, whether it is so or not, and which may properly be called 'natural'; not in the sense in

which the term 'natural' would imply that such a system
ever did exist or could exist independently of force exercised
by society over individuals, but 'natural' because necessary to
the end which it is the vocation of human society to realise.

10. The 'jus naturæ,' thus understood, is at once distinguished from the sphere of moral duty, and relative to it.
It is distinguished from it because admitting of enforcement
by law. Moral duties do not admit of being so enforced.
The question sometimes put, whether moral duties should
be enforced by law, is really an unmeaning one; for they
simply cannot be enforced. They are duties to act, it is
true, and an act can be enforced : but they are duties to act
from certain dispositions and with certain motives, and these
cannot be enforced. Nay, the enforcement of an outward
act, the moral character of which depends on a certain
motive and disposition, may often contribute to render that
motive and disposition impossible : and from this fact arises
a limitation to the proper province of law in enforcing
acts, which will have to be further considered below. When
obligations then are spoken of in this connection, as part of
the 'jus naturæ' correlative to rights, they must always be
understood not as moral duties, not as relative to states of
will, but as relative to outward acts, of which the performance or omission can and should be enforced. There is a
moral duty to discharge such obligations, and to do so in a
certain spirit, but the obligation is such as that with which
law has to do or may have to do, is relative to an outward
act merely, and does not amount to a moral duty. There is
a moral duty in regard to obligations, but there can be no
obligation in regard to moral duties. Thus the 'jus naturæ'
—the system of rights and obligations, as it should become
no less than as it actually is maintained—is distinct from
morality in the proper sense. But it is relative to it. This
is implied in saying that there is a moral duty in regard to
actual obligations, as well as in speaking of the system of
rights and obligations as it should become. If such language is justifiable, there must be a moral ground both for
conforming to, and for seeking to develope and improve,
established 'Recht'; a moral ground which can only lie in
the moral end served by that established system.

11. Thus we begin the ethical criticism of law with two
principles:—(1) that nothing but external acts can be

matter of 'obligation' (in the restricted sense) ; and (2)
that, in regard to that which can be made matter of obligation, the question what should be made matter of obligation
—the question how far rights and obligations, as actually
established by law, correspond to the true 'jus naturæ'—
must be considered with reference to the moral end, as
serving which alone law and the obligations imposed by law
have their value.[1]

12. Before proceeding, some remarks have to be made as
to what is implied in these principles. (a) Does the law, or
is it possible that it should, confine its view to external acts?
What exactly is meant by an external act? In the case of
obligations which I am legally punishable for disregarding,
the law, in deciding whether punishment is or is not due,
takes account of much beside the external act; and this implies that much beside external action is involved in legal
obligation. In the case where the person or property of
another is damaged by me, the law does not inquire merely
whether the act of damage was done, and done by means of
my bodily members, but whether it was done intentionally;
and if not done with the direct intention of inflicting the
damage, whether the damage arose in a manner that might
have been foreseen out of something which I did intend to
do : whether, again, if it was done quite accidentally the

---

[1] There are two definitions of ' Recht'
or 'jus naturæ,' quoted by Ulrici
(*Naturrecht*, p. 219), which embody the
truths conveyed in these statements.
(1) Krause defines ' Recht' as ' das
organische Ganze der äusseren Bedingungen des Vernunftlebens,' 'the organic
whole of the outward conditions necessary to the rational life.' (2) Henrici
says that ' Recht' is ' was der Idee der
Unverletzbarkeit der materiellen we-
sentlichen Bedingungen des moralischen
Menschenthums, d. h. der menschlichen
Persönlichkeit nach ihrer Existenz und
ihrer Vervollkommnung, oder der un-
veräusserlichen Menschengüter im
äusserlichen Verkehr entspricht': i.e.
'Right is what' (or, 'that is properly
matter of legal obligation which') 'in
the outward intercourse of men corresponds to the idea of the inviolability
of the essential material conditions of
a moral humanity, i.e. of the human
personality in respect of its existence
and its perfection;' or, more simply,

'Right is that which is really necessary
to the maintenance of the material conditions essential to the existence and
perfection of human personality.' Cf.
Trendelenburg, *Naturrecht*, § 46. 'Das
Recht ist im sittlichen Ganzen der In-
begriff derjenigen allgemeinen Bestimmungen des Handelns, durch welche
es geschieht dass das sittliche Ganze
und seine Gliederung sich erhalten und
weiter bilden kann.' Afterwards he
emphasises the words 'des Handelns,'
and adds : ' Zwar kann das Handeln
nicht ohne den Willen gedacht werden,
der zum Grunde liegt: aber die Recht-
bestimmungen sind nicht Bestimmungen
des Willens als solchen, was dem innern
Gebiet, der Ethik der Gesinnung,
anheimfallen würde. Der Wille der
nicht Handlung wird entzieht sich dem
Recht. Wenn das Recht Schuld und
Versehen, *dolus* und *culpa*, in sein
Bereich zieht, so sind sie als innere aber
charakteristische Beschaffenheiten des
Handelns anzusehen.'

accident was due to culpable negligence. This, however, does not show that the law can enforce or prevent anything but external action, but only that it is *action* which it seeks to enforce or prevent, for without intention there is no action. We talk indeed of a man acting against his will, but if this means acting against intention it is what it is impossible to do. What I call an act done against my will is either (1) an act done by someone else using my body, through superior force, as a means : in which case there is an act, but it is not mine (e.g. if another uses my hand to pull the trigger of a gun by which someone is shot) ; or (2) a natural event in which my limbs are affected in a certain way which causes certain results to another person (e.g. if the rolling of a ship throws me against another person who is thus thrown into the water) ; or (3) an act which I do under the influence of some strong inducement (e.g. the fear of death), but which is contrary to some strong wish. In this case the act is mine, but mine because I intend it; because it is not against my will as = intention. In saying, then, that the proper, because the only possible, function of law is to enforce the performance of or abstinence from external actions, it is implied that its function is to produce or prevent certain intentions, for without intention on the part of someone there is no act.

13. But if an act necessarily includes intention, what is the nature of the restriction implied in calling it external ? An external action is a determination of will as exhibited in certain motions of the bodily members which produce certain effects in the material world ; not a determination of the will as arising from certain motives and a certain disposition. All that the law can do is to enjoin or forbid determinations of will as exhibited in such motions, &c. It does indeed present a motive, for it enforces its injunctions and prohibitions primarily by fear, by its threat of certain consequences if its commands are disobeyed. This enforcement is not an exercise of physical force in the strict sense, for in this sense no force can produce an action, since it cannot produce a determination of will ; and the only way in which the law or its administrators employ such force is not in the production but in the prevention of action (as when a criminal is locked up or the police prevent mischievous persons from assaulting us or breaking into our houses). But though, in enforcing its commands by threats, the law is presenting a motive, and

thus, according to our distinction, affecting action on its inner side, it does this solely for the sake of the external act. It does not regard the relation of the act to the motive fear as of any intrinsic importance. If the action is performed without this motive ever coming into play under the influence of what the moralist counts higher motives, the purpose of the law is equally satisfied. Indeed, it is always understood that its purpose is most thoroughly served when the threat of pains and penalties has ceased to be necessary, and the obligations correlative to the relations of individuals and of societies are fulfilled from other motives. Its business is to maintain certain conditions of life—to see that certain actions are done which are necessary to the maintenance of those conditions, others omitted which would interfere with them. It has nothing to do with the motive of the actions or omissions, on which, however, the moral value of them depends.

14. It appears, then, that legal obligations—obligations which can possibly form the subject of positive law—can only be obligations to do or abstain from certain acts, not duties of acting from certain motives, or with a certain disposition. It is not a question whether the law should or should not oblige to anything but performance of outward acts. It simply cannot oblige to anything else, because the only means at its command for obtaining the fulfilment of obligations are (1) threats of pain and offers of reward, by means of which it is possible indeed to secure the general performance of certain acts, but not their performance from the motive even of fear of the pain threatened or hope of the reward offered, much less from any higher motive; (2) the employment of physical force, (a) in restraining men disposed to violate obligations, (b) in forcibly applying the labour or the property of those who violate obligations to make good the breach, so far as is possible; (as, e.g., when the magistrate forestalls part of a man's wages to provide for a wife whom he has deserted, or when the property of a debtor is seized for the benefit of his creditors.)

15. Only outward acts, then, can be matter of legal obligation; but what sort of outward acts should be matter of legal obligation? The answer to this question arises out of the above consideration of the means which law employs to obtain the fulfilment of obligations, combined with the view

of law as relative to a moral end, i.e. the formation of a
society of persons, acting from a certain disposition, from
interest in the society as such. Those acts only should be matter
of legal injunction or prohibition of which the performance
or omission, irrespectively of the motive from which it proceeds, is so necessary to the existence of a society in which the
moral end stated can be realised, that it is better for them to
be done or omitted from that unworthy motive which consists
in fear or hope of legal consequences than not to be done at all.

16. We distinguish, then, the system of rights actually
maintained and obligations actually enforced by legal
sanctions ('Recht' or 'jus') from the system of relations
and obligations which *should be* maintained by such sanctions
('Naturrecht'); and we hold that those actions or omissions
should be made obligations which, when made obligations,
serve a certain moral end; that this end is the ground or
justification or rationale of legal obligation; and that thus
we obtain a general rule, of both positive and negative application, in regard to the proper matter or content of legal
obligation. For since the end consists in action proceeding
from a certain disposition, and since action done from apprehension of legal consequences does not proceed from that
disposition, no action should be enjoined or prohibited by
law of which the injunction or prohibition interferes with
actions proceeding from that disposition, and every action
should be so enjoined of which the performance is found to
produce conditions favourable to action proceeding from that
disposition, and of which the legal injunction does not interfere with such action.

17. Does this general rule give any real guidance in the
difficulties which practically arise in regard to the province
of law—as to what should be required by law, and what left
to the inclination of individuals? What cases are there or
have there been of enactments which on this principle we
can pronounce wrong? Have attempts ever been made by
law to enforce acts as virtuous which lose their virtue when
done under fear of legal penalties? It would be difficult, no
doubt, to find instances of attempts to enforce by law actions
of which we should say that the value lies in the disposition
from which they are done, actions, e.g. of disinterested
kindness, because the clear conception of virtue as depending not on outward results, but on disposition, is but

slowly arrived at, and has never been reflected in law. But without any strictly moral object at all, laws have been made which check the development of the moral disposition. This has been done (a) by legal requirements of religious observance and profession of belief, which have tended to vitiate the religious source of morality; (b) by prohibitions and restraints, unnecessary, or which have ceased to be necessary, for maintaining the social conditions of the moral life, and which interfere with the growth of self-reliance, with the formation of a manly conscience and sense of moral dignity,—in short, with the moral autonomy which is the condition of the highest goodness; (c) by legal institutions which take away the occasion for the exercise of certain moral virtues (e.g. the Poor-law which takes away the occasion for the exercise of parental forethought, filial reverence, and neighbourly kindness).

18. Laws of this kind have often been objected to on the strength of a one-sided view of the function of laws; the view, viz., that its only business is to prevent interference with the liberty of the individual. And this view has gained undue favour on account of the real reforms to which it has led. The laws which it has helped to get rid of were really mischievous, but mischievous for further reasons than those conceived of by the supporters of this theory. Having done its work, the theory now tends to become obstructive, because in fact advancing civilisation brings with it more and more interference with the liberty of the individual to do as he likes, and this theory affords a reason for resisting all positive reforms, all reforms which involve an action of the state in the way of promoting conditions favourable to moral life. It is one thing to say that the state in promoting these conditions must take care not to defeat its true end by narrowing the region within which the spontaneity and disinterestedness of true morality can have play; another thing to say that it has no moral end to serve at all, and that it goes beyond its province when it seeks to do more than secure the individual from violent interference by other individuals. The true ground of objection to 'paternal government' is not that it violates the 'laissez faire' principle and conceives that its office is to make people good, to promote morality, but that it rests on a misconception of morality. The real function of government being to

maintain conditions of life in which morality shall be
possible, and morality consisting in the disinterested per
formance of self-imposed duties, 'paternal government' does
its best to make it impossible by narrowing the room for
the self-imposition of duties and for the play of disinterested
motives.

19. The question before us, then, is, In what ways and
how far do the main obligations enforced and rights maintained by law in all civilised societies contribute to the moral
end described; viz. to establish those conditions of life in
which a true, i.e. a disinterested or unselfish morality shall
be possible? The answer to this question will be a theory of
the 'jus naturæ'; i.e. it will explain how far positive law is
what it should be, and what is the ground of the duty to
obey it; in other words, of political obligation. There are
two things from which such a theory must be distinguished.
(1) It is not an inquiry into the process by which actual
law came to be what it is; nor (2) is it an inquiry how far
actual law corresponds to and is derived from the exercise
of certain original or natural rights. (1) It is not the
former, because the process by which the law of any nation
and the law in which civilised nations agree has come to
be what it is, has not been determined by reference to that
end to which we hold that law ought to be directed and
by reference to which we criticise it. That is to say, the
process has not been determined by any such conscious
reference on the part of the agents in the process. No
doubt a desire for social good as distinct from private
pleasure, for what is good on the whole as distinct from
what is good for the moment, has been a necessary condition
of it; but (a), as an agent in the development of law, this
has not reached the form of a conception of moral good
according to that definition of it by which the value of law
is to be estimated; and (b) in bringing law to its present
state it has been indistinguishably blended with purely
selfish passions and with the simple struggle for existence.

20. (2) A true theory of 'jus naturæ,' a rationale of law
or ideal of what it should be, is not to be had by inquiring
how far actual law corresponds to, and is derived from, the
exercise of certain original or natural rights, if that is taken
to mean that we know, or can ascertain, what rights are
natural on grounds distinct from those on which we deter-

mine what laws are justifiable, and that then we can proceed
to ascertain what laws are justifiable by deduction from
such rights. ' Natural rights,' so far as there are such things,
are themselves relative to the moral end to which perfect
law is relative. A law is not good because it enforces
' natural rights,' but because it contributes to the realisation
of a certain end. We only discover what rights are natural
by considering what powers must be secured to a man in
order to the attainment of this end. These powers a perfect
law will secure to their full extent. Thus the consideration
of what rights are ' natural ' (in the only legitimate sense)
and the consideration what laws are justifiable form one and
the same process, each presupposing a conception of the
moral vocation of man.

21. The doctrine here asserted, that all rights are relative
to moral ends or duties, must not be confused with the
ordinary statement that every right implies a duty, or that
rights and duties are correlative. This of course is true in
the sense that possession of a right by any person both
implies an obligation on the part of someone else, and is
conditional upon the recognition of certain obligations on
the part of the person possessing it. But what is meant is
something different, viz. that the claim or right of the
individual to have certain powers secured to him by society,
and the counter-claim of society to exercise certain powers
over the individual, alike rest on the fact that these powers
are necessary to the fulfilment of man's vocation as a moral
being, to an effectual self-devotion to the work of developing
the perfect character in himself and others.

22. This, however, is not the ground on which the claim
in question has generally been asserted. Apart from the
utilitarian theory, which first began to be applied politically
by Hume, the ordinary way of justifying the civil rights of
individuals (i.e. the powers secured to them by law as
against each other), as well as the rights of the state against
individuals (i.e. the powers which, with the general approval
of society, it exercises against them), has been to deduce
them from certain supposed prior rights, called natural rights.
In the exercise of these natural rights, it has been supposed,
men with a view to their general interest established political
society. From that establishment is derived both the system
of rights and obligations maintained by law as between

man and man, and the right of the state to the submission of its subjects. If the question, then, is raised,
why I ought to respect the legal rights of my neighbours,
to pay taxes, or have my children vaccinated, serve in the
army if the state requires it, and generally submit to the
law, the answer according to this theory will be that if I
fail to do so, I shall directly or indirectly be violating the
natural rights of other men; directly in those cases where
the legal rights of my neighbours are also natural rights, as
they very well may be (e.g. rights of liberty or personal
safety); indirectly where this is not the case, because,
although the rights of the state itself are not natural, and
many rights exercised by individuals would not only not be
secured but would not exist at all but for legal enactment,
yet the state itself results from a covenant which originally,
in the exercise of their natural rights, men made with each
other, and to which all born under the state and sharing
the advantages derived from it must be considered parties.
There is a natural right, therefore, on the part of each
member of a state to have this compact observed, with a corresponding obligation to observe it; and this natural right
of all is violated by any individual who refuses to obey the
law of the state or to respect the rights, not in themselves
natural, which the state confers on individuals.

23. This, on the whole, was the form in which the ground
of political obligation, the justification of established rights,
was presented throughout the seventeenth century, and in
the eighteenth till the rise of the 'utilitarian' theory of
obligation. Special adaptations of it were made by Hobbes
and others. In Hobbes, perhaps (of whom more later), may
be found an effort to fit an anticipation of the utilitarian
theory of political obligation into the received theory which
traced political obligation, by means of the supposition of a
primitive contract, to an origin in natural right. But in
him as much as anyone the language and framework of
the theory of compact is retained, even if an alien doctrine
may be read between the lines. Of the utilitarian theory of
political obligation more shall be said later. It may be presented in a form in which it would scarcely be distinguishable
from the doctrine just now stated, the doctrine, viz., that
the ground of political obligation, the reason why certain
powers should be recognised as belonging to the state and

certain other powers as secured by the state to individuals, lies in the fact that these powers are necessary to the fulfilment of man's vocation as a moral being, to an effectual self-devotion to the work of developing the perfect character in himself and others. Utilitarianism proper, however, recognises no vocation of man but the attainment of pleasure and avoidance of pain. The only reason why civil rights should be respected—the only justification of them—according to it, would be that more pleasure is attained or pain avoided by the general respect for them; the ground of our consciousness that we ought to respect them, in other words their ultimate sanction, is the fear of what the consequences would be if we did not. This theory and that which I deem true have one negative point in common. They do not seek the ground of actual rights in a prior natural right, but in an end to which the maintenance of the rights contributes. They avoid the mistake of identifying the inquiry into the ultimate justifiability of actual rights with the question whether there is a prior right to the possession of them. The right to the possession of them, if properly so called, would not be a mere power, but a power recognised by a society as one which should exist. This recognition of a power, in some way or other, as that which should be, is always necessary to render it a right. Therefore when we had shown that the rights exercised in political society were derived from prior 'natural' rights, a question would still remain as to the ground of those natural rights. We should have to ask why certain powers were recognised as powers which should be exercised, and thus became these natural rights.

24. Thus, though it may be possible and useful to show how the more seemingly artificial rights are derived from rights more simple and elementary, how the rights established by law in a political society are derived from rights that may be called natural, not in the sense of being prior to society, but in the sense of being prior to the existence of a society governed by written law or a recognised sovereign, still such derivation is no justification of them. It is no answer to the question why they should be respected; because this question remains to be asked in regard to the most primitive rights themselves. Political or civil rights, then, are not to be explained by derivation from natural rights, but in regard to both political and natural rights, in any sense

in which there can be truly said to be natural rights, the question has to be asked, how it is that certain powers are recognised by men in their intercourse with each other as powers that should be exercised, or of which the possible exercise should be secured.

25. I have tried to show in lectures on morals that the conception expressed by the 'should be' is not identical with the conception of a right possessed by some man or men, but one from which the latter conception is derived. It is, or implies on the part of whoever is capable of it, the conception of an ideal, unattained condition of himself, as an absolute end. Without this conception the recognition of a power as a right would be impossible. A power on the part of anyone is so recognised by others, as one which should be exercised, when these others regard it as in some way a means to that ideal good of themselves which they alike conceive : and the possessor of the power comes to regard it as a right through consciousness of its being thus recognised as contributory to a good in which he too is interested. No one therefore can have a right except (1) as a member of a society, and (2) of a society in which some common good is recognised by the members of the society as their own ideal good, as that which should be for each of them. The capacity for being determined by a good so recognised is what constitutes personality in the ethical sense ; and for this reason there is truth in saying that only among persons, in the ethical sense, can there come to be rights ; (which is quite compatible with the fact that the logical disentanglement of the conception of rights precedes that of the conception of the legal person ; and that the conception of the moral person, in its abstract and logical form, is not arrived at till after that of the legal person).

Conversely, everyone capable of being determined by the conception of a common good as his own ideal good, as that which unconditionally should be (of being in that sense an end to himself), in other words, every moral person, is capable of rights ; i.e. of bearing his part in a society in which the free exercise of his powers is secured to each member through the recognition by each of the others as entitled to the same freedom with himself. To say that he is capable of rights, is to say that he ought to have them, in that sense of 'ought' in which it expresses the relation of man to an end conceived as absolutely good, to an end which, whether desired or no, is conceived as intrinsically desirable. The moral capacity implies a consciousness on the part of the subject of the capacity that its realisation is an end desirable in itself, and rights are the condition of realising it. Only through the possession of rights can the power of the individual freely to make a common good his own have reality given to it. Rights are what may be called the negative realisation of this power. That is, they realise it in the sense of providing for its free exercise, of securing the treatment of one man by another as equally free with himself, but they do not realise it positively, because their possession does not imply that in any active way the individual makes a common good his own. The possession of them, however, is the condition of this positive realisation of the moral capacity, and they ought to be possessed because this end (in the sense explained) ought to be attained.

26. Hence on the part of every person ('person' in the moral sense explained) the claim, more or less articulate and reflected on, to rights on his own part is co-ordinate with his recognition of rights on the part of others. The capacity to conceive a common good as one's own, and to regulate the exercise of one's powers by reference to a good which others recognise, carries with it the consciousness that powers should be so exercised; which means that there should be rights, that powers should be regulated by mutual recognition. There ought to be rights, because the moral personality,—the capacity on the part of an individual for making a common good his own,—ought to be developed; and it is developed through rights; i.e. through the recognition by members of a society of powers in each other contributory to a common good, and the regulation of those powers by that recognition.

27. In saying that only among 'persons' can there come to be rights, and that every 'person' should have rights, I have been careful to explain that I use 'person' in the moral, not merely in the legal, sense. In dealing, then, with such phrases as 'jura personarum' and 'personal rights,' we must keep in view the difference between the legal and ethical sense of the proposition that all rights are personal, or subsist as between persons. In the legal sense, so far as it is true,—and it is so only if 'person' is used in the sense

of Roman law,—it is an identical proposition. A person
means a subject of rights and nothing more. Legal personality is derived from the possession of right, not *vice versa*.
Like other identical propositions, its use is to bring out and
emphasise in the predicate what is included in the understood connotation of the subject; to remind us that when we
speak of rights we imply the existence of parties, in English
phraseology, capable of suing and being sued. In the ethical
sense, it means that rights are derived from the possession
of personality as = a rational will (i.e. the capacity which
man possesses of being determined to action by the conception of such a perfection of his being as involves the perfection of a society in which he lives), in the sense (*a*) that
only among beings possessed of rational will can there come
to be rights, (*b*) that they fulfil their idea, or are justifiable,
or such rights as should be rights, only as contributing to
the realisation of a rational will. It is important to bear
this distinction in mind in order that the proposition in its
ethical sense, which can stand on its own merits, may not
derive apparent confirmation from a juristic truism.

28. The moral idea of personality is constantly tending to
affect the legal conception of the relation between rights and
persons. Thus the 'jura personarum,' which properly =
either rights arising out of ' status,' or rights which not only
(like all rights) reside in someone having a legal status and
are available against others having a legal status, but are
exercised over, or in respect of, someone possessed of such
status (e.g. a wife or a servant), come to be understood as
rights derived from the human personality or belonging to
man as man. It is with some such meaning that English
writers on law speak of rights to life and liberty as personal
rights. The expression might seem pleonastic, since no right
can exist except as belonging to a person in the legal sense.
They do not use the phrase either pleonastically or in the
sense of the Roman lawyers' ' jura personarum ' above, but
in the sense that these rights are immediately derived from,
or necessarily attach to, the human personality in whatever
that personality is supposed to consist. There is no doubt,
however, that historically the conception of the moral person,
in any abstract form, is not arrived at till after that of the
legal person has been thus disentangled and formulated; and
further that the abstract conception of the legal person, as

the sustainer of rights, is not arrived at till long after rights have been actually recognised and established. But the disentanglement or abstract formulation of the conception of moral personality is quite a different thing from the action of the consciousness in which personality consists.

29. The capacity, then, on the part of the individual of conceiving a good as the same for himself and others, and of being determined to action by that conception, is the foundation of rights ; and rights are the condition of that capacity being realised. No right is justifiable or should be a right except on the ground that directly or indirectly it serves this purpose. Conversely every power should be a right, i.e. society should secure to the individual every power, that is necessary for realising this capacity. Claims to such powers as are directly necessary to a man's acting as a moral person at all —acting under the conception of a good as the same for self and others—may be called in a special sense personal rights (though they will include more than Stephen includes under that designation) ; they may also be called, if we avoid misconceptions connected with these terms, 'innate' or 'natural' rights. They are thus distinguished from others which are (1) only indirectly necessary to the end stated, or (2) are so only under special conditions of society ; as well as from claims which rest merely on legal enactment and might cease to be enforced without any violation of the 'jus naturæ.'

30. The objection to calling them 'innate' or 'natural,' when once it is admitted on the one side that rights are not arbitrary creations of law or custom but that there are certain powers which ought to be secured as rights, on the other hand that there are no rights antecedent to society, none that men brought with them into a society which they contracted to form, is mainly one of words. They are 'innate' or 'natural' in the same sense in which according to Aristotle the state is natural ; not in the sense that they actually exist when a man is born and that they have actually existed as long as the human race, but that they arise out of, and are necessary for the fulfilment of, a moral capacity without which a man would not be a man. There cannot be innate rights in any other sense than that in which there are innate duties, of which, however, much less has been heard. Because a group of beings are capable each of conceiving an absolute good of

himself and of conceiving it to be good for himself as identical with, and because identical with, the good of the rest of the group, there arises for each a consciousness that the common good should be the object of action, i.e. a duty, and a claim in each to a power of action that shall be at once secured and regulated by the consciousness of a common good on the part of the rest, i.e. a right. There is no ground for saying that the right arises out of a primary human capacity, and is thus 'innate,' which does not apply equally to the duty.

31. The dissociation of innate rights from innate duties has gone along with the delusion that such rights existed apart from society. Men were supposed to have existed in a state of nature, which was not a state of society, but in which certain rights attached to them as individuals, and then to have formed societies by contract or covenant. Society having been formed, certain other rights arose through positive enactment; but none of these, it was held, could interfere with the natural rights which belonged to men antecedently to the social contract or survived it.

Such a theory can only be stated by an application to an imaginary state of things, prior to the formation of societies as regulated by custom or law, of terms that have no meaning except in relation to such societies. 'Natural right,' as = right in a state of nature which is not a state of society, is a contradiction. There can be no right without a consciousness of common interest on the part of members of a society. Without this there might be certain powers on the part of individuals, but no recognition of these powers by others as powers of which they allow the exercise, nor any claim to such recognition; and without this recognition or claim to recognition there can be no right.

B. *SPINOZA*

32. SPINOZA is aware of this. In the *Tractatus Politici*,
II. 4, he says, 'Per *jus* itaque *naturæ* intelligo . . . ipsam
naturæ potentiam.' . . . 'Quicquid unusquisque homo ex
legibus suæ naturæ agit, id summo naturæ jure agit, tantum-
que in naturam habet juris, quantum potentia valet.' If
only, seeing that the 'jus naturæ' was mere 'potentia,' he
had denied that it was 'jus' at all, he would have been on
the right track. Instead of that, however, he treats it as
properly 'jus,' and consistently with this regards all 'jus'
as mere 'potentia': nor is any 'jus humanum' according
to him guided by or the product of reason. It arises, in
modern phrase, out of the 'struggle for existence.' As
Spinoza says, 'homines magis cæca cupiditate quam ratione
ducuntur; ac proinde hominum naturalis potentia sive jus non
ratione, sed quocumque appetitu quo ad agendum determi-
nantur, quoque se conservare conantur, definiri debet' (II. 5).
The 'jus civile' is simply the result of the conflict of natural
powers, which = natural rights, which arises from the effort
of every man to gratify his passions and 'suum esse conservare.' Man is simply a 'pars naturæ,' the most crafty of the
animals. 'Quatenus homines ira, invidia aut aliquo odii
affectu conflictantur, eatenus diverse trahuntur et invicem
contrarii sunt, et propterea eo plus timendi, quo plus possunt,
magisque callidi et astuti sunt, quam reliqua animalia; et
quia homines ut plurimum his affectibus natura sunt obnoxii,
sunt ergo homines ex natura hostes' (II. 14). Universal
hostility means universal fear, and fear means weakness. It
follows that in the state of nature there is nothing fit to be
called 'potentia' or consequently 'jus'; 'atque adeo con-
cludimus jus naturæ vix posse concipi nisi ubi homines jura
habent communia, qui simul terras, quas habitare et colere
possunt, sibi vindicare, seseque munire, vimque omnem repel-

lere et ex communi omnium sententia vivere possunt. Nam (per art. 13 hujus cap.) quo plures in unum sic conveniunt, eo omnes simul plus juris habent' (15). The collective body, i.e., has more 'jus in naturam,' i.e. 'potentiam,' than any individual could have singly (13). In the advantage of this increased 'jus in naturam' the individual shares. On the other hand (16), 'Ubi homines jura communia habent omnesque una veluti mente ducuntur, certum est (per art. 13 hujus cap.) eorum unumquemque tanto minus habere juris, quanto reliqui simul ipso potentiores sunt, hoc est, illum revera jus nullum in naturam habere præter id, quod ipsi commune concedit jus. Ceterum quicquid ex communi consensu ipsi imperatur, teneri exsequi vel (per art. 4 hujus cap.) jure ad id cogi.' This 'jus' by which the individual's actions are now to be regulated, is still simply 'potentia.' 'Hoc jus, quod multitudinis potentia definitur, imperium appellari solet' (17). It is not to be considered anything different from the 'jus naturæ.' It is simply the 'naturalis potentia' of a certain number of men combined; 'multitudinis quæ una veluti mente ducitur' (III. 2). Thus in the 'status civilis' the 'jus naturæ' of the individual in one sense disappears, in another does not. It disappears in the sense that the individual member of the state has no mind to act or power to act against the mind of the state. Anyone who had such mind or power would not be a member of the state. He would be an enemy against whose 'potentia' the state must measure its own. On the other hand, 'in statu civili,' just as much as 'in statu naturali,' 'homo ex legibus suæ naturæ agit suæque utilitati consulit' (3). He exercises his 'naturalis potentia' for some natural end of satisfying his wants and preserving his life as he did or would do outside the 'status civilis.' Only in the 'status civilis' these motives on the part of individuals so far coincide as to form the 'una veluti mens' which directs the 'multitudinis potentia.'

According to this view, any member of a state will have just so much 'jus,' i.e. 'potentia,' against other members as the state allows him. If he can exercise any 'jus' or 'potentia' against another 'ex suo ingenio,' he is so far not a member of the state and the state is so far imperfect. If he could exercise any 'jus' or 'potentia' against the state itself, there would be no state, or, which is the same, the state would not be 'sui juris.'

33. Is there then no limit to the 'jus' which the state may exercise? With Spinoza this is equivalent to the question, is there no limit to the 'potentia' which it can exercise? As to this, he suggests three considerations.

(1). Its power is weakened by any action against right reason, because this must weaken the 'animorum unio' on which it is founded. 'Civitatis jus potentia multitudinis, quæ una veluti mente ducitur, determinatur. At hæc animorum unio concipi nulla ratione posset, nisi civitas id ipsum maxime intendat, quod sana ratio omnibus hominibus utile esse docet' (III. 7).

(2). The 'right' or 'power' of the state depends on its power of affecting the hopes and fears of individual citizens. . . . 'Subditi eatenus non sui, sed civitatis juris sint, quatenus ejus potentiam seu minas metuunt, vel quatenus statum civilem amant (per art. 10 præced. cap.). Ex quo sequitur, quod ea omnia, ad quæ agenda nemo præmiis aut minis induci potest, ad jura civitatis non pertineant' (III. 8). Whatever cannot be achieved by rewards and threats, is beyond the power and therefore beyond the 'right' of the state. Examples are given in the same section.

(3). 'Ad civitatis jus ea minus pertinere, quæ plurimi indignantur' (III. 9). Severities of a certain kind lead to conspiracies against the state, and thus weaken it. 'Sicut unusquisque civis sive homo in statu naturali, sic civitas eo minus sui juris est, quo majorem timendi causam habet.'

Just so far then as there are certain things which the state cannot do, or by doing which it lessens its power, so far there are things which it has no 'right' to do.

34. Spinoza proceeds to consider the relation of states or sovereign powers to each other. Here the principle is simple. They are to each other as individuals in the state of nature, except that they will not be subject to the same weaknesses. 'Nam quandoquidem (per art. 2 hujus cap.) jus summæ potestatis nihil est præter ipsum naturæ jus, sequitur duo imperia ad invicem sese habere, ut duo homines in statu naturali, excepto hoc, quod civitas sibi cavere potest, ne ab alia opprimatur, quod homo in statu naturali non potest, nimirum qui quotidie somno, sæpe morbo aut animi ægritudine, et tandem senectute gravatur, et præter hæc aliis incommodis est obnoxius, a quibus civitas securam se reddere potest' (III. 11). In other words, '. . . duæ civitates

natura hostes sunt. Homines enim in statu naturali hostes
sunt. Qui igitur jus naturæ extra civitatem retinent, hostes
manent' (III. 13). The 'jura belli' are simply the powers
of any one state to attack or defend itself against another.
The ' jura pacis,' on the other hand, do not appertain to any
single state, but arise out of the agreement of two at least.
They last as long as the agreement, the ' fœdus,' lasts; and
this lasts as long as the fear or hope, which led to its being
made, continues to be shared by the states which made it.
As soon as this ceases to be the case, the agreement is
necessarily at an end, ' nec dici potest, quod dolo vel perfidia
agat, propterea quod fidem solvit, simulatque metus vel spei
causa sublata est, quia hæc conditio unicuique contrahentium
æqualis fuit, ut scilicet quæ prima extra metum esse potest,
sui juris esset, eoque ex sui animi sententia uteretur, et præterea quia nemo in futurum contrahit nisi positis præceden-
tibus circumstantiis ' (III. 14).

35. It would seem to follow from the above that a state
can do no wrong, in the sense that there are no rights that
it can violate. The same principle is applicable to it as
to the individual. ' In statu naturali non dari peccatum,
vel si quis peccat, is sibi, non alteri peccat: . . . nihil
absolute naturæ jure prohibetur, nisi quod nemo potest' (II.
18). A state is to any other state, and to its subjects, as
one individual to another ' in statu naturali.' A wrong, a
'peccatum,' consists in a violation by individuals of the
'commune decretum.' There can be no ' peccare ' on the
part of the ' commune decretum ' itself. But ' non id omne,
quod jure fieri dicimus, optime fieri affirmamus. Aliud
namque est agrum jure colere, aliud agrum optime colere ;
aliud, inquam, est sese jure defendere, conservare, judicium
ferre, &c., aliud sese optime defendere, conservare, atque
optimum judicium ferre; et consequenter aliud est jure
imperare et reipublicæ curam habere, aliud optime imperare et
rempublicam optime gubernare. Postquam itaque de jure
cujuscumque civitatis in genere egimus, tempus est, ut de
optimo cujuscumque imperii statu agamus ' (V. 1). Hence
a further consideration ' de optimo cujusque imperii statu.'
This is guided by reference to the ' finis status civilis,' which
is ' pax vitæque securitas.' Accordingly that is the best
government under which men live in harmony, and of which
the rights are kept inviolate. Where this is not the case,

the fault lies with the government, not with any 'subditorum malitia.' 'Homines enim civiles non nascuntur, sed fiunt. Hominum præterea naturales affectus ubique iidem sunt' (V. 2).

The end is not fully attained where men are merely kept in order by fear. Such a state of things is not peace but merely absence of war. 'Pax enim non belli privatio, sed virtus est, quæ ex animi fortitudine oritur[1]; est namque obsequium constans voluntas id exsequendi, quod ex communi civitatis decreto fieri debet' (V. 4).

The 'peace,' then, which it is the end of the state to obtain, consists in rational virtue; in a common mind, governed by desire on the part of each individual for perfection of being in himself and others. The harmony of life, too, which is another way of expressing its object, is to be understood in an equally high sense. The life spoken of is one 'quæ maxime ratione, vera mentis virtute et vita, definitur.'

The 'imperium' which is to contribute to this end must clearly be one 'quod multitudo libera instituit, non autem id, quod in multitudinem jure belli acquiritur.' Between the two forms of 'imperium' there may be no essential difference in respect of the 'jus' which belongs to each, but there is the greatest in respect of the ends which they serve as well as in the means by which they have to be maintained (V. 6).

36. This conclusion of Spinoza's doctrine of the state does not seem really consistent with the beginning. At the outset, no motives are recognised in men but such as render them 'natura hostes.' From the operation of these motives the state is supposed to result. Each individual finds that the war of all against all is weakness for all. Consequently the desire on the part of each to strengthen himself, which is a form of the universal effort 'suum esse conservare,' leads to combination, it being discovered that 'homini nihil homine utilius' (*Eth.* IV. 18. Schol.). But we are expressly told that the civil state does not bring with it other

---

[1] For the definition of 'fortitudo,' see *Ethics*, III. 59, Schol. 'Omnes actiones quæ sequuntur ex affectibus qui ad mentem referuntur, quatenus intelligit, ad fortitudinem refero, quam in animositatem et generositatem distinguo. Nam per animositatem intelligo cupiditatem, qua unusquisque conatur suum esse ex solo rationis dictamine conservare. Per generositatem . . . cupiditatem qua unusquisque ex solo rationis dictamine conatur reliquos homines juvare et sibi amicitia jungere.'

motives than those operative 'in statu naturali.' 'Homo
namque tam in statu naturali quam civili ex legibus suæ
naturæ agit, suæque utilitati consulit.' But then it appears
that there supervenes or may supervene on such motives
'constans voluntas id exsequendi quod ex communi civitatis
decreto fieri debet,' and that not of a kind which seeks to
carry out the 'commune decretum' as a means of escaping
pain or obtaining pleasure, for it is said to arise from the
'animi fortitudo' which rests on reason ('ad mentem
refertur quatenus intelligit') and includes 'generositas'
defined as above. It is also said that the true object of
'imperium' is 'vitam concorditer transigere' or 'vitam
colere' in a sense of 'vita' in which it 'maxime ratione
. . . definitur.' And as the 'imperium' established for
this end is one which 'multitudo libera instituit,' it seems [1]
to be implied that there is a desire for such an end on the
part of the people. It is not explained how such desires
should arise out of the conflict of 'naturales potentiæ' or out
of the impulses which render men 'natura hostes.' On the
other hand, if the elements of them already exist in the impulses which lead to the formation of the 'status civilis,' the
reasons for saying that men are 'natura hostes' disappear,
and we get a different view of 'jus,' whether 'naturale' or
'civile,' from that which identifies it simply with 'potentia.'
Some power of conceiving and being interested in a good *as
common*, some identification of the 'esse' of others with
the 'suum esse' which every man, as Spinoza says, seeks to
preserve and promote, must be supposed in those who form
the most primitive social combinations, if these are to issue
in a state directed to such ends and maintained by such a
'constans voluntas' as Spinoza describes. And it is the
interest of men in a common good, the desire on the part of
each which he thinks of others as sharing, for a good which
he conceives to be equally good for them, that transforms
mere 'potentia' into what may fitly be called 'jus,' i.e. a
power claiming recognition as exercised or capable of being
exercised for the common good.

[1] Certainly this is so, if we apply
to the 'libera multitudo' the definition
of freedom applied to the 'liber homo.'
'Hominem eatenus *liberum* omnino voco,
quatenus ratione ducitur, quia eatenus
ex causis, quæ per solam eius naturam
possunt adæquate intelligi, ad agendum
determinatur, tametsi ex iis necessario
ad agendum determinetur. Nam liber-
tas agendi necessitatem non tollit, sed
ponit' (II. 11).

37. If this qualification of 'potentia' which alone renders it 'jus' had been apprehended by Spinoza, he would have been entitled to speak of a 'jus naturale' as preceding the 'jus civile,' i.e. of claims to the recognition of powers and the actual customary recognition of such, as exercised for a common good, preceding the establishment of any regular institutions or general laws for securing their exercise. As it is, the term 'jus naturale' is with him really unmeaning. If it means no more than 'potentia,' why call it 'jus'? 'Jus' might have a meaning distinct from that of 'potentia' in the sense of a power which a certain 'imperium' enables one man to exercise as against another. This is what Spinoza understands by 'jus civile.' But there is no need to qualify it as 'civile,' unless 'jus' may be employed with some other qualification and with a distinctive meaning. But the 'jus naturale,' as he understands it, has no meaning other than that of 'potentia,' and his theory as it stands would have been more clearly expressed if instead of 'jus naturale' and 'jus civile' he had spoken of 'potentia' and 'jus,' explaining that the latter was a power on the part of one man against others, maintained by means of an 'imperium' which itself results from a combination of 'powers.' He himself in one passage shows a consciousness of the impropriety of speaking of 'jus' except with reference to a community; 'jus naturæ, quod humani generis proprium est, vix posse concipi, nisi ubi homines jura habent communia, qui simul terras, quas habitare et colere possunt, sibi vindicare, seseque munire, vimque omnem repellere et ex communi omnium sententia vivere possunt' (II. 15). He takes no notice, however, of any forms of community more primitive than that of the state. The division into the 'status naturalis' and the 'status civilis' he seems to treat as exhaustive, and the 'status naturalis' he regards, after the manner of his time, as one of pure individualism, of simple detachment of man from man, or of detachment only modified by conflict. From such a 'status naturalis,' lacking both the natural and the rational principles of social development (the natural principle, i.e. the interest in others arising primarily from family ties, and the rational principle, i.e. the power of conceiving a good consisting in the more perfect being of the individual and of those in whom he is interested), no process could be traced to the 'status civilis.' The two 'status' stand

over against each other with an impassable gulf between.
'Homines civiles non nascuntur, sed fiunt.' They are so
made, he seems to hold, by the action of the 'imperium' upon
them. But how is the 'imperium' to be made? Men must
first be, if not 'civiles,' yet something very different from
what they are in the 'status naturalis,' between which and
the 'status civilis' Spinoza recognises no middle term, before any 'imperium' which could render them 'civiles' could
be possible.

38. The cardinal error of Spinoza's 'Politik' is the admission of the possibility of a right in the individual apart
from life in society, apart from the recognition by members
of a society of a correlative claim upon and duty to each
other, as all interested in one and the same good. The error
was the error of his time, but with Spinoza it was confirmed
by his rejection of final causes. The true conception of
'right' depends on the conception of the individual as being
what he really is in virtue of a function which he has to fulfil
relatively to a certain end, that end being the common well-
being of a society. A 'right' is an ideal attribute ('ideal'
in the sense of not being sensibly verifiable, not reducible to
any perceivable fact or facts) which the individual possesses so
far as this function is in some measure freely fulfilled by
him—i.e. fulfilled with reference to or for the sake of the
end—and so far as the ability to fulfil it is secured to him
through its being recognised by the society as properly belonging to him. The essence of right lies in its being not simply
a power producing sensible effects, but a power relative to an
insensible function and belonging to individuals only in so far
as each recognises that function in himself and others. It
is not in so far as I *can* do this or that, that I have a right to
do this or that, but so far as I recognise myself and am recognised by others as able to do this or that for the sake
of a common good, or so far as in the consciousness of myself
and others I have a function relative to this end. Spinoza,
however, objects to regard anything as determined by relation
to a final cause. He was not disposed therefore to regard individuals as being what they are in virtue of functions relative
to the life of society, still less as being what they are in
virtue of the recognition by each of such functions in himself and others. He looked upon man, like everything else in
nature, as determined by material and efficient causes, and

as himself a material and efficient cause. But as such he has no 'rights' or 'duties,' but only 'powers.'

39. It was because Plato and Aristotle conceived the life of the πόλις so clearly as the τέλος of the individual, relation to which makes him what he is—the relation in the case of the πολίτης proper being a conscious or recognised relation —that they laid the foundation for all true theory of 'rights.' It is true that they have not even a word for 'rights.' The claims which in modern times have been advanced on behalf of the individual against the state under the designation 'natural rights' are most alien from their way of thinking. But in saying that the πόλις was a 'natural' institution and that man was φύσει πολιτικός, Aristotle, according to the sense which he attached to πόλις, was asserting the doctrine of 'natural rights' in the only sense in which it is true. He regards the state (πόλις) as a society of which the life is maintained by what its members do for the sake of maintaining it, by functions consciously fulfilled with reference to that end, and which in that sense imposes duties; and at the same time as a society from which its members derive the ability, through education and protection, to fulfil their several functions, and which in that sense confers rights. It is thus that the πολίτης μετέχει τοῦ ἄρχειν καὶ τοῦ ἄρχεσθαι. Man, being φύσει πολίτης,—being already in respect of capacities and tendencies a member of such a society, existing only in κοινωνίαι which contain its elements,—has 'naturally' the correlative duties and rights which the state imposes and confers. Practically it is only the Greek man that Aristotle regards as φύσει πολίτης, but the Greek conception of citizenship once established was applicable to all men capable of a common interest. This way of conceiving the case, however, depends on the 'teleological' view of man and the forms of society in which he is found to live, i.e. on the view of men as being what they are in virtue of non-sensible functions, and of certain forms of life determined by relation to more perfect forms which they have the capacity or tendency to become.

40. Spinoza, like Bacon, found the assumption of ends which things were meant to fulfil in the way of accurate inquiry into what things are (materially) and do. He held Plato and Aristotle cheap as compared with Democritus and

Epicurus (*Epist.* LX. 13).   Accordingly he considers the individual apart from his vocation as a member of society, the state apart from its office as enabling the individual to fulfil that vocation.   Each, so considered, is merely a vehicle of so much power (natural force).   On the other hand, he recognises a difference between a higher and lower, a better and worse, state of civil society, and a possibility of seeking the better state because it is understood to be better.   And this is to admit the possibility of the course of human affairs being affected by the conception of a final cause.   It is characteristic of Spinoza that while he never departs from the principle 'homo naturæ pars,' he ascribes to him the faculty of understanding the order of nature, and of conforming to it or obeying it in a new way on account of that understanding.   In other words, he recognised the distinction called by Kant the distinction between determination according to law and determination according to the consciousness of law; though in his desire to assert the necessity of each kind of determination he tends to disguise the distinction and to ignore the fact that, if rational determination (or the determination by a conception of a law) is a part of nature, it is so in quite a different sense from determination merely according to laws of nature.   As he puts it, the clear understanding that we are parts of nature, and of our position in the universe of things, will yield a new character.   We shall only then desire what is ordained for us and shall find rest in the truth, in the knowledge of what is necessary.   This he regards as the highest state of the individual, and the desire to attain it he evidently considers the supreme motive by which the individual should be governed.   The analogue in political life to this highest state of the individual is the direction of the 'imperium' by a 'libera multitudo' to the attainment of 'pax vitæque securitas' in the high sense which he attaches to those words in *Tract. Pol.* cap. V.[1]

---

[1] Cp. *Eth.* IV. *Appendix,* xxxii. 'Ea quæ nobis eveniunt contra id, quod nostræ utilitatis ratio postulat, æquo animo feremus, si conscii simus nos functos nostro officio fuisse, et potentiam, quam habemus, non potuisse se eo usque extendere, ut eadem vitare possemus, nosque partem totius naturæ esse, cujus ordinem sequimur. Quod si clare et distincte intelligamus, pars illa nostri, quæ intelligentia definitur, hoc est, pars melior nostri, in eo plane acquiescet et in ea acquiescentia perseverare conabitur. Nam quatenus intelligimus, nihil appetere nisi id, quod necessarium est, nec absolute nisi in veris acquiescere possumus; adeoque quatenus hæc recte intelligimus, eatenus

41. The conclusion, then, is that Spinoza did really, though not explicitly, believe in a final cause determining human life. That is to say, he held that the conception of an end consisting in the greater perfection of life on the part of the individual and the community might, and to some extent did, determine the life of the individual and the community. He would have said no doubt that this end, like every good, existed only in our consciousness; that it was ' nihil positivum in rebus in se consideratis ' (*Ethics*, **IV.** Preface); but an existence of the end in human consciousness, determining human action, is a sufficiently real existence, without being ' positivum in rebus.' But he made the mistake of ignoring the more confused and mixed forms in which the conception of this end operates; of recognising it only in the forms of the philosophic ' amor Dei,' or in the wisdom of the exceptional citizen, whom alone he would admit ' ratione duci.' And in particular he failed to notice that it is the consciousness of such an end to which his powers may be directed, that constitutes the individual's claim to exercise them as rights, just as it is the recognition of them by a society as capable of such direction which renders them actually rights; in short that, just as according to him nothing is good or evil but thinking makes it so, so it is only thinking that makes a might a right,—a certain conception of the might as relative to a social good on the part at once of the person or persons exercising it, and of a society which it affects.

conatus melioris partis nostri cum ordine totius naturæ convenit.' *Eth.* IV. Preface . . . ' Per *bonum* . . . intelligam id, quod certo scimus medium esse, ut ad exemplar humanæ naturæ, quod nobis proponimus, magis magisque accedamus. . . . Deinde homines *perfectiores* aut *imperfectiores* dicemus, quatenus ad hoc idem exemplar magis aut minus accedunt.'

C. HOBBES

42. ALL the more fruitful elements in Spinoza's political doctrine are lacking in that of Hobbes, but the principle of the two theories is very much the same. Each begins with the supposition of an existence of human individuals, unaffected by society, and each struggling for existence against the rest, so that men are 'natura hostes.' Each conceives 'jus naturale' as = 'potentia naturalis.' But Spinoza carries out this conception much more consistently. He does not consider that the natural right, which is might, ceases to exist or becomes anything else when a multitude combine their natural rights or mights in an 'imperium.' If the ostensible 'imperium' comes into collision with the powers of individuals, single or combined, among those who have hitherto been subject to it, and proves the weaker, it *ipso facto* ceases to be an 'imperium.' Not having superior power, it no longer has superior right to the 'subditi.' It is on this principle, as we have seen, that he deals with the question of limitations to the right of a sovereign. Its rights are limited because its powers are so. Exercised in certain ways and directions they defeat themselves. Thus as he puts it in *Epist.* L. (where he points out his difference from Hobbes), 'Supremo magistratui in qualibet urbe non plus in subditos juris, quam juxta mensuram potestatis, qua subditum superat, competere statuo.' Hobbes, on the other hand, supposes his sovereign power to have an absolute right to the submission of all its subjects, singly or collectively, irrespectively of the question of its actual power against them. This right he considers it to derive from a covenant by which individuals, weary of the state of war, have agreed to devolve their 'personæ,' in the language of Roman law, upon some individual or collection of individuals, which is henceforward to represent them, and to be considered as acting with their combined powers. This covenant being in the nature of the case irrevocable, the sovereign derives from it an indefeasible right to direct the actions of all members of the society over which it is sovereign.

43. The doctrine may be found in *Leviathan*, Part II., chapter 17. In order 'to erect such a common power as may be able to defend them from the invasion of foreigners and the injuries of one another,' men 'confer all their power and strength upon one man or upon one assembly of men,' . . . i.e. 'appoint one man or assembly of men to bear their person. . . . This is more than consent and concord; it is a real unity of them all in one and the same person, made by covenant of every man with every man, in such a manner as if every man should say to every man, 'I authorise, and give up my right of governing myself to this man or this assembly of men, on condition that thou give up thy right to him and authorise all his actions in like manner.' This done, the multitude so united in one person is called a commonwealth, in Latin *civitas* . . . which (to define it) is one person, of whose acts a great multitude by mutual covenant one with another have made themselves everyone the author, to the end he may use the strength and means of them all, as he shall think expedient, for their peace and common defence. And he that carrieth this person is called sovereign, and said to have sovereign power; and everyone besides, his subject.'

44. In order to understand the form in which the doctrine is stated, we have to bear in mind the sense in which 'persona' is used by the Roman lawyers, as=either a complex of rights, or the subject (or possessor) of those rights, whether a single individual or a corporate body. In this sense of the word, a man's person is separable from his individual existence as a man. 'Unus homo sustinet plures personas.' A magistrate, e.g.,would be one thing in respect of what he is in himself, another thing in respect of his 'persona' or complex of rights belonging to him as a magistrate, and so too a monarch. On the same principle, a man, remaining a man as before, might devolve his 'persona,' the complex of his rights, on another. A son, when by the death of his father according to Roman law he was delivered from 'patria potestas' and became in turn head of a family,

acquired a 'persona' which he had not before, the 'persona' which had previously belonged to the father. Again, to take a modern instance, the fellows of a college, as a corporation, form one 'persona,' but each of them would bear other 'persons,' if, e.g., they happened to be magistrates, or simply in respect of their rights as citizens. Thus 'one person' above = one sustainer of rights; while in the second passage, . . . 'carrieth this person,' it rather = the rights sustained.

45. Hobbes expressly states that the sovereign 'person' may be an *assembly* of men, but the natural associations of the term, when the sovereign is spoken of as a person, favour the development of a monarchical doctrine of sovereignty.

Sovereign power is attained either by acquisition or institution.   By acquisition, when a man makes his children and their children, or a conqueror his enemies, to submit under fear of death.   By institution, when men agree among themselves to submit to some man or assembly ' on confidence to be protected against all others.'   Hobbes speaks (II. 17, end) as if there were two ways by which a commonwealth and a sovereign defined as above could be brought into existence, but clearly a sovereign by acquisition is not a sovereign in the sense explained.   He does not ' carry a person of whose acts a great multitude by *mutual covenant* one with another, have made themselves everyone the author, to the end he may use the strength and means of them all, as he shall think expedient, for their peace and common defence.'   And what Hobbes describes in the sequel (c. 18) are, as he expressly says, rights of sovereigns by institution; but he seems tacitly to assume that every sovereign may claim the same, though he could hardly have supposed that the existing sovereignties were in their origin other than sovereignties by acquisition.

' A commonwealth is said to be instituted, when a multitude of men covenant, everyone with everyone, that to whatsoever man or assembly of men shall be given by the major part the right to represent the person of them all, everyone, as well he that voted for it as he that voted against it, shall authorise all the actions and judgments of that man or assembly of men, in the same manner as if they were his own, to the end to live peaceably amongst themselves, and to be protected against other men' (c. 18).   Here

a distinction is drawn between the covenant of all with all
to be bound by the act of the majority in appointing a sovereign, and that act of appointment itself which is not a
covenant of all with all. The natural conclusion would be
that it was no violation of the covenant if the majority
afterwards transferred the sovereign power to other hands.
But in the sequel Hobbes expressly makes out such a trans-
ference to be a violation of the original compact. This is an
instance of his desire to vindicate the absolute right of a *de
facto* monarch.

46. Throughout these statements we are moving in a
region of fiction from which Spinoza keeps clear. Not only
is the supposition of the devolution of wills or powers on a
sovereign by a covenant historically a fiction (about that no
more need be said) ; the notion of an obligation to observe
this covenant, as distinct from a compulsion, is inconsistent
with the supposition that there is no right other than power
prior to the act by which the sovereign power is established.
If there is no such right antecedent to the establishment of
the sovereign power, neither can there be any after its establishment except in the sense of a power on the part of individuals which the sovereign power enables them to exercise.
This power, or 'jus civile,' cannot itself belong to the
sovereign, who enables individuals to exercise it. The only
right which can belong to the sovereign is the 'jus naturale,'[1]
consisting in the superiority of his power, and this right
must be measured by the inability of the subjects to resist.
If they *can* resist, the right has disappeared. In a successful resistance, then, to an ostensibly sovereign power, there
can on the given supposition be no wrong done to that
power. To say that there is, would be a contradiction in
terms. Is such resistance, then, a violation of the 'jus
civile' as between the several subject citizens ? In the
absence of a sovereign power, no doubt, the 'jus civile'
(according to the view in question, which makes it depend
on the existence of an 'imperium') would cease to exist.
But then a successful resistance would simply show that
there was no longer such a sovereign power. It would not

---

[1] 'The 'jus naturale' is the liberty
each man hath to use his own power
as he will himself for the preservation
of his own nature ; that is to say of his
own life ; and consequently of doing
anything which in his own judgment
and reason he shall conceive to be the
aptest means thereunto.' (*Lev.,* I. 14.)

itself be a violation of 'jus civile,' but simply a proof that the conditions of 'jus civile' were no longer present. It might at the same time be a step to re-establishing them if, besides being a proof that the old 'imperium' no longer exists, it implied such a combination of powers as suffices to establish a new one.

47. No obligation, then, as distinct from compulsion, to submit to an ostensibly sovereign power can consistently be founded on a theory according to which right either = simple power, or only differs from it, in the form of 'jus civile,' through being a power which an 'imperium' enables individuals to exercise as against each other. Hobbes could not, indeed, have made out his doctrine (of the absolute submission to the sovereign) with any plausibility, if he had stated with the explicitness of Spinoza that 'jus naturale' = 'naturalis potentia.' That it is so is implied in the account of the state of things preceding the establishment of sovereignty as one of 'bellum omnium contra omnes'; for where there is no recognition of a common good, there can be no right in any other sense than power. But where there are no rights but natural power, no obligatory covenant can be made. In order, however, to get a sovereignty, to which there is a perpetual obligation of submission, Hobbes has to suppose a covenant of all with all, preceding the establishment of sovereignty, and to the observance of which, therefore, there cannot be an obligation in the sense that the sovereign punishes for the non-observance (the obligation corresponding to 'jus civile' in Spinoza's sense), but which no one can ever be entitled to break. As the obligatoriness of this covenant, then, cannot be derived from the sovereignty which is established through it, Hobbes has to ascribe it to a 'law of nature' which enjoins 'that men perform their covenants made' (*Lev.*, I. 15). Yet in the immediate sequel of this passage he says expressly, 'The nature of justice consisteth in the keeping of valid covenants, but the validity of covenants begins not but with the constitution of a civil power, sufficient to compel men to keep them; and then it is also that propriety begins.' On this principle the covenant by which a civil power is for the first time constituted cannot be a valid covenant. The men making it are not in a position to make a valid covenant at all. The 'law of nature,' to which alone Hobbes

can appeal according to his principles, as the source of the
obligatoriness of the covenant of all with all, he defines as a
'precept or general rule, found out by reason, by which a
man is forbidden to do that which is destructive of his life,
or taketh away the means of preserving the same ; and to
omit that by which he thinketh it may best be preserved'
(I. 14). When a law of nature, however, is said to command
or forbid, we must not understand those terms in that sense
which, according to Hobbes, could only be derived from
the establishment of an 'imperium.' This 'law of nature,'
therefore, is merely an expression in a general form of the
instinct by which, as Spinoza says, every living creature ' in
suo esse perseverare conatur,' as guided by a calculation
of consequences (for no meaning but this can be given to
'reason' according to Hobbes). The prohibition, then, by
this law of nature of a breach of that covenant of all with
all, by which a sovereign power is supposed to be established,
can properly mean nothing more than that it is everyone's
interest to adhere to it. This, however, could only be a
conditional prohibition, conditional, in particular, on the
way in which the sovereign power is exercised. Hobbes
tries to show that it must always be for the advantage of
all to obey it, because not to do so is to return to the state of
universal war ; but a successful resistance to it must be *ipso
facto* an establishment of a new combined power which
prevents the 'bellum omnium contra omnes' from returning.
At any rate, an obligation to submit to the established
'imperium,' measured by the self-interest of each in doing
so, is quite a different thing from the obligation which
Hobbes describes in terms only appropriate (according to
his own showing) to contracts between individuals enforced
by a sovereign power.

48. It would seem that Hobbes' desire to prove all resistance to established sovereignty unjustifiable leads him to
combine inconsistent doctrines. He adopts the notion that
men are ' natura hostes,' that 'jus naturale ' = mere power,
because it illustrates the benefit to man's estate derived from
the establishment of a supreme power and the effects of the
subversion of such power once established, which he assumes
to be equivalent to a return to a state of nature. But this
notion does not justify the view that a rebellion, which is
strong enough to succeed, is wrong. For this purpose he has

to resort to the representation of the sovereign as having a right distinct from power, founded on a contract of all with all, by which sovereignty is established. This representation is quite alien to Spinoza, with whom sovereignty arises, it is true, when 'plures in unum conveniunt,' but in the sense of combining their powers, not of contracting. But after all, the fiction of this contract will not serve the purpose which Hobbes wants it to serve. The sovereignty established by the contract can only have a *natural* right to be maintained inviolate, for all other right presupposes it, and cannot be presupposed by it. If this natural right means mere power, then upon a successful rebellion it disappears. If it means anything else it must mean that there are natural rights of men, other than their mere power, which are violated by its subversion. But if there are such rights, there must equally be a possibility of collision between the sovereign power and these natural rights, which would justify a resistance to it.

49. It may be asked whether it is worth while to examine the internal consistency of a theory which turns upon what is admitted to be historically a fiction, the supposition of a contract of all with all. There are fictions and fictions however. The supposition that some event took place which as a matter of history did not take place may be a way of conveying an essentially true conception of some moral relation of man. The great objection to the representation of the right of a sovereign power over subjects, and the rights of individuals which are enforced by this 'imperium,' as having arisen out of a contract of all with all, is that it conveys a false notion of rights. It is not merely that the possibility of such a contract being made presupposes just that state of things—a *régime* of recognised and enforced obligations—which it is assumed to account for. Since those who contract must already have rights, the representation of society with its obligations as formed by contract implies that individuals have certain rights, independently of society and of their functions as members of a society, which they bring with them to the transaction. But such rights abstracted from social function and recognition could only be powers, or (according to Hobbes' definition) liberties to use powers, which comes to the same; i.e. they would not be rights at all; and from no combination or devolution of them could any right

in the proper sense, anything more than a combined power, arise.

50. Thus the only logical development of that separation of right from social duty which is implied in the doctrine of ' social contract,' is that of Spinoza. Happily the doctrine has not been logically developed by those whose way of thinking has been affected by it. The reduction of political right—the right of the state over its subjects—to superior power, has not been popularly accepted, though the general conception of *national* right seems pretty much to identify it with power. Among the enlightened, indeed, there has of late appeared a tendency to adopt a theory very like that of Spinoza, without the higher elements which we noticed in Spinoza; to consider all right as a power attained in that ' struggle for existence' to which human ' progress' is reduced. But for one person, who, as a matter of speculation, considers the right of society over him to be a disguised might, there are thousands who, as a matter of practice, regard their own right as independent of that correlation to duty without which it is merely a might. The popular effect of the notion that the individual brings with him into society certain rights which he does not derive from society,—which are other than claims to fulfil freely (i.e. for their own sake) certain functions towards society,—is seen in the inveterate irreverence of the individual towards the state, in the assumption that he has rights against society irrespectively of his fulfilment of any duties to society, that all ' powers that be ' are restraints upon his natural freedom which he may rightly defy as far as he safely can.

D. LOCKE

51. It was chiefly Rousseau who gave that cast to the
doctrine of the origin of political obligation in contract, in
which it best lends itself to the assertion of rights apart from
duties on the part of individuals, in opposition to the counter-
fallacy which claims rights for the state irrespectively of its
fulfilment of its function as securing the rights of individuals.
It is probably true that the *Contrat Social* had great effect
on the founders of American independence, an effect which
appears in the terms of the Declaration of Independence
and in preambles to the constitutions of some of the original
American states.   But the essential ideas of Rousseau are
to be found in Locke's *Treatise of Civil Government,* which
was probably well known in America for half a century
before Rousseau was heard of.[1]   Locke again constantly
appeals to Hooker's first book on *Ecclesiastical Polity,*[2] and
Grotius[3] argues in exactly the same strain.

Hooker, Grotius, Hobbes, Locke, and Rousseau only
differ in their application of the same conception ; viz. that
men live first in a state of nature, subject to a law of
nature, also called the law of reason ; that in this state they
are in some sense free and equal ; that 'finding many inconveniences' in it they covenant with each other to establish a

---

[1] Locke, *Civil Government,* chap. vii.
sec. 87. 'Man, being born with a
title to perfect freedom, and an uncontrolled enjoyment of all the rights
and privileges of the law of nature,
equally with any other man or number
of men in the world, hath by nature a
power not only to preserve his life,
liberty, and estate against . . . other
men ; but to judge of and punish the
breaches of that law in others. . . .
There, and there only, is political society
where every one of the members hath
quitted this natural power, resigned it
up into the hands of the community in

all cases that exclude him not from
appealing for protection to the law established by it.'

[2] 'Laws human, of what kind so-
ever, are available by consent,' Hooker,
Eccl. Pol. I. 10 (quoted by Locke, *l. c.*
chap. xi. sec. 134). 'To be commanded
we do consent, when that society, where-
of we be a part, hath at any time before
consented, without revoking the same
after by the like universal agreement.'
Hooker ; *ibid.*

[3] *De jure belli et pacis,* Proleg. secs.
15 and 16.

government—a covenant which they are bound by the 'law
of nature' to observe—and that out of this covenant the
obligation of submission to the 'powers that be' arises.
Spinoza alone takes a different line : he does not question
the state of nature or the origin of government in a combination of men who find the state of nature 'inconvenient';
but he regards this combination as one of powers directed to
a common end, and constituting superior force, not as a
covenant which men are bound by the law of nature to
observe.

52. The common doctrine is so full of ambiguities that
it readily lends itself to opposite applications. In the first
place 'state of nature' may be understood in most different
senses. The one idea common to all the writers who suppose
such a state to have preceded that of civil society is a
negative one. It was a state which was *not* one of political
society, one in which there was no civil government; i.e.
no supreme power, exercised by a single person or plurality
of persons, which could compel obedience on the part of all
members of a society, and was recognised as entitled to do so
by them all, or by a sufficient number of them to secure
general obedience. But was it one of society at all? Was
it one in which men had no dealings with each other except
in the way of one struggling to make another serve his will
and to get for himself what the other had, or was it one
in which there were ties of personal affection and common
interest, and recognised obligations, between man and man?
Evidently among those who spoke of a state of nature, there
were very various and wavering conceptions on this point.
They are apt to make an absolute opposition between the
state of nature and the political state, and to represent men
as having suddenly contracted themselves out of one into
the other. Yet evidently the contract would have been
impossible unless society in a form very like that distinctively called political had been in existence beforehand.
If political society is to be supposed to have originated in a
pact at all, the difference between it and the preceding state
of nature cannot, with any plausibility, be held to have been
much more than a difference between a society regulated by
written law and officers with defined power and one regulated
by customs and tacitly recognised authority.

53. Again, it was held that in a state of nature men were

'free and equal.' This is maintained by Hobbes as much as by the founders of American independence. But if freedom is to be understood in the sense in which most of these writers seem to understand it, as a power of executing, of giving effect to, one's will, the amount of freedom possessed in a state of nature, if that was a state of detachment and collision between individuals, must have been very small. Men must have been constantly thwarting each other, and (in the absence of that 'jus in naturam,' as Spinoza calls it, which combination gives) thwarted by powers of nature. In such a state those only could be free, in the sense supposed, who were *not* equal to the rest; who, in virtue of superior power, could use the rest. But whether we suppose an even balance of weaknesses, in subjection to the crushing forces of nature, or a dominion of few over many by means of superior strength, in such a state of nature no general pact would be possible. No equality in freedom is possible except for members of a society of whom each recognises a good of the whole which is also his own, and to which the free co-operation of all is necessary. But if such society is supposed in the state of nature—and otherwise the 'pact' establishing political society would be impossible—it is already in principle the same as political society.

54. It is not always certain whether the writers in question considered men to be actually free and equal in the state of nature, or only so according to the 'law of nature,' which might or might not be observed. (Hobbes represents the freedom and equality in the state of nature as actual, and this state as being for that reason 'bellum omnium contra omnes.') They all, however, implicitly assume a *consciousness* of the law of nature in the state of nature. It is thus not a law of nature in the sense in which we commonly use the term. It is not a law according to which the agents subject to it act necessarily but without consciousness of the law. It is a law of which the agent subject to it has a consciousness, but one according to which he may or may not act; i.e. one according to which he *ought* to act. It is from it that the obligation to submission to civil government, according to all these writers, is derived. But in regard to such a law, two questions have to be asked: firstly, how can the consciousness of obligation arise without recognition by the individual of claims on the part of others—social claims

in some form or other—which may be opposed to his momentary inclinations? and secondly, given a society of men capable of such a consciousness of obligation, constituting a law according to which the members of the society are free and equal, in what does it differ from a political society? If these questions had been fairly considered, it must have been seen that the distinction between a political society and a state of nature, governed by such a law of nature, was untenable; that a state of things out of which political society could have arisen by compact, must have been one in which the individual regarded himself as a member of a society which has claims on him and on which he has claims, and that such society is already in principle a political society. But the ambiguity attending the conception of the law of nature prevented them from being considered. When the writers in question spoke of a law of nature, to which men in the state of nature were subject, they did not make it clear to themselves that this law, as understood by them, could not exist at all without there being some recognition or consciousness of it on the part of those subject to it. The designation of it as 'law of nature' or 'law of God' helped to disguise the fact that there was no imponent of it, in the sense in which a law is imposed on individuals by a political superior. In the absence of such an imponent, unless it is either a uniformity in the relations of natural events or an irresistible force —and it is not represented in either of these ways in juristic writings—it can only mean a recognition of obligation arising in the consciousness of the individual from his relations to society. But this not being clearly realised, it was possible to represent the law of nature as antecedent to the laws imposed by a political superior, without its being observed that this implied the antecedence of a condition of things in which the result supposed to be obtained through the formation of political society—the establishment, viz. of reciprocal claims to freedom and equality on the part of members of a society—already existed.

55. In fact, the condition of society in which it could properly be said to be governed by a law of nature, i.e. by an obligation of which there is no imponent but the consciousness of man, an obligation of which the breach is not punished by a political superior, is not antecedent to political society, but one which it gradually tends to produce. It is

the radical fault of the theory which finds the origin of political society in compact, that it has to reverse the true process. To account for the possibility of the compact of all with all, it has to assume a society subject to a law of nature, prescribing the freedom and equality of all. But a society governed by such a law as a law of nature, i.e. with no imponent but man's consciousness, would have been one from which political society would have been a decline, one in which there could have been no motive to the establishment of civil government. Thus this theory must needs be false to itself in one of two ways. Either it is false to the conception of a law of nature, with its prescription of freedom and equality, as governing the state of things prior to the compact by which political society is established, only introducing the law of nature as the ground of the obligatoriness of that compact, but treating the state of nature as one of universal war in which no reciprocal claims of any sort were recognised, (so Hobbes); or just so far as it realises the conception of a society governed by a law of nature, as equivalent to that spontaneous recognition by each of the claims of all others, without which the covenant of all with all is in fact unaccountable, it does away with any appearance of necessity for the transition from the state of nature to that of political society and tends to represent the latter as a decline from the former. This result is seen in Rousseau; but to a great extent Rousseau had been anticipated by Locke. The broad differences between Locke and Hobbes in their development of the common doctrine, are (1) that Locke denies that the state of nature is a state of war, and (2) that Locke distinguishes the act by which political society is established from that by which the government, legislative and executive, is established, and is consequently able to distinguish the dissolution of the political society from the dissolution of the government (*Civ. Gov.* Chapter XIX. § 211).

56. The 'state of nature' and the 'state of war' 'are so far distant as a state of peace, good-will, mutual assistance and preservation, and a state of enmity, malice, violence, and mutual destruction, are from one another. Men living together, according to reason, without a common superior on earth with authority to judge between them, is properly the state of nature. But force, or a declared design of force, upon the person of another, where there is no common

superior on earth to appeal to for relief, is the state of war '
(*Civ. Gov.* III. § 19). In the state of nature, however, when the
state of war has once begun, there is not the same means of
terminating it as in civil society.

The right of war may belong to a man, 'though he be in
society and a fellow-subject,' when his person or property is
in such immediate danger that it is impossible to appeal for
relief to the common superior. 'But when the actual force
is over, the state of war ceases between those that are in
society . . . because there lies the remedy of appeal for the
past injury and to prevent future harm.' In the state of
nature, when the state of war has once begun, it continues
until the aggressor offers peace and reparation. The state
of war, though not proper to the state of nature, is a frequent
incident of it, and to avoid it is one great reason of men's
putting themselves into society (*ib.* § 21). The state of
nature is not one that is altogether over and done with.
'All rulers of independent governments all through the
world are in a state of nature.' The members of one state
in dealing with those of another are in a state of nature, and
the law of nature alone binds them. 'For truth and keeping
of faith belongs to men as men, and not as members of
society' (*Civ. Gov.* II. § 14). 'All men are naturally in that
state and remain so till by their own consents they make
themselves members of some politic society' (*ib.* § 15).

57. The antithesis, as put above, between the state of
nature and the state of war, can only be maintained on the
supposition that the 'law of nature' is observed in a state of
nature. Locke does not explicitly state that this is the case.
If it were so, it would not appear how the state of war
should arise in the state of nature. But he evidently
thought of the state of nature as one in which men recognised the law of nature, though without fully observing it.
He quotes with approval from Hooker language which
implies that not only is the state of nature a state of
equality, but that in it there is such consciousness of
equality with each other on the part of men that they
recognise the principle 'do as you would be done by'
(*Civ. Gov.* II. § 5). With Hobbes, in the supposed state of
nature the 'law of nature' is emphatically *not* observed,
and hence it is a state of war. As has been pointed out
above, a 'law of nature' in the sense in which these writers

use the term, as a law which obliges but yet has no imponent in the shape of a sovereign power, is, as Locke says (§ 136), 'nowhere to be found but in the minds of men'; it can only have its being in the consciousness of those subject to it. If therefore we are to suppose a state of nature in which such a law of nature exists, it is more consistent to conceive it in Locke's way than in that of Hobbes; more con- sistent to conceive it as one in which men recognise duties to each other than as a 'bellum omnium contra omnes.'

58. As to the second point, from his own conception of what men are in the state of nature, and of the ends for which they found political societies, Locke derives certain necessary limitations of what the supreme power in a commonwealth may rightfully do. The prime business of the political society, once formed, is to establish the legis- lative power. This is 'sacred and unalterable in the hands where the community have once placed it' (*Civ. Gov.* XI. § 134); 'unalterable,' that is, as we gather from the sequel, by anything short of an act of the community which origin- ally placed it in these hands. But as men in a state of nature have 'no arbitrary power' over each other (which must mean that according to the 'law of nature' they have no such power), so they cannot transfer any such power to the community nor it to the legislature. No legislature can have the right to destroy, enslave, or designedly impoverish the subjects. And as no legislature can be entitled to do anything which the individual in the state of nature would not by the law of nature be entitled to do, so its great business is to declare the law of nature in general terms and administer it by known authorised judges. The state of nature, Locke seemed to think, would have done very well, but for the inconvenience of every man being judge in his own case of what the law of nature requires. It is to remedy this inconvenience by establishing (1) a settled law, received by common consent, (2) a known and indifferent judge, (3) a power to enforce the decisions of such a judge, that political society is formed.

Hence a legislature violates the 'trust that is put in it' by society unless it observes the following rules: (1) it is to govern 'by promulgated established laws,' not to be varied to suit particular interests; (2) these laws are to be designed only for the good of the people; (3) it must not raise taxes but by consent of the people through themselves or their deputies; (4) it neither 'must, nor can, transfer the power of making laws to anybody else, or place it anywhere but where the people have' (*Civ. Gov.* XI. § 142).

59. Thus 'the legislative being only a fiduciary power to act for certain ends, there remains still in the people a supreme power to remove or alter the legislature.' Subject to this ultimate 'sovereignty' (a term which Locke does not use) of the people, the legislative is necessarily the supreme power, to which the executive is subordinate. An appearance to the contrary can only arise in cases where (as in England) the supreme executive power is held by a person who has also a share in the legislative. Such a person may 'in a very tolerable sense be called supreme.' It is not, however, to him as supreme legislator (which he is not, but only a participator in supreme legislation) but to him as supreme executor of the law that oaths of allegiance are taken. It is only as executing the law that he can claim obedience, his executive power being, like the power of the legislative, 'a fiduciary trust placed in him' to enforce obedience to law and that only (*Civ. Gov.* XIII. § 151). This distinction of the supreme power of the people from that of the supreme executive, corresponding to a distinction between the act of transferring individual powers to a society and the subsequent act by which that society establishes a particular form of government, enables Locke to distinguish what Hobbes had confounded, the dissolution of government and the dissolution of political society.

60. He gets rid of Hobbes' notion, that because the 'covenant of all with all,' by which a sovereignty is established, is irrevocable, therefore the government once established is unalterable. He conceives the original pact merely as an agreement to form a civil society, which must indeed have a government, but not necessarily always the same government. The pact is a transfer by individuals of their natural rights to a society, and can only be cancelled through the dissolution of the society by foreign conquest. The delegation by the society of legislative and executive powers to a person or persons is a different matter. The society always retains the right, according to Locke, of resuming the powers thus delegated, and must exercise the right in the event either of the legislative being altered,

(placed in different hands from those originally intended), of
a collision between its executive and legislative officers, or of
a breach between different branches of the legislature (when
as in England there are such different branches), or when
legislative and executive or either of them ' act contrary to
their trust.' He thus in effect vindicates the right of revolution, ascribing to a ' sovereign people ' the attributes which
Hobbes assigned to a ' person,' single or corporate, on which
the people forming a society were supposed by an irrevocable
act to have devolved their powers. In other words, he considered the whole civil society in all cases to have the rights
which Hobbes would only have allowed it to possess where
the government was not a monarchy or aristocracy but a
democracy; i.e. where the supreme ' person ' upon which
all devolve their several ' personæ ' is an ' assembly of all
who will come together.' As such a democracy did not then
exist in Europe, any more than it does now, except in some
Swiss cantons, the practical difference between the two
views was very great. Both Locke and Hobbes wrote with
a present political object in view, Hobbes wishing to condemn the Rebellion, Locke to justify the Revolution. For
practical purposes, Locke's doctrine is much the better; but
if Hobbes' translation of the irrevocableness of the covenant
of all with all into the illegitimacy of resistance to an established government in effect entitles any tyrant [1] to do as
he likes, on the other hand, it is impossible upon Locke's
theory to pronounce when resistance to a *de facto* government is legitimate or otherwise. It would be legitimate
according to him when it is an act of the ' sovereign people '
(not that Locke uses the phrase), superseding a government
which has been false to its trust. But this admitted, all
sorts of questions arise as to the means of ascertaining what
is and what is not an act of the ' sovereign people.'

61. The rapid success of the revolution without popular
disorder prevented Locke's theory from becoming of importance, but in the presence of such sectarian enthusiasm as
existed in Hobbes' time it would have become dangerous.
It would not any more than that of Hobbes justify resistance
to ' the powers that be ' on the part of any body of men
short of the civil society acting as a whole, i.e. by a majority.

[1] According to Hobbes, tyranny = 'monarchy misliked'; oligarchy = 'aristocracy
misliked.'

The sectaries of the time of the Rebellion, in pleading a natural or divine right to resist the orders of the government, would have been as much condemned by Locke's theory as by that of Hobbes. But who can say when any popular action by which established powers, legislative or executive, are resisted or altered is an act of the ' sovereign people,' of the civil society acting as a whole, or no. Where government is democratic, in Hobbes' sense, i.e. vested in an assembly of all who will come together, the act of the ' sovereign people ' is unmistakeable. It is the act of the majority of such an assembly. But in such a case the difficulty cannot arise. There can be no withdrawal by the sovereign people of power from its legislative or executive representatives, since it has no such representatives. In any other case it would seem impossible to say whether any resistance to, or deposition of, an established legislative or executive is the act of the majority of the society or no Any sectary or revolutionary may plead that he has the ' sovereign people ' on his side. If he fails, it is not certain that he has them not on his side ; for it may be that, though he has the majority of the society on his side, yet the society has allowed the growth within it of a power which prevents it from giving effect to its will. On the other hand, if the revolution succeeds, it is not certain that it had the majority on its side when it began, though the majority may have come to acquiesce in its result. In short, on Locke's principle that any particular government derives its authority from an act of the society, and society by a like act may recall the authority, how can we ever be entitled to say that such an act has been exercised ?

62. It is true that there is no greater difficulty about supposing it to be exercised in the dissolution than in the establishment of a government, indeed not so much ; but the act of first establishing a government is thrown back into an indefinite past. It may easily be taken for granted without further inquiry into the conditions of its possibility. On the other hand, as the act of legitimately dissolving a government or superseding one by another has to be imagined as taking place in the present, the inquiry into the conditions of its possibility cannot well be avoided. If we have once assumed with Hobbes and Locke, that the authority of government is derived from a covenant of all with all,

—either directly or mediately by a subsequent act in which
the covenanted society delegates its powers to a representative or representatives,—it will follow that a like act is required
to cancel it; and the difficulties of conceiving such an act
under the conditions of the present are so great, that
Hobbes' view of the irrevocableness of the original act by
which any government was established has much to say
for itself. If the authority of any government—its claim on
our obedience—is held to be derived not from an original
covenant, or from any covenant, but from the function which
it serves in maintaining those conditions of freedom which
are conditions of the moral life, then no act of the people in
revocation of a prior act need be reckoned necessary to
justify its dissolution. If it ceases to serve this function, it
loses its claim on our obedience. It is a παρέκβασις. (Here
again the Greek theory, deriving the authority of government not from consent but from the end which it serves, is
sounder than the modern.) Whether or no any particular
government has on this ground lost its claim and may be
rightly resisted, is a question, no doubt, difficult for the
individual to answer with certainty. In the long run, however, it seems generally if not always to answer itself. A
government no longer serving the function described—which,
it must be remembered, is variously served according to
circumstances—brings forces into play which are fatal to it.
But if it is difficult upon this theory for the individual to
ascertain, as a matter of speculation, whether resistance to
an established government is justified or no, at any rate
upon this theory such a justification of resistance is possible.
Upon Locke's theory, the condition necessary to justify it—
viz. an act of the whole people governed—is one which, anywhere except in a Swiss canton, it would be impossible to
fulfil. For practical purposes, Locke comes to a right result
by ignoring this impossibility. Having supposed the reality
of one impossible event,—the establishment of government
by compact or by the act of a society founded on compact,—
he cancels this error in the result by supposing the possibility of another transaction equally impossible, viz. the
collective act of a people dissolving its government.

63. It is evident from the chapter (XIX.) on the 'dissolution of government' that he did not seriously contemplate
the conditions under which such an act could be exercised.

What he was really concerned about was to dispute 'the right divine to govern wrong' on the part of a legislative as much as on the part of an executive power; to maintain the principle that government is only justified by being for the good of the people, and to point out the difference between holding that some government is necessarily for the good of the people, and holding that any particular government is for their good, a difference which Hobbes had ignored. In order to do this, starting with the supposition of an actual deed on the part of a community establishing a government, he had to suppose a reserved right on the part of the community by a like deed to dissolve it. But in the only particular case in which he contemplates a loss by the legislature of its representative character, he does not suggest the establishment of another by an act of the whole people. He saw that the English Parliament in his time could not claim to be such as it could be supposed that the covenanting community originally intended it to be. 'It often comes to pass,' he says, 'in governments where part of the legislative consists of representatives chosen by the people, that in tract of time this representation becomes very unequal and disproportionate to the reasons it was first established upon. . . . The bare name of a town, of which there remains not so much as the ruins, where scarce so much housing as a sheepcote, or more inhabitants than a shepherd is to be found, sends as many representatives to the grand assembly of law-makers, as a whole county, numerous in people, and powerful in riches. This strangers stand amazed at, and everyone must confess needs a remedy; though most think it hard to find one, because the constitution of the legislative being the original and supreme act of the society antecedent to all positive laws in it, and depending wholly on the people, no inferior power can alter it. And therefore the people, when the legislative is once constituted, having, in such a government as we have been speaking of, no power to act as long as the government stands, this inconvenience is thought incapable of a remedy' (Chapter XIII. § 157). The only remedy which he suggests is not an act of the sovereign people, but an exercise of prerogative on the part of the executive, in the way of redistributing representation, which would be justified by 'salus populi suprema lex.'

E. ROUSSEAU

64. THAT ' sovereignty of the people,' which Locke looks upon as held in reserve after its original exercise in the establishment of government, only to be asserted in the event of a legislature proving false to its trust, Rousseau supposes to be in constant exercise. Previous writers had thought of the political society or commonwealth, upon its formation by compact, as instituting a sovereign. They differed chiefly on the point whether the society afterwards had or had not a right of displacing an established sovereign. Rousseau does not think of the society, *civitas* or commonwealth, as thus instituting a sovereign, but as itself in the act of its formation becoming a sovereign and ever after continuing so.

65. In his conception of a state of nature, Rousseau does not differ from Locke. He conceives the motive for passing out of it, however, somewhat differently and more after the manner of Spinoza. With Locke the motive is chiefly a sense of the desirability of having an impartial judge, and efficient enforcement of the law of nature. According to Rousseau, some pact takes place when men find the hindrances to their preservation in a state of nature too strong for the forces which each individual can bring to bear against them. This recalls Spinoza's view of the ' jus in naturam ' as acquired by a combination of the forces of individuals in civil society.

66. The ' problem of which the social contract is a solution ' Rousseau states thus : ' To find a form of association which protects with the whole common force the person and property of each associate, and in virtue of which everyone, while uniting himself to all, only obeys himself and remains as free as before.' (*Contrat Social*, I, vi.) The terms of the contract which solves this problem Rousseau states thus :

'Each of us throws into the common stock his person and all his faculties under the supreme direction of the general will; and we accept each member as an individual part of the whole. . . . There results from this act of association, in place of the several persons of the several contracting parties, a collective moral body, composed of as many members as there are voices in the assembly, which body receives from this act its unity, its common self, its life, and its will. . . . It is called by its members a *state* when it is passive, a *sovereign* when it is active, a *power* when compared with similar bodies. The associates are called collectively a *people*, severally *citizens* as sharing in the sovereign authority, *subjects* as submitted to the laws of the state.' (*Ib.*) Each of them is under an obligation in two relations, 'as a member of the sovereign body towards the individuals, and as a member of the state towards the sovereign.' All the subjects can by a public vote be placed under a particular obligation towards the sovereign, but the sovereign cannot thus incur an obligation towards itself. It cannot impose any law upon itself which it cannot cancel. Nor is there need to restrict its powers in the interest of the subjects. For the sovereign body, being formed only of the individuals which constitute it, can have no interest contrary to theirs. 'From the mere fact of its existence, it is always all that it ought to be' (since, from the very fact of its institution, all merely private interests are lost in it). On the other hand, the will of the individual (his particular interest as founded upon his particular desires) may very well conflict with that general will which constitutes the sovereign. Hence the social pact necessarily involves a tacit agreement, that anyone refusing to conform to the general will shall be forced to do so by the whole body politic; in other words, 'shall be forced to be free,' since the universal conformity to the general will is the guarantee to each individual of freedom from dependence on any other person or persons. (I, vii.)

67. The result to the individual may be stated thus. He exchanges the natural liberty to do and get what he can, a liberty limited by his relative strength, for a liberty at once limited and secured by the general will; he exchanges the mere possession of such things as he can get, a possession which is the effect of force, for a property founded on a positive title, on the guarantee of society. At the same

time he becomes a moral agent. Justice instead of instinct
becomes the guide of his actions. For the moral slavery to
appetite he substitutes the moral freedom which consists in
obedience to a self-imposed law. Now for the first time it
can be said that there is anything which he *ought* to do, as
distinguished from that which he is *forced* to do. (I, viii.)

68. Such language makes it clear that the sovereignty
of which Rousseau discusses the origin and attributes, is
something essentially different from the supreme coercive
power which previous writers on the 'jus civile' had in
view. A contemporary of Hobbes had said that

> 'there's on earth a yet auguster thing,
> Veiled though it be, than Parliament and King.'

It is to this ' auguster thing,' not to such supreme power as
English lawyers held to be vested in ' Parliament and King,'
that Rousseau's account of the sovereign is really applicable.
What he says of it is what Plato or Aristotle might have
said of the θεῖος νοῦς, which is the source of the laws and
discipline of the ideal polity, and what a follower of Kant
might say of the 'pure practical reason,' which renders the
individual obedient to a law of which he regards himself, in
virtue of his reason, as the author, and causes him to treat
humanity equally in the person of others and in his own
always as an end, never merely as a means. But all the
while Rousseau himself thinks that he is treating of the
sovereign in the ordinary sense; in the sense of some power
of which it could be reasonably asked how it was established
in the part where it resides, when and by whom and in
what way it is exercised. A reader of him who is more or
less familiar with the legal conception of sovereignty, but
not at all with that of practical reason or of a 'general will,'
a common ego, which wills nothing but what is for the
common good, is pretty sure to retain the idea of supreme
coercive power as the attribute of sovereignty, and to ignore
the attribute of pure disinterestedness, which, according to
Rousseau, must characterise every act that can be ascribed to
the sovereign.

69. The practical result is a vague exaltation of the prerogatives of the sovereign people, without any corresponding
limitation of the conditions under which an act is to be
deemed that of the sovereign people. The justifiability of
laws and acts of government, and of the rights which these

confer, comes to be sought simply in the fact that the people wills them, not in the fact that they represent a true 'volonté générale,' an impartial and disinterested will for the common good. Thus the question of what really needs to be enacted by the state in order to secure the conditions under which a good life is possible, is lost sight of in the quest for majorities; and as the will of the people in any other sense than the measure of what the people will tolerate is really unascertainable in the great nations of Europe, the way is prepared for the sophistries of modern political management, for manipulating electoral bodies, for influencing elected bodies, and procuring plébiscites.

70. The incompatibility between the ideal attributes which Rousseau ascribes to the sovereign and any power that can actually be exercised by any man or body of men becomes clearer as we proceed. He expressly distinguishes 'sovereignty' from power, and on the ground of this distinction holds that it cannot be alienated, represented, or divided. 'Sovereignty being simply the exercise of the general will can never be alienated, and the sovereign, who is only a collective being, can only be represented by himself. Power can be transmitted, but not will.' (II, i.) In order to the possibility of a representation of the general will, there must be a permanent accord between it and the individual will or wills of the person or persons representing it. But such *permanent* accord is impossible. (*Ib.*) Again, a general will is from the nature of the case indivisible. It is commonly held to be divided, not, indeed, in respect of its source, but in respect of the objects to which its acts are directed, e.g. into legislative and executive powers; into rights of taxation, of war, of justice, &c. But this supposed division of sovereign powers or rights implies that 'what are only emanations from the sovereign authority are taken to be parts of it.' (II, ii.) The only exercise of sovereign power, properly so called, is in legislation, and there is no proper act of legislation except when the whole people comes to a decision with reference to the whole people. Then the matter decided on is as general as the will which decides on it; and this is what constitutes a law. (II, vi.) By this consideration several questions are answered. Whose office is it to make laws? It is that of the general will, which can neither be alienated nor represented. Is the prince above the law?

The answer is, He is a member of the state, and cannot be so. Can the law be unjust? No one can be unjust to himself: therefore not the whole people to the whole people. How can we be free and yet subject to the laws? The laws are the register of our own will. (*Ib.*) Laws, in short, are properly those general ' conditions of civil association ' which the associates impose on themselves. Where either of the specified conditions is lacking, where either it is not the universal will from which an ordinance proceeds or it is not the whole people to which it relates, it is not a law but a decree, not an act of sovereignty but of magistracy. (*Ib.*)

71. This leads to a consideration of the nature and institution of magistracy or government. (III, i.) The government is never the same as the sovereign. The two are distinguished by their functions, that of the one being legislative, that of the other executive. Even where the people itself governs, its acts of government must be distinguished from its acts of sovereignty, the former having a particular, the latter a general, reference. Government is the exercise according to law of the executive power, and the ' prince ' or ' magistrate ' is the man or body of men charged with this administration; ' a body intermediary between the subjects and the sovereign, charged with the execution of the laws, and with the maintenance of civil and political freedom ' (*Ib.*) Where all or most of the citizens are magistrates, or charged with the supreme functions of government, we have a democracy; where a few, an aristocracy; where one is so charged, a monarchy. (III, iii.) The differences depend, not as Hobbes and others had supposed, on the quarter where the sovereignty resides—for it must always reside in the whole body of people—but on that in which government resides. The idea of government is that the dominant will of the prince should be the general will or law, that it should be simply the public force by which that general will is brought to bear on individuals or against other states, serving the same purpose in the state as the union of soul and body in the individual (III, i.); and this idea is most likely to be satisfied under a democracy. There, the general will (if there *is* a general will, which the democracy is no guarantee for there being, according to Rousseau's distinction between the ' volonté générale ' and ' volonté de tous,' of which more hereafter) cannot fail to coincide with the

dominant will of the government. The prevalence of particular interests may prevent there being a will at all of the kind which Rousseau would count general or truly sovereign, but they cannot be more prevalent in the magistracy, constituted by the whole people, than in the same people acting in the way of legislation. In a democracy, therefore, the will of the sovereign, so far as there is a sovereign in the proper sense, necessarily finds expression in the will of the magistracy. On the other hand, though under either of the other forms of government there is danger of collision between sovereign and government, yet the force of the government is greater than in a democracy. It is greatest when the government is a monarchy, because under all other forms there is more or less discrepancy between the individual wills of the several persons composing the government, as directed to the particular good of each, and the corporate will of the government of which the object is its own efficiency, and under a monarchy this source of weakness is avoided. (III, ii.) As there is more need of force in the government in proportion to the number of subjects whose particular wills it has to control, it follows that monarchy is best suited to the largest, democracy to the smallest states. (III, iii.)

72. As to the institution of government, Rousseau maintains strenuously that it is not established by contract. 'There is only one contract in the state, viz. that of the original association; and this excludes every other. No other public contract can be imagined which would not be a violation of the first.' (III, xvi.) Even when government is vested in an hereditary body, monarchic or aristocratic, this is merely a provisional arrangement, made and liable to be reversed by the sovereign, whose officers the governors are. The act by which government is established is twofold, consisting firstly of the passing of a law by the sovereign, to the effect that there shall be a government; secondly, of an act in execution of this law, by which the governors—the 'magistrates'—are appointed. But it may be asked, How can the latter act, being one not of sovereignty but of magistracy (for it has a particular reference in the designation of the governors), be performed when as yet there is no government? The answer is that the people resolves itself from a sovereign body into a body of magistrates, as the English

Parliament resolves itself constantly from a legislative body into a committee. In other words, by a simple act of the general will a democracy is for the time established, which then proceeds either to retain the government in its own hands, or to place it in those of an officer, according to the form in which the sovereign has decided to establish the government. (III, xvii.) Acts similar to that by which the government was originally constituted need to be periodically repeated in order to prevent the government from usurping the functions of the sovereign, i.e. the function of legislation. (Could this usurpation occur under a democracy?) In order that the sovereignty may not fall into abeyance, it must be exercised, and it can only be exercised in assemblies of the whole people. These must be held periodically, and at their opening two questions ought to be submitted; one, whether it pleases the sovereign to maintain the present form of government; the other, whether it pleases the people to leave the administration in the hands of those at present charged with it. (III, xviii.) Such assemblies are entitled to revise and repeal all previously enacted laws. A law not so repealed the sovereign must be taken tacitly to confirm, and it retains its authority. But as the true sovereign is not any law but the general will, no law, even the most fundamental, can be exempt from liability to repeal. Even the social pact itself might legitimately be dissolved, by agreement of all the citizens assembled. (*Ib.*) (Whether unanimity is necessary for the purpose is not specified.) Without such assemblies there can be no exercise of the general will (which, as before stated, cannot be represented), and consequently no freedom. The English people, e.g., is quite mistaken in thinking itself free. It is only free while the election of members of Parliament is going on. As soon as they are elected, it is in bondage, it is nothing. In the short moments of its freedom it makes such a bad use of it that it well deserves to lose it. (III, xv.)

73. It appears from the above that, according to Rousseau, the general will, which is the true sovereign, can only be exercised in assemblies of the whole people. On the other hand, he does not hold that an act of such an assembly is necessarily an act of the general will. After telling us that the ' general will is always right, and always tends to the public good,' he adds, ' but it does not follow that the delibe-

rations of the people have always the same rectitude. . . .
There is often a great difference between the will of all and
the general will. The latter only looks to the common interest; the other looks to private interests, and is only a sum
of the wills of individuals.' (II, iii.) Again (II, iv.), 'that
which generalises the will is not so much the number of voices
as the common interest which unites them.' He holds apparently that in the assembly of the whole people, if they had
sufficient information, and if no minor combinations of particular interests were formed within the entire body, the difference between the wills of individuals would neutralise each
other, and the vote of the whole body would express the true
general will. But in fact in all assemblies there is at least a
liability to lack of information and to the formation of cliques;
and hence it cannot be held that the vote of the assembly
necessarily expresses the general will. Rousseau, however,
does not go so far as to say that unless the law is actually such
as contributes to the common good, it is not an expression
of the general will. The general will, according to him,
always aims at or wills the common good, but is liable to
be mistaken as to the means of attaining it. ' It is always
right, but the judgment which guides it is not always
enlightened. . . . Individuals see the good which they reject;
the public wills the good which it does not see.' (II, vi.)
Hence the need of a guide in the shape of a great lawgiver.
Apparently, however, the possible lack of enlightenment on
the part of the general will does not, in Rousseau's view,
prevent its decisions from being for the public good. In
discussing the ' limits of the sovereign power ' he maintains
that there can be no conflict between it and the natural
right of the individual, because, ' although it is only that
part of his power, his goods, his freedom, of which the use
is important to the community, that the individual transfers
to the sovereign by the social pact, yet the sovereign alone
can be judge of the importance '; and the sovereign ' cannot
lay on the subjects any constraint which is not for the good
of the community.' ' Under the law of reason ' (which is thus
identified with the general will) ' nothing is done without a
cause, any more than under the law of nature.' (II, iv.)

74. But though even an unenlightened general will is
the general will still, and (as we are left to infer) cannot in
its decisions do otherwise than promote the public good,

Rousseau distinctly contemplates the possibility of the general will being so overpowered by particular interests that it finds no expression in the votes of a popular assembly, though the assembly be really one of a whole people, and the vote of the majority is duly taken. (IV, i.) In such cases it is not that the general will is 'annihilated or corrupted; it is always constant, unalterable, and pure.' Even in the individual whose vote is governed by his private interest the general will is not extinct, nor is he unaware either of what the public good requires or of the fact that what is for the public good is also for his own. But his share in the public evil to which he knows that his vote will contribute, seems nothing by the side of the special private good which he hopes to gain. By his vote, in short, he does not answer the question, Is so and so for the advantage of the state? but, Is it for the advantage of this particular man or party? (*Ib.*)

75. The test of the dominance of the general will in assemblies of the people is an approach to unanimity. ' Long debates, discussions, tumult, indicate the ascendency of particular interests and the decline of the state.' (IV, ii.) Rousseau, however, does not venture to say that absolute unanimity in the assembly is necessary to an expression of the general will, or to give a law a claim upon the obedience of the subjects. This would have been to render effectual legislation impossible. Upon the theory, however, of the foundation of legitimate sovereignty in consent, the theory that the natural right of the individual is violated unless he is himself a joint imponent of the law which he is called to obey, it is not easy to see what rightful claim there can be to the submission of a minority. Rousseau so far recognises the difficulty that he requires unanimity in the original compact. (IV, ii.) If among those who are parties to it there are others who oppose it, the result is simply that the latter are not included in it. ' They are strangers among the citizens.' But this does not explain how they are to be rightfully controlled, on the principle that the only rightful control is founded on consent; or, if they are not controlled, what is the value of the 'social compact.' How can the object of the pact be attained while those who are bound by it have these 'strangers' living among them who are not bound by it, and who, not being bound by it, cannot be

rightfully controlled? The difficulty must recur with each
generation of the descendants of those who were parties to
the original pact. The parties to the pact, it is true, have
no right to resist the general will, because the pact is *ex
hypothesi* to the effect that each individual, in all things of
common concern, will take the general will for his own.
The true form, therefore, of the question upon which each
party to the pact should consider himself to be voting in
the assembly is, as Rousseau puts it, not 'Is the proposed
measure what I wish for, or what I approve, or no?' but
'Is it in conformity with the general will?' If, having
voted upon this question, he finds himself in a minority, he
is bound to suppose that he is mistaken in his views of the
general will, and to accept the decision of the majority as
the general will which, by the pact, he is bound to obey.
So far all is consistent; though how the individual is to be
answered if he pleads that the vote of the assembly has
been too much biassed by particular interests to be an
expression of the general will, and that therefore it is not
binding on him, does not appear.

76. But after the first generation of those who were
parties to the supposed original compact, what is to settle
whether anyone is a party to it or no? Rousseau faces the
question, but his only answer is that when once the state
is instituted, consent is implied in residence; ' to dwell on the
territory is to submit to the sovereignty.' (IV, ii.) This
answer, however, will scarcely stand examination. Rousseau
himself does not consider that residence in the same region
with the original parties to the pact renders those so
resident also parties to it. Why should it do so, when the
pact has descended to a later generation? It may be
argued of course that everyone residing in a settled society,
which secures him in his rights of person and property, has
the benefit of the society from the mere fact of his residence
in it, and is therefore morally bound to accept its laws. But
this is to abandon the doctrine of obligation being founded
on consent. Residence in a territory governed by a certain
sovereign can only be taken to imply consent to the rule of
that sovereign, if there is any real possibility of relinquish-
ing it, and this there can scarcely ever be.

77. Rousseau certainly carried out the attempt to recon-
cile submission to government with the existence of natural

rights antecedent to the institution of government, by the hypothesis of a foundation of government in consent, more consistently than any other writer; and his result shows the hopelessness of the attempt. To the consistency of his theory he sacrifices every claim to right on the part of any state except one in which the whole body of citizens directly legislates, i.e. on the part of nearly all states then or now existing; and finally he can only justify the control of the minority by the majority in any state whatever by a subterfuge. It does not follow, however, because the doctrine of natural rights and the consequent conception of government as founded on compact are untenable, that there is no truth in the conception of the state or sovereign as representing a general will, and as authorised or entitled to obedience on that account. It is this conception, as the permanently valuable thing in Rousseau, that we have now further to consider.

78. The first remark upon it which suggests itself is that, as Rousseau puts the matter, there may be an independent political society in which there is no sovereign power at all, or in which, at any rate, it is not exercised. The sovereign is the general will. But the general will can only be exercised through the assembly of a whole people. The necessary conditions of its exercise, then, in Rousseau's time, were only fulfilled in the Swiss cantons and (perhaps) in the United Provinces. In England they were fulfilled in a way during the time of a general election. But even where these conditions were fulfilled, it did not follow that the general will was put in force. It might be overpowered, as in the Roman *comitia*, by particular interests. Is it then to be understood that, according to Rousseau, either there can be independent states without any sovereignty in actual exercise, or that the European states of his time, and equally the great states of the present day (for in none of these is there any more exercise of the general will than in the England of his time), are not properly states at all?

79. We may try to answer this question by distinguishing sovereign *de facto* from sovereign *de jure*, and saying that what Rousseau meant was that the general will, as defined by him and as exercised under the conditions which he prescribes, was the only sovereign *de jure*, but that he would have recognised in the ordinary states of his time a sove-

reign *de facto*; and that in the same way, when he describes
the institution of government as arising out of a twofold
act consequent on the original pact (an act in which the
sovereign people first decides that there shall be a government, and then, not as a sovereign people, but as a democratic magistracy, decides in what hands the government
shall be placed), he does not conceive himself to be describ-
ing what has actually taken place, but what is necessary to
give a government a moral title to obedience. Whether
Rousseau himself had this distinction in view is not always
clear. At the outset he states his object thus: 'Man is born
free, and everywhere he is in fetters. How has this change
come about? I do not know. What can render it legitimate? That is a question which I deem myself able to
answer.' (I, i.) The answer is the account of the establishment of a sovereign by social pact. It might be inferred
from this that he considered himself in the sequel to be
delineating transactions to the actual occurrence of which
he did not commit himself, but which, if they did occur,
would constitute a duty as distinct from a physical necessity
of submission on the part of subjects to a sovereign, and to
which some equivalent must be supposed, in the shape of a
tacit present convention on the part of the members of a
state, if their submission is to be matter of duty as distinct
from physical necessity, or is to be explained as a matter
of right by the ostensible sovereign. This, however, would
merely be an inference as to his meaning. His actual
procedure is to describe transactions, by which the sovereignty of the general will was established, and by which
it in turn established a government, as if they had actually
taken place. Nor is he content with supposing a tacit
consent of the people as rendering subjection legitimate.
The people whose submission to law is to be 'legitimate'
must actually take part in sovereign legislative assemblies.
It is very rarely that he uses language which implies the
possibility of a sovereign power otherwise constituted. He
does indeed speak [1] of the possibility of a prince (in the

---

[1] 'If it happened that the prince had
a private will more active than that of
the sovereign, and that he made use of
the public force placed in his hands as
the instrument of this private will,
there would result, so to speak, two
sovereignties, one *de jure*, the other *de
facto*; but from that moment the social
union would disappear, and the body
politic would be dissolved.' (III, i.)
'When the prince ceases to administer
the state according to the laws, and

special meaning of the term, as representing the head of the executive) usurping sovereignty, and speaks of the sovereignty thus usurped as existing *de facto*, not *de jure*; but in no other connection (so far as I have observed) does he speak of anything short of the ' volonté générale ' exercised through the vote of an assembled people as sovereign at all. And the whole drift of his doctrine is to show that no sovereign, otherwise constituted, had any claim on obedience. There was no state in Europe at his time in which his doctrine would not have justified rebellion, and even under existing representative systems the conditions are not fulfilled which according to him are necessary to give laws the claim on our obedience which arises from their being an expression of the general will. The only system under which these conditions could be fulfilled would be one of federated self-governing communes, small enough to allow each member an active share in the legislation of the commune. It is probably the influence of Rousseau that has made such a system the ideal of political enthusiasts in France.

usurps the sovereign power . . . then the state in the larger sense is dissolved, and there is formed another within it, composed only of the members of the government . . . the social pact is broken . . . and all the ordinary citizens return as a matter of right to their state of natural liberty, and are merely forced, but not obliged, to obey.' (III, x.)

F. SOVEREIGNTY AND THE GENERAL WILL

ROUSSEAU AND AUSTIN

80. THE questions then arise (1) whether there is any truth in Rousseau's conception of sovereignty as founded upon a 'volonté générale' in its application to actual sovereignty. Does anything like such a sovereignty exist in the societies properly called political? (2) Is there any truth in speaking of a sovereignty *de jure* founded upon the 'volonté générale'? (3) If there is, are we to hold with Rousseau that this 'will' can only be exercised through the votes of a sovereign people?

81. (1) The first question is one which, if we take our notions of sovereignty from such writers as Austin, we shall be at first disposed decidedly to negative. Austin is considered a master of precise definition. We may begin, therefore, by looking to his definition of sovereignty and the terms connected with it. His general definition of law runs as follows : 'A law, in the most general and comprehensive acceptation in which the term, in its literal meaning, is employed, may be said to be a rule laid down for the guidance of an intelligent being by an intelligent being having power over him.'[1] These rules are of two kinds : (1) laws set by God to men, or the law of nature; and (2) laws set by men to men, or human law. We are only concerned with the latter, the human laws. These are again distinguished into two classes, according as they are or are not established by political superiors. 'Of the laws or rules set by men to men, some are established by *political* superiors, sovereign and subject; by persons exercising supreme and subordinate *government,* in independent nations, or independent political societies' (pp. 88 and 89). 'The aggregate of the rules established by political superiors is frequently styled *positive*

[1] *Lectures on Jurisprudence*, vol. i. p. 88 (edit. of 1869, in two vols.)

law, or law existing *by position*' (p. 89). This is distinguished from 'positive morality.' Laws are further explained as a species of commands. A command is a signification of desire, distinguished by the fact that the party to whom it is addressed is liable to evil from the party expressing the desire in case he does not comply with it (p. 91). This liability to evil forms the sanction of the command. Where a command 'obliges *generally* to acts or forbearances of *a class*, it is a law' (p. 95). 'Every positive law, or every law simply and strictly so called, is set by a sovereign person or a sovereign body of persons to a member or members of the independent political society wherein that person or body is sovereign or supreme. Or (changing the expression) it is set by a monarch, or sovereign member, to a person or persons in a state of subjection to its author. Even though it sprung directly from another fountain or source, it *is* a positive law, or a law strictly so called, by the institution of that present sovereign in the character of political superior. Or (borrowing the language of Hobbes) the legislator is he, not by whose authority the law was first made, but by whose authority it continues to be a law' (pp. 225 and 226).

'The notions of sovereignty and independent political society may be expressed concisely thus. If a *determinate* human superior, *not* in a habit of obedience to a like superior, receive *habitual* obedience from the *bulk* of a given society, that determinate superior is sovereign in that society, and the society (including the superior) is a society political and independent' (p. 226).

'In order that a given society may form a society political and independent, the two distinguishing marks which I have mentioned above must unite. The *generality* of the given society must be in a *habit* of obedience to a *determinate* and *common* superior ; whilst that determinate person, or determinate body of persons, must *not* be habitually obedient to a determinate person or body. It is the union of that positive with this negative mark which renders that certain superior sovereign or supreme, and which renders that given society (including that certain superior) a society political and independent ' (p. 227).

82. It may be remarked in passing that, according to the above, while every law implies a sovereign, from whom directly or indirectly (through a subordinate political supe-

rior) it proceeds, it is not necessary to a sovereign that his commands should take the form of laws, as opposed to 'particular or occasional commands.' A superior might signify his desires only in the form of such particular and occasional commands, and yet there might be a habit of obedience to him, and he might not be habitually obedient to any other person or body; in which case he would be a 'sovereign.'

83. Austin's doctrine seems diametrically opposite to one which finds the sovereign in a 'volonté générale,' because (a) it only recognises sovereignty in a *determinate* person or persons, and (b) it considers the essence of sovereignty to lie in the power, on the part of such determinate persons, to put compulsion without limit on subjects, to make them do exactly as it pleases.[1] The 'volonté générale,' on the other hand, it would seem, cannot be identified with the will of any determinate person or persons; it can, indeed, according to Rousseau, only be expressed by a vote of the whole body of subject citizens; but when you have got them together, there is no certainty that their vote does express it; and it does not—at any rate necessarily—command any power of compulsion, much less unlimited power. Rousseau expressly

---

[1] Cf. Maine's statement of Austin's doctrine in *The Early History of Institutions*, pp. 349 and 350 : 'There is in every independent political community —that is, in every political community not in the habit of obedience to a superior above itself—some single person or some combination of persons which has the power of compelling the other members of the community to do exactly as it pleases. This single person or group—this individual or this collegiate sovereign (to employ Austin's phrase) may be found in every independent political community as certainly as the centre of gravity in a mass of matter. If the community be violently or voluntarily divided into a number of separate fragments, then, as soon as each fragment has settled down (perhaps after an interval of anarchy) into a state of equilibrium, the sovereign will exist, and with proper care will be discoverable in each of the now independent portions. The sovereignty over the North American colonies of Great Britain had its seat in one place before they became the United States, in another place afterwards; but in both cases there was a discoverable sovereign somewhere. This sovereign, this person or combination of persons, universally occurring in all independent political communities, has in all such communities one characteristic, common to all the shapes sovereignty may take, the possession of irresistible force, not necessarily exerted, but capable of being exerted. According to the terminology preferred by Austin, the sovereign, if a single person, is or should be called a monarch ; if a small group, the name is an oligarchy ; if a group of considerable dimensions, an aristocracy ; if very large and numerous, a democracy. Limited monarchy, a phrase perhaps more fashionable in Austin's day than it is now, is abhorred by Austin, and the government of Great Britain he classes with aristocracies. That which all the forms of sovereignty have in common is the power (the power but not necessarily the will) to put compulsion without limit on subjects or fellow-subjects.'

contemplates the possibility of the executive power conflicting with and overbearing the general will. Indeed, according to his view, it was the ordinary state of things; and though this view may be exaggerated, no one could maintain that the 'general will,' in any intelligible sense of the words, had always unlimited force at its command.

84. The two views thus seem mutually exclusive, but perhaps it may be by taking each as complementary to the other that we shall gain the truest view of sovereignty as it actually exists. In those states of society in which obedience is habitually rendered by the bulk of society to some determinate superior, single or corporate, who, in turn, is independent of any other superior, the obedience is so rendered because this determinate superior is regarded as expressing or embodying what may properly be called the general will, and is virtually conditional upon the fact that the superior is so regarded. It is by no means an unlimited power of compulsion that the superior exercises, but one dependent in the long run, or dependent for the purpose of insuring an *habitual* obedience, upon conformity to certain convictions on the part of the subjects as to what is for their general interest. As Maine says (*Early History of Institutions*, p. 359), 'the vast mass of influences, which we may call for shortness moral, perpetually shapes, limits, or forbids the actual direction of the forces of society by its sovereign.' Thus, quite apart from any belief in the right of revolution, from the view that the people in any state are entitled to an ultimate sovereignty, or are sovereign *de jure*, and may withdraw either legislative or executive power from the hands in which it has been placed in the event of its being misused, it may fairly be held that the ostensible sovereign—the determinate person or persons to whom we can point and say that with him or them lies the ultimate power of exacting habitual obedience from the people—is only able to exercise this power in virtue of an assent on the part of the people, nor is this assent reducible to the fear of the sovereign felt by each individual. It is rather a common desire for certain ends—specially the 'pax vitæque securitas'—to which the observance of law or established usage contributes, and in most cases implies no conscious reference on the part of those whom it influences to any supreme coercive power at all. Thus when it has been ascertained in regard to any

people that there is some determinate person or persons to whom, in the last resort, they pay habitual obedience, we may call this person or persons sovereign if we please, but we must not ascribe to him or them the real power which governs the actions and forbearances of the people, even those actions and forbearances (only a very small part) which are prescribed by the sovereign. This power is a much more complex and less determinate, or less easily determinable, thing; but a sense of possessing common interests, a desire for common objects on the part of the people, is always the condition of its existence. Let this sense or desire—which may properly be called general will—cease to operate, or let it come into general conflict with the sovereign's commands, and the habitual obedience will cease also.

85. If, then, those who adopt the Austinian definition of a sovereign mean no more than that in a thoroughly developed state there must be some determinate person or persons, with whom, in the last resort, lies the recognised power of imposing laws and enforcing their observance, over whom no legal control can be exercised, and that even in the most thorough democracy, where laws are passed in the assembly of the whole people, it is still with determinate persons, viz. a majority of those who meet in the assembly, that this power resides, they are doubtless right. So far they only need to be reminded that the thoroughly developed state, as characterised by the existence of such definite sovereignty, is even among civilised people but imperfectly established. It is perfectly established (1) where customary or 'common' or 'judge-made' law, which does not proceed from any determinate person or persons, is either superseded by express enactments that do proceed from such person or persons, or (as in England) is so frequently trenched upon by statute law that it may fairly be said only to survive upon sufferance, or to be itself virtually enacted by the sovereign legislature; and (2) where no question of right can be raised between local legislatures or authorities and the legislature claiming to be supreme, as in America before the war of secession, and as might perhaps be found to be the case in Germany now, if on certain educational and ecclesiastical matters the imperial legislature came to be at issue with the local legislatures. But though the organisation

of the state, even in civilised and independent nations, is not everywhere complete, it no doubt involves the residence with determinate persons, or a body or bodies, of supreme i.e. legally uncontrolled power to make and enforce laws. The term 'sovereign' having acquired this definite meaning, Rousseau was misleading his readers when he ascribed sovereignty to the general will. He could only be understood as meaning, and in fact understood himself to mean, that there was no legitimate sovereign except in the most thorough democracy, as just described.

86. But the Austinians, having found their sovereign, are apt to regard it as a much more important institution than—if it is to be identified with a determinate person or persons—it really is ; they are apt to suppose that the sovereign, with the coercive power (i.e. the power of operating on the fears of the subjects) which it exercises, is the real determinant of the habitual obedience of the people, at any rate of their habitual obedience in respect of those acts and forbearances which are prescribed by law. But, as we have seen, this is not the case. It then needs to be pointed out that if the sovereign power is to be understood in this fuller, less abstract sense, if we mean by it the real determinant of the habitual obedience of the people, we must look for its sources much more widely and deeply than the 'analytical jurists' do ; that it can no longer be said to reside in a determinate person or persons, but in that impalpable congeries of the hopes and fears of a people, bound together by common interests and sympathy, which we call the general will.

87. It may be objected that this view of the general will, as that on which habitual obedience to the sovereign really depends, is at best only applicable to 'self-governing' communities, not to those under a despotic sovereign. The answer is that it is applicable in all forms of society where a sovereign in the sense above defined (as a determinate person or persons with whom in the last resort lies the recognised power of imposing laws and enforcing their observance) really exists, but that there are many where there cannot fairly be said to be any such sovereign at all ; in other words, that in all organised communities the power which practically commands the habitual obedience of the people in respect of those acts and forbearances which are

enjoined by law or authoritative custom, is one dependent on the general will of the community, but this power is often not sovereign in the sense in which the ruler of an independent state is sovereign. It may very well be that there is at the same time another power merely coercive, a power really operating on people simply through their fears, to which obedience is rendered, and which is not in turn representative of a general will; but where this is the case we shall find that such power is only in contact with the people, so to speak, at one or two points; that their actions and forbearances, as determined by law and custom, are in the main independent of it; that it cannot in any proper sense be said to be a sovereign power over them; at any rate, not in the sense in which we speak of King, Lords, and Commons as sovereign in England.

88. Maine has pointed out (*Early History of Institutions,* Lecture XIII.) that the great despotic empires of ancient times, excluding the Roman, of which more shall be said directly, and modern empires in the East were in the main tax-collecting institutions. They exercise coercive force over their subjects of the most violent kind for certain purposes at certain times, but they do not impose laws as distinct from 'particular and occasional commands,' nor do they judicially administer or enforce a customary law. In a certain sense the subjects render them habitual obedience, i.e. they habitually submit when the agents of the empire descend on them for taxes and recruits, but in the general tenor of their lives their actions and forbearances are regulated by authorities with which the empire never interferes,—with which probably it could not interfere without destroying itself. These authorities can scarcely be said to reside in a determinate person or persons at all, but, so far as they do so, they reside mixedly in priests or exponents of customary religion, in heads of families acting within the family, and in some village-council acting beyond the limits of the family. Whether, in such a state of things, we are to consider that there is a sovereign power at all, and, if so, where it is to be considered to reside, are chiefly questions of words. If complete uncontrolledness by a stronger power is essential to sovereignty, the local authorities just spoken of are not sovereign. The conquering despot could descend on them and sweep them away, leaving anarchy in their place, and he

does compel them to be put in exercise for a particular purpose, that of raising tribute or sometimes recruits. On the other hand, these authorities, which represent a general will of the communities, form the power which determines such actions and forbearances of the individual as do not proceed from natural inclination. The military ruler, indeed, is sovereign in the sense of possessing irresistible coercive power, but in fact this power is only exercised within narrow limits, and not at all in any legislative or judicial way. If exercised beyond these limits and in conflict with customary law, the result would be a general anarchy. The truest way of expressing the state of the case is to say that, taking the term 'sovereign' in the sense which we naturally associate with it, and in which it is used by modern European writers on sovereignty, there is under such conditions no sovereign, but that the practical regulation of life, except during intervals of military violence and anarchy, rests with authorities representing the general will, though these are to a certain extent interfered with by an alien force.

89. The same account is applicable to most cases of foreign dominion over a people with any organised common life of their own. The foreign power is not sovereign in the sense of being a maker or maintainer of laws. Law-making, under such conditions, there is properly none. The subject people inherits laws, written or unwritten, and maintains them for itself, a certain shelter from violence being afforded by the foreign power. Such, in the main, was the condition of North Italy, for instance, under Austrian domination. Where this is the case, the removal of the coercive power of the foreigner need not involve anarchy, or any violation of established rights (such as Hobbes supposes to follow necessarily from the deposition of an actual sovereign). The social order does not depend on the foreign dominion, and may survive it. The question whether in any particular case it actually can do so must depend on the possibility of preventing further foreign aggression, and on the question whether there is enough national unity in the subject people to prevent them from breaking up into hostile communities when the foreign dominion is removed.

90. It is otherwise where the foreign power is really a law-making and law-maintaining one, and is sovereign in

that proper sense, as was the Roman Empire. But just so far as the Roman Empire was of this sovereign, i.e. law-making and law-maintaining, character, it derived its permanence, its hold on the 'habitual obedience' of its subjects, from the support of the general will. As the empire superseded customary or written laws of conquered countries, it conferred rights of Roman citizenship, a much more perfect system of protection in action and acquisition than the conquered people had generally possessed before. Hence, while nothing could be further removed from what Rousseau would have counted liberty than the life of the citizens of the Roman Empire, for they had nothing to do with making the laws which they obeyed, yet probably there was never any political system more firmly grounded on the good-will of the subjects, none in the maintenance of which the subjects felt a stronger interest. The British power in India exercises a middle function between that of the Roman Empire and that of the mere tax-collecting and recruit-raising empire with which the Roman Empire has just been contrasted. It presents itself to the subject people in the first place as a tax-collector. It leaves the customary law of the people mostly untouched. But if only to a very small extent a law-making power, it is emphatically a law-maintaining one. It regulates the whole judicial administration of the country, but applies its power generally only to enforce the customary law which it finds in existence. For this reason an 'habitual obedience' may fairly be said to be rendered by the Indian people to the English government, in a sense in which it could not be said to be rendered to a merely tax-collecting military power; but the 'habitual obedience' is so rendered only because the English government presents itself to the people, not merely as a tax-collector, but as the maintainer of a customary law, which, on the whole, is the expression of the general will. The same is true in principle of those independent states which are despotically governed, in which, i.e., the ultimate legislative power does not reside, wholly or in part, with an assembly representing the people, or with the people themselves ; e.g. Russia. It is not the absolute coercive power of the Czar which determines the habitual obedience of the people. This coercive power, if put to the test as a *coercive* power, would probably be found very far from absolute.

The habitual obedience is determined by a system of law, chiefly customary, which the administration controlled by the Czar enforces against individuals, but which corresponds to the general sense of what is equitable and necessary. If a despotic government comes into anything like habitual conflict with the unwritten law which represents the general will, its dissolution is beginning.

91. The answer, then, to the question whether there is any truth in Rousseau's conception of sovereignty as founded upon a ' volonté générale,' in its application to actual sovereignty, must depend on what we mean by ' sovereign.' The essential thing in political society is a power which guarantees men rights, i.e. a certain freedom of action and acquisition conditionally upon their allowing a like freedom in others. It is but stating the same condition otherwise to speak of a power which guarantees the members of the society these rights, this freedom of action and acquisition, impartially or according to a general will or law. What is the lowest form in which a society is fit to be called political, is hard to say. The political society is more complete as the freedom guaranteed is more complete, both in respect of the persons enjoying it and of the range of possible action and acquisition over which it extends. A family or a nomad horde could not be called a political society, on account of the narrow range of the political freedom which they severally guarantee. The nomad horde might indeed be quite as numerous as a Greek state, or as the sovereign canton of Geneva in Rousseau's time; but in the horde the range within which reciprocal freedom of action and acquisition is guaranteed to the individual is exceedingly small. It is the power of guaranteeing rights, defined as above, which the old writers on sovereignty and civil government supposed to be established by covenant of all with all, translating the common interest which men have in the maintenance of such a power into an imaginary historical act by which they instituted it. It was this power that they had chiefly in view when they spoke of sovereignty.

92. It is to be observed, however, that the power may very well exist and serve its purpose where it is not sovereign in the sense of being exempt from any liability of being interfered with by a stronger coercive power, such as that of a tax-collecting military ruler. The occasional interference of

the military ruler is so far a drawback to the efficiency with which freedom of action and acquisition is guaranteed, but does not nullify the general maintenance of rights. On the other hand, when the power by which rights are guaranteed is sovereign (as it is desirable that it should be) in the special sense of being maintained by a person or persons, and wielding coercive force not liable to control by any other human force, it is not this coercive force that is the important thing about it, or that determines the habitual obedience essential to the real maintenance of rights. That which determines this habitual obedience is a power residing in the common will and reason of men, i.e. in the will and reason of men as determined by social relations, as interested in each other, as acting together for common ends. It is a power which this universal rational will exercises over the inclinations of the individual, and which only needs exceptionally to be backed by coercive force.

93. Thus, though it may be misleading to speak of the general will as anywhere either actually or properly sovereign, because the term 'sovereign' is best kept to the ordinary usage in which it signifies a determinate person or persons charged with the supreme coercive function of the state, and the general will does not admit of being vested in a person or persons, yet it is true that the institutions of political society—those by which equal rights are guaranteed to members of such a society—are an expression of, and are maintained by, a general will. The sovereign should be regarded, not in abstraction as the wielder of coercive force, but in connection with the whole complex of institutions or political society. It is as their sustainer, and thus as the agent of the general will, that the sovereign power must be presented to the minds of the people if it is to command habitual loyal obedience ; and obedience will scarcely be habitual unless it is loyal, not forced. If once the coercive power, which must always be an incident of sovereignty, becomes the characteristic thing about it in its relation to the people governed, this must indicate one of two things ; either that the general interest in the maintenance of equal rights has lost its hold on the people, or that the sovereign no longer adequately fulfils its function of maintaining such rights, and thus has lost the support derived from the general sense of interest in supporting it. It may be

doubted whether the former is ever really the case; but whatever explanation of the case may be the true one, it is certain that when the idea of coercive force is that predominantly associated with the law-imposing and law-enforcing power, then either a disruption of the state or a change in the sources of sovereignty must sooner or later take place. In judging, however, whether this is the case, we must not be misled by words. In England, e.g., from the way in which many people speak of 'government,' we might suppose that it was looked on mainly as the wielder of coercive force; but it would be a mistake on that account to suppose that English people commonly regard the laws of the country as so much coercion, instead of as an institution in the maintenance of which they are interested. When they speak disapprovingly of 'government,' they are not thinking of the general system of law, but of a central administrative agency, which they think interferes mischievously with local and customary administration.

94. It is more true, then, to say that law, as the system of rules by which rights are maintained, is the expression of a general will than that the general will is the sovereign. The sovereign, being a person or persons by whom in the last resort laws are imposed and enforced, in the long run and on the whole is an agent of the general will, contributes to realise that will. Particular laws may, no doubt, be imposed and enforced by the sovereign, which conflict with the general will; not in the sense that if all the subject people could be got together to vote upon them, a majority would vote against them,—that might be or might not be,— but in the sense that they tend to thwart those powers of action, acquisition, and self-development on the part of the members of the society, which there is always a general desire to extend (though the desire may not be enlightened as to the best means to the end), and which it is the business of the law to sustain and extend. The extent to which laws of this kind may be intruded into the general ' corpus juris ' without social disruption it is impossible to specify. Probably there has never been a civilised state in which they bore more than a very small proportion to the amount of law which there was the strongest general interest in maintaining. But, so far as they go, they always tend to lessen the ' habitual obedience ' of the people, and thus to make the

sovereign cease to be sovereign. The hope must be that this will result in the transfer of sovereignty to other hands before a social disruption ensues; before the general system of law has been so far perverted as to lose its hold on the people. Of the possibility of a change in sovereignty without any detraction from the law-abiding habits of the people, France has lately given a conspicuous example. Here, however, it must be remembered that a temporary foreign conquest made the transition easier.

95. (2) After what has been said, we need not dwell long on the second question raised [1] concerning Rousseau's theory: Is there any truth in speaking of a sovereignty ' de jure ' founded upon the ' volonté générale '? It is a distinction which can only be maintained so long as either ' sovereign ' is not used in a determinate sense, or by ' jus ' is understood something else than law or right established by law. If by ' sovereign ' we understand something short of a person or persons holding the supreme law-making and law-enforcing power, e.g. an English king who is often called sovereign, we might say that sovereignty was exercised ' de facto ' but not ' de jure ' when the power of such a ' sovereign ' was in conflict with, or was not sanctioned by, the law as declared and enforced by the really supreme power. Thus an English king, so far as he affected to control the army or raise money without the co-operation of Parliament, might be said to be sovereign ' de facto ' but not ' de jure '; only, however, on the supposition that the supreme law-making and law-enforcing power does not belong to him, and thus that he is called ' sovereign ' in other than the strict sense. If he were sovereign in the full sense ' de facto,' he could not fail to be so ' de jure,' i.e. legally. In such a state of things, if the antagonism between king and parliament continued for any length of time, it would have to be admitted that there was no sovereign in the sense of a supreme law-making and law-enforcing power; that sovereignty in this sense was in abeyance, and that anarchy prevailed. Or the same thing might be explained by saying that sovereignty still resided ' de jure ' with the king and parliament, though not ' de facto ' exercised by them; but if we use such language, we must bear in mind that we are qualifying ' sovereignty ' by an epithet which neutralises its

[1] [Above, sec. 80.]

meaning as an actually supreme power. If, however, the king succeeded in establishing such a power on a permanent footing, he would have become sovereign in the full sense, and there would be no ground for saying, as before, that he was not sovereign ' de jure ' ; for the qualifications ' de jure ' and ' not de jure,' in that sense in which they might be applied to a power which is not supreme, are equally inapplicable to the power of making and enforcing law which is supreme. The monarch's newly established supremacy may be in conflict with laws that were previously in force, but he has only to abolish those laws in order to render it legal. If, then, it is still to be said to be not ' de jure,' it must be because ' jus ' is used for something else than law or right established by law; viz. either for ' natural right ' (if we admit that there is such a thing), and ' natural right ' as not merely = natural power ; or for certain claims which the members of the subject community have come to recognise as inherent in the community and in themselves as members of it, claims regarded as the foundation of law, not as founded upon it, and with which the commands of the sovereign conflict. But even according to this meaning of ' jus,' a sovereign in the strict Austinian sense, that is not so ' de jure,' is in the long run an impossibility. ' Habitual obedience ' cannot be secured in the face of such claims.

96. But whether or no in any qualified sense of ' sovereign ' or ' jus,' a sovereign that is not so ' de jure ' is possible, once understand by ' sovereign ' the determinate person or persons with whom the ultimate law-imposing and law-enforcing power resides, and by ' jus ' law, it is then obviously a contradiction to speak of a sovereign ' de jure ' as distinguished from one ' de facto.' The power of the ultimate imponent of law cannot be derived from, or limited by, law. The sovereign may no doubt by a legislative act of its own lay down rules as to the mode in which its power shall be exercised, but if it is sovereign in the sense supposed, it must always be open to it to alter these rules. There can be no illegality in its doing so. In short, in whatever sense ' jus ' is derived from the sovereign, in that sense no sovereign can hold his power ' de jure.' So Spinoza held that ' imperium ' was ' de jure ' indeed, but ' de jure naturali ' (' jus naturale ' = natural power), which is the

same as 'de jure divino'; only powers exercised in subordination to 'imperium' are 'de jure civili.' So Hobbes said that there could be no 'unjust law.' A law was not a law unless enacted by a sovereign, and 'the just' being that to which the sovereign obliges, the sovereign could not enact the unjust, though it might enact the inequitable and the pernicious, the 'inequitable' presumably meaning that which conflicts with a law of nature, the 'pernicious' that which tends to weaken individuals or society. Rousseau retains the same notion of the impeccability of the sovereign, but on different grounds. Every act of the sovereign is according to him 'de jure,' not because all right is derived from a supreme coercive power and the sovereign is that power, but because the sovereign is the general will, which is necessarily a will for the good of all. The enactment of the sovereign could as little, on this view, be 'inequitable' or 'pernicious' as it could be 'unjust.' But this view necessitates a distinction between the sovereign, thus conceived, and the actually supreme power of making and enforcing law as it exists anywhere but in what Rousseau considered a perfect state. Rousseau indeed generally avoids calling this actually supreme power 'sovereign,' though he cannot, as we have seen, altogether avoid it; and since, whatever he liked to call it, the existence of such a power in forms which according to him prevented its equivalence to the general will was almost everywhere a fact, his readers would naturally come to think of the actually supreme power as sovereign 'de facto,' in distinction from something else which was sovereign 'de jure.' And further, under the influence of Rousseau's view that the only organ of the general will was an assembly of the whole people, they would naturally regard such an assembly as sovereign 'de jure,' and any other power actually supreme as merely sovereign 'de facto.' This opposition, however, really arises out of a confusion in the usage of the term 'sovereign'; out of inability on the one side to hold fast the identification of sovereign with general will, on the other to keep it simply to the sense of the supreme law-making and law-enforcing power. If 'sovereign' = 'general will,' the distinction of 'de facto' and 'de jure' is inapplicable to it. A certain desire either is or is not the general will. A certain interest is or is not an interest in the

common good. There is no sense in saying that such desire
or interest is general will ' de jure' but not ' de facto,' or
vice versa. On the other hand, if ' sovereign ' = the supreme
law-making and law-enforcing power, the distinction is
equally inapplicable to it. If any person or persons have
this power at all, they cannot be said to have it merely ' de
facto ' while others have it ' de jure.'

97. It may be urged with much truth that the actual
possession of such power by a determinate person or persons
is rather a convenient hypothesis of writers on jurisprudence
than an actual fact; and, as we have seen, the actual condition of things at certain times in certain states may
conveniently be expressed by saying that there was a
sovereign ' de facto ' that was not so ' de jure,' or *vice versa*;
but only on the supposition that ' sovereign ' is not taken
necessarily in the full sense of a supreme law-making and
law-enforcing power. In a state of things that can be so
described, however, there is no ' sovereignty' at all in the
sense of an actually supreme power of making and enforcing
law resident in a determinate person or persons. Sovereignty in this sense can only exist ' de facto '; and when it
so exists, it is obvious that no other can in the same sense
exist ' de jure.' It may be denied indeed in particular cases
that an actually supreme power of making and enforcing
law is exercised ' de jure,' in a sense of that phrase already
explained (see section 95). Reasons were given for doubting
whether a power could really maintain its sovereign attributes if conflicting with ' jus,' in the sense thus explained.
But supposing that it could, the fact that it was not exercised ' de jure ' would not entitle us to say that any other
person or persons were sovereign ' de jure,' without altering
the meaning of ' sovereign.' If any one has supreme power
' de facto,' that which any one else has cannot be supreme
power. The qualification of a power as held not ' de facto '
but ' de jure ' is one which destroys its character as supreme,
i.e. as sovereign in the sense before us.

98. It is only through trying to combine under the term
' sovereign' the notions of the general will and of supreme
power that we are led to speak of the people as sovereign
' de jure,' if not ' de facto.' There would be no harm indeed
in speaking of the general will as sovereign, if the natural
association of ' sovereign' with supreme coercive power

could be got rid of; but as this cannot be, when once we have pronounced the general will ' sovereign,' we are pretty sure to identify the general will with a vote of the majority of citizens. A majority of citizens *can* be conceived as exercising a supreme coercive power, but a general will, in the sense of an unselfish interest in the common good which in various degrees actuates men in their dealings with each other, cannot be so conceived. Thus for the sovereignty, in an impalpable and unnatural sense, of the general will, we get a sovereignty, in the natural and demonstrable sense, of the multitude. But as the multitude is not everywhere supreme, the assertion of its sovereignty has to be put in the form that it is sovereign ' de jure.' The truth which underlies this proposition is that an interest in common good is the ground of political society, in the sense that without it no body of people would recognise any authority as having a claim on their common obedience. It is so far as a government represents to them a common good that the subjects are conscious that they ought to obey it, i.e. that obedience to it is a means to an end desirable in itself or absolutely. This truth is latent in Rousseau's doctrine of the sovereignty of the general will, but he confounds with it the proposition that no government has a claim on obedience, but that which originates in a vote passed by the people themselves who are called on to obey (a vote which must be unanimous in the case of the original compact, and carried by a majority in subsequent cases).

99. This latter doctrine arises out of the delusion of natural right. The individual, it is thought, having a right, not derived from society, to do as he likes, can only forego that right by an act to which he is a party. Therefore he has a right to disregard a law unless it is passed by an assembly of which he has been a member, and by the decision of which he has expressly or tacitly agreed to be bound. Clearly, however, such a natural right of the individual would be violated under most popular sovereignties no less than under one purely monarchical, if he happened to object to the decision of the majority; for to say, as Rousseau says, that he has virtually agreed, by the mere fact of residence in a certain territory, to be bound by the votes of the majority of those occupying that territory, is a mere trick to save appearances. But in truth there is no such natural

right to do as one likes irrespectively of society. It is on the relation to a society, to other men recognising a common good, that the individual's rights depend, as much as the gravity of a body depends on relations to other bodies. A right is a power claimed and recognised as contributory to a common good. A right against society, in distinction from a right to be treated as a member of society, is a contradiction in terms. No one, therefore, has a right to resist a law or ordinance of government, on the ground that it requires him to do what he does not like, and that he has not agreed to submit to the authority from which it proceeds; and if no one person has such a right, no number of persons have it. If the common interest requires it, no right can be alleged against it. Neither can its enactment by popular vote enhance, nor the absence of such vote diminish, its right to be obeyed. Rousseau himself well says that the proper question for each citizen to ask himself in regard to any proposal before the assembly is not, Do I like or approve it? but, Is it according to the general will? which is only another way of asking, Is it according to the general interest? It is only as the organ of this general interest that the popular vote can endow any law with the right to be obeyed; and Rousseau himself, if he could have freed himself from the presuppositions of natural right, might have admitted that, as the popular vote is by no means necessarily an organ of the general interest, so the decree of a monarch or of an aristocratic assembly, under certain conditions, might be such an organ.

100. But it may be asked, Must not the individual judge for himself whether a law is for the common good? and if he decides that it is not, is he not entitled to resist it? Otherwise, not only will laws passed in the interest of individuals or classes, and against the public good, have a claim to our absolute and permanent submission, but a government systematically carried on for the benefit of a few against the many can never be rightfully resisted. To the first part of this question we must of course answer 'yes,' without qualification. The degree to which the individual judges for himself of the relation between the common good and the laws which cross the path of his ordinary life, is the measure of his intelligent, as distinguished from a merely instinctive, recognition of rights in others and in the state;

and on this recognition again depends his practical understanding of the difference between mere powers and rights
as recognised by himself. Supposing then the individual
to have decided that some command of a 'political superior'
is not for the common good, how ought he to act in regard
to it? In a country like ours, with a popular government
and settled methods of enacting and repealing laws, the
answer of common sense is simple and sufficient. He should
do all he can by legal methods to get the command cancelled,
but till it is cancelled he should conform to it. The common
good must suffer more from resistance to a law or to the
ordinance of a legal authority, than from the individual's
conformity to a particular law or ordinance that is bad,
until its repeal can be obtained. It is thus the social duty of
the individual to conform, and he can have no right, as we
have seen, that is against his social duty; no right to anything or to do anything that is not involved in the ability to
do his duty.

101. But difficulties arise when either (1) it is a case of
disputed sovereignty, and in consequence the legal authority
of the supposed command is doubtful; or (2) when the
government is so conducted that there are no legal means of
obtaining the repeal of a law; or (3) when the whole system
of a law and government is so perverted by private interests
hostile to the public that there has ceased to be any common
interest in maintaining it; or (4),—a more frequent case,—
when the authority from which the objectionable command
proceeds is so easily separable from that on which the maintenance of social order and the fabric of settled rights
depends, that it can be resisted without serious detriment to
this order and fabric. In such cases, may there not be a
right of resistance based on a 'higher law' than the command of the ostensible sovereign?

102. (1) As to cases where the legal authority of the
supposed command is doubtful. In modern states the definition of sovereignty,—the determination of the person or
persons with whom the supreme power of making and
enforcing law legally resides,—has only been arrived at by
a slow process. The European monarchies have mostly arisen
out of the gradual conversion of feudal superiority into
sovereignty in the strict sense. Great states, such as
Germany and Italy, have been formed by the combination

of independent or semi-dependent states. In England the unity of the state goes back much further than anywhere else, but in England it was but gradually that the residence of sovereignty jointly in king, lords, and commons came to be practically established, and it is still founded merely on a customary law. In the United States, with a written constitution, it required all Austin's subtlety to detect where sovereignty lay, and he places it where probably no ordinary citizen of the United States had ever thought of it as residing, viz. ' in the states' governments as forming one aggregate body: meaning by a state's government, not its ordinary legislature, but the body of citizens which appoints its ordinary legislature, and which, the union apart, is properly sovereign therein.' He bases this view on the provision in the constitution, according to which amendments to it are only valid ' when ratified by the legislature in three-fourths of the several states, or by convention in three-fourths thereof.' (I, p. 268.) But no ordinary citizen of the United States probably ever thought of sovereignty except as residing either in the government of his state or in the federal government consisting of congress and president, or sometimes in one way, sometimes in the other. In other countries, e.g. France, where since Louis XIV the quarter in which sovereignty resides has at any given time been easily assignable, there have since the revolution been such frequent changes in the ostensible sovereign that there might almost at any time have been a case for doubting whether the ostensible sovereign had such command over the habitual obedience of the people as to be a sovereign in that sense in which there is a social duty to obey the sovereign, as the representative of the common interest in social order; whether some prior sovereignty was not really still in force. For these various reasons there have been occasions in the history of all modern states at which men, or bodies of men, without the conscious assertion of any right not founded upon law, might naturally deem themselves entitled to resist an authority which on its part claimed a right—a legally established power—to enforce obedience, and turned out actually to possess the power of doing so.

103. In such cases the truest retrospective account to be given of the matter will often be, that at the time there was

nothing amounting to a right on either side. A right is a power of which the exercise by the individual or by some body of men is recognised by a society, either as itself directly essential to a common good, or as conferred by an authority of which the maintenance is recognised as so essential. But in cases of the kind described the authorities, appealed to on each side as justifying respectively compulsion and resistance, often do not command a sufficiently general recognition of their being necessary to the common good to enable them to confer rights of compulsion or resistance. One or other of them may be coming to do so, or ceasing to do so, but rights, though on the one hand they are eternal or at least coeval with human society, on the other hand take time to form themselves in this or that particular subject and to transfer themselves from one subject to another; (just as one may hold reason to be eternal, and yet hold that it takes time for this or that being to become rational.) Hence in periods of conflict between local or customary and imperial or written law, between the constituent powers of a sovereignty, such as king and parliament in England, of which the relation to each other has not become accurately defined, between a falling and a rising sovereign in a period of revolution, between federal and state authorities in a composite state, the facts are best represented by saying that for a time there may be no right on either side in the conflict, and that it is impossible to determine precisely the stage at which there comes to be such a right on the one side as implies a definite resistance to right on the other. This of course is not to be taken to mean that in such periods rights in general are at an end. It is merely that right is in suspense on the particular point at issue between the conflicting powers. As we have seen, the general fabric of rights in any society does not depend on the existence of a definite and ascertained sovereignty, in the restricted sense of the words; on the determination of a person or persons in whom supreme power resides; but on the control of the conduct of men according to certain regular principles by a society recognising common interests; and though such control may be more or less weakened during periods of conflict of the kind supposed, it never ceases.

104. It does not follow, however, because there may often not be strictly a right on either side in such periods of

conflict, that there is not a good and an evil, a better and a
worse, on one side or the other. Of this we can only judge
by reference to the end, whatever it be, in which we conceive
the good of man to consist. There may be clear ground for
saying, in regard to any conflict, that one side rather than
the other *ought* to have been taken, not because those on one
side were, those on the other were not, entitled to say that
they had a right to act as they did, but because the common
good of a nation or mankind was clearly promoted by one
line of action, not by the other. E.g. in the American war
of secession, though it would be difficult to say that a man
had not as much a right to fight for his seceding state as
for the Union, yet as the special interest of the seceding
states was that of maintaining slavery, there was reason for
holding that the side of the Union, not that of the seceding
states, was the one which ought to be taken. On the other
hand, it does not follow that in a struggle for sovereignty
the good of man is more served by one of the competing
powers than by the other. Good may come out of the
conflict without one power contributing more to it than the
other. There may thus be as little ground retrospectively
for saying that one side or the other ought to have been
taken, as that men had a right to take one and not the
other. At the same time, as regards the individual, there
is no reason for doubting that the better the motive which
determines him to take this side or that, the more he is
actuated in doing so by some unselfish desire for human
good, the more free he is from egotism, and that conceit or
opinionatedness which is a form of egotism, the more good
he will do whichever side he adopts.

105. It is in such cases as we have been considering that
the distinction between sovereign 'de facto' and sovereign
'de jure' arises. It has a natural meaning in the mouths
of those who, in resisting some coercive power that claims
their obedience, can point to another determinate authority
to which they not only consider obedience due, but to which
such obedience in some considerable measure is actually
rendered; a meaning which it has not when all that can be
opposed to sovereign 'de facto' is either a 'general will,' or
the mere name of a fallen dynasty exercising no control
over men in their dealings with each other. But where this
opposition can be used with a natural meaning, it is a truer

account of the matter (as we have seen) to say that sovereignty is in abeyance. The existence of competing powers, each affecting to control men in the same region of outward action, and each having partisans who regard it alone as entitled to exercise such control, implies that there is not that unity of supreme control over the outward actions of men which constitutes sovereignty and which is necessary to the complete organisation of a state. The state has either not reached complete organisation, or is for the time disorganised, the disorganisation being more or less serious according to the degree to which the everyday rights of men (their ordinary freedom of action and acquisition) are interfered with by this want of unity in the supreme control.

106. In such a state of things, the citizen has no rule of 'right' (in the strict sense of the word) to guide him. He is pretty sure to think that one or other of the competing powers has a right to his obedience because, being himself interested (not necessarily selfishly interested) in its support, he does not take account of its lacking that general recognition as a power necessary to the common good which is requisite in order to give it a right. But we looking back may see that there was no such right. Was there then nothing to direct him either way? Simply, I should answer, the general rule of looking to the moral good of mankind, to which a necessary means is the organisation of the state, which again requires unity of supreme control, in the common interest, over the outward actions of men. The citizen ought to have resisted or obeyed either of the competing authorities, according as by doing so he contributed most to the organisation of the state in the sense explained. It must be admitted that without more knowledge and foresight than the individual can be expected to possess, this rule, if he had recognised it, could have afforded him no sure guidance; but this is only to say that there are times of political difficulty in which the line of conduct adopted may have the most important effect, but in which it is very hard to know what is the proper line to take. On the other side must be set the consideration that the man who brings with him the character most free from egotism to the decision even of those questions of conduct, as to which established rules of right and wrong are of no avail, is most sure on the whole to take the line which yields the best results.

107. We come next to the question of the possible duty of resistance in cases where no law, acknowledged or half-acknowledged, written or customary, can be appealed to against a command (general or particular) contrary to the public good; where no counter-sovereignty, in the natural sense of the words, can be alleged against that of the imponent of the law; and where at the same time, from the people having no share, direct or indirect, in the government, there is no means of obtaining a repeal of the law by legal means. I say the 'duty' of resistance because, from the point of view here adopted, there can be no 'right,' unless on the ground that it is for the common good, and if so, there is a duty. In writings of the seventeenth and eighteenth centuries, starting with the assumption of natural rights, the question was never put on its proper footing. It was not asked, When, for the sake of the common good, the citizen ought to resist the sovereign? but, What sort of injury to person or property gave him a natural right to resist? Now there is sense in inquiring upon what sort and amount of provocation from government individuals inevitably will resist; how (in Spinoza's language) that 'indignatio' is excited which leads them 'in unum conspirare'; but there is none in asking what gives them a right to resist, unless we suppose a wrong done to society in their persons; and then it becomes a question not of right merely, but of duty, whether the wrong done is such as to demand resistance. Now when the question is thus put, no one presumably would deny that under certain conditions there might be a duty of resistance to sovereign power.

108. It is important, however, that instead of discussing the right of a majority to resist, we should discuss the duty of resistance as equally possible for a minority and a majority. There can be no right of a majority of citizens, as such, to resist a sovereign. If by law, written or customary, the majority of citizens possess or share in the sovereign power, then any conflict that may arise between it and any power cannot be a conflict between it and the sovereign. The majority may have a right to resist such a power, but it will not be a right to resist a *sovereign*. If, on the other hand, the majority of citizens have no share by law or custom in the supreme law-making and law-enforcing power, they never can have a right, simply as a majority, to resist that power.

In such a case, there may arise a social duty to resist, and the exercise of men's powers in fulfilment of that duty may be sustained by such a general recognition of its being for the public good, as to become a right; but the resistance may be a duty before a majority of the citizens approve it, and does not necessarily become a duty when a majority of them do approve it; while that general recognition of its exercise as being for the common good, through which the power of resistance becomes a right, must be something more habitual and sustained and penetrating than any vote of a majority can convey. Incidentally, however, the consideration of the attitude of the mass of the people in regard to a contemplated resistance to established government must always be most important in determining the question whether the resistance should be made. It should be made, indeed, if at all, not because the majority approve it, but because it is for the public good; but account must be taken of the state of mind of the majority in considering whether it is for the public good or no. The presumption must generally be that resistance to a government is not for the public good when made on grounds which the mass of the people cannot appreciate; and it must be on the presence of a strong and intelligent popular sentiment in favour of resistance that the chance of avoiding anarchy, of replacing the existing government by another effectual for its purpose, must chiefly depend. On the other hand, it is under the worst governments that the public spirit is most crushed; and thus in extreme cases there may be a duty of resistance in the public interest, though there is no hope of the resistance finding efficient popular support. (An instance is the Mazzinian outbreaks in Italy.) Its repeated renewal and repeated failure may afford the only prospect of ultimately arousing the public spirit which is necessary for the maintenance of a government in the public interest. And just as there may thus be a duty of resistance on the part of a hopeless minority, so on the other side resistance even to a monarchic or oligarchic government is not justified by the fact that a majority, perhaps in some temporary fit of irritation or impatience, is ready to support it, if, as may very well be, the objects for which government subsists—the general freedom of action and acquisition and self-development—are likely to suffer from an overthrow of the government in the popular interest.

109. No precise rule, therefore, can be laid down as to the conditions under which resistance to a despotic government becomes a duty. But the general questions which the good citizen should ask himself in contemplating such resistance will be, (a) What prospect is there of resistance to the sovereign power leading to a modification of its character or an improvement in its exercise without its subversion? (b) If it is overthrown, is the temper of the people such, are the influences on which the general maintenance of social order and the fabric of recognised rights depend so far separable from it, that its overthrow will not mean anarchy? (c) If its overthrow does lead to anarchy, is the whole system of law and government so perverted by private interests hostile to the public, that there has ceased to be any common interest in maintaining it?

110. Such questions are so little likely to be impartially considered at a time when resistance to a despotic government is in contemplation, and, however impartially considered, are so intrinsically difficult to answer, that it may seem absurd to dwell on them. No doubt revolutionists do and must to a great extent 'go it blind.' Such beneficent revolutions as there have been could not have been if they did not. But in most of those questions of right and wrong in conduct, which have to be settled by consideration of the probable effects of the conduct, the estimate of effects which regulates our approval or disapproval upon a retrospective survey, and according to which we say that an act should or should not have been done, is not one which we could expect the agent himself to have made. The effort to make it would have paralysed his power of action.

111. In the simple cases of moral duty, where there is no real doubt as to the effects of this or that action, and danger arises from interested self-sophistication, we can best decide for ourselves whether we ought to act in this way or that by asking whether it is what is good in us—a disinterested or unselfish motive—that moves us to act in this way or that; and in judging of the actions of others, where the issues and circumstances are simple, the moral question, the question of 'ought' or 'ought not,' is often best put in the form, How far was the action such as could

represent a good character? That indeed is the form in which the question should always be put, when the nature of the case admits it; since, as argued elsewhere [*Prol. to Ethics*, II, i and ii], it is only in its relation to character that action is in the full sense good or bad. But where the probable effects of a certain line of action are at the time of taking it very obscure, we cannot be sure that relatively the best character will lead a man to take the line which turns out best in the result, or that because a line of action has turned out well in result, the character of the man who adopted it was good. This being so, in judging of the act retrospectively we have to estimate it by the result simply, in abstraction from the character of the agent. Thus in looking back upon a revolutionary outbreak we can only judge whether it was vindicated by the result. If in the light of the result it appears that conditions were not present under which it would have furthered rather than interfered with the true objects of government, we judge that it should not have been made; if otherwise, we approve it,—judge that the persons concerned in it were doing their duty in acting as they did. But whether they were really doing their duty in the full sense of the term in acting as they did in a case when the outbreak was successful, or not doing it in a case where it failed, is what we simply cannot tell; for this depends on the state of character which their action represented, and that is beyond our ken.

112. Such is the necessary imperfection under which all historical judgments labour, though historians are not apt to recognise it and would be thought much more dull if they did. They would have fewer readers if they confined themselves to the analysis of situations, which may be correctly made, and omitted judgments on the morality of individuals for which, in the proper sense, the data can never be forthcoming. We scarcely have them for ourselves (except that we know that we are none of us what we should be), still less for our intimate acquaintance; not at all for men whom we only know through history, past or present. In regard to them, we can only fall back on the generalisation, that the best man—the man most disinterestedly devoted to the perfecting of humanity, in some form or other, in his own person or that of others—is more likely to act in a way that is good as measured by its results, those results again being

estimated with reference to an ideal of character, and that this is so even under circumstances of political complication. Appearances to the contrary, appearances of harm done from good motives, may be met by the considerations, (1) that there is often much egotism in what calls itself conscientiousness, and that the 'conscientious' motives which lead to mischievous acts may not be in the highest sense disinterested; (2) that to what we call the consequences of an action many influences contribute besides the action which we call the cause, and if evil seems to clog the consequences of action pure in motive, this may be due to other influences connected with motives less worthy, while the consequences which in the rough we call bad might have been worse but for the intervention of the purely-motived action; (3) that the beneficent results are often put to the credit of the actions of selfish men when they should rather be credited to influences more remote and complex, without which those actions would have been impossible or had no good effect, and which have arisen out of unselfish activities. We see the evil in a course of events and lay the blame on someone who should have acted differently, and whom perhaps we take as an instance of how good men cause mischief; but we do not see the greater evil which would otherwise have ensued.

In regard to the questions stated above as those which the good citizen should set himself in contemplation of a possible rebellion, though they are questions to which it is impossible for a citizen in the heat of a revolutionary crisis to give a sufficient answer, and which in fact can only be answered after the event, yet they represent objects which the good citizen will set before himself at such times; and in proportion to the amount of good citizenship, as measured by interest in those objects, interest in making the best of existing institutions, in maintaining social order and the general fabric of rights, interest which leads to a *bona fide* estimate of the value of the existing government in its relation to public good, will be the good result of the political movement.

G. WILL, NOT FORCE, IS THE BASIS OF THE STATE.

113. LOOKING back on the political theories which we have discussed, we may see that they all start with putting the question to be dealt with in the same way, and that their errors are very much due to the way in which they put it. They make no inquiry into the development of society and of man through society. They take no account of other forms of community than that regulated by a supreme coercive power, either in the way of investigating their historical origin and connection, or of considering the ideas and states of mind which they imply or which render them possible. They leave out of sight the process by which men have been clothed with rights and duties, and with senses of right and duty, which are neither natural nor derived from a sovereign power. They look only to the supreme coercive power on the one side and to individuals, to whom natural rights are ascribed, on the other, and ask what is the nature and origin of the right of that supreme coercive power as against these natural rights of individuals. The question so put can only be answered by some device for representing the individuals governed as consenting parties to the exercise of government over them. This they no doubt are so long as the government is exercised in a way corresponding to their several wishes ; but, so long as this is the case, there is no interference with their ' natural liberty ' to do as they like. It is only when this liberty is interfered with, that any occasion arises for an explanation of the compatibility of the sovereign's right with the natural right of the individual ; and it is just then that the explanation by the supposition that the right of the sovereign is founded on consent, fails. But the need of the fictitious explanation arises from a wrong way of putting the question ; the power which regulates our

conduct in political society is conceived in too abstract a way
on the one side, and on the other are set over against it, as
the subjects which it controls, individuals invested with all
the moral attributes and rights of humanity. But in truth
it is only as members of a society, as recognising common
interests and objects, that individuals come to have these
attributes and rights; and the power, which in a political
society they have to obey, is derived from the development
and systematisation of those institutions for the regulation
of a common life without which they would have no rights
at all.

114. To ask why I am to submit to the power of the
state, is to ask why I am to allow my life to be regulated
by that complex of institutions without which I literally
should not have a life to call my own, nor should be able
to ask for a justification of what I am called on to do. For
that I may have a life which I can call my own, I must not
only be conscious of myself and of ends which I present to
myself as mine; I must be able to reckon on a certain freedom
of action and acquisition for the attainment of those ends,
and this can only be secured through common recognition
of this freedom on the part of each other by members of a
society, as being for a common good. Without this, the
very consciousness of having ends of his own and a life which
he can direct in a certain way, a life of which he can make
something, would remain dormant in a man.   It is true that
slaves have been found to have this consciousness in high
development; but a slave even at his lowest has been partly
made what he is by an ancestral life which was not one of
slavery pure and simple, a life in which certain elementary
rights were secured to the members of a society through
their recognition of a common interest. He retains certain
spiritual aptitudes from that state of family or tribal freedom.
This, perhaps, is all that could be said of most of the
slaves on plantations in modern times; but the slavery of the
ancient world, being mainly founded on captivity in war, was
compatible with a considerable amount of civilisation on the
part of the slaves at the time when their slavery began. A
Jewish slave, e.g., would carry with him into slavery a
thoroughly developed conception of right and law. Slavery,
moreover, implies the establishment of some regular system
of rights in the slave-owning society. The slave, especially

the domestic slave, has the signs and effects of this system all about him. Hence such elementary consciousness of rights—of powers that are his own to make the best of—as the born slave may inherit from an ancestral life of freedom, finds a stimulus to its inward development, though no opportunity for outward exercise, in the habits and ideas of civilised life with which a common language enables the slave to become conversant, and which, through the sympathy implied in a common language, he to some extent makes his own. Thus the appearance in slaves of the conception that they should be masters of themselves, does not conflict with the proposition that only so far as a certain freedom of action and acquisition is secured to a body of men through their recognition of the exercise of that freedom by each other as being for the common good, is there an actualisation of the individual's consciousness of having life and ends of his own. The exercise, manifestation, expression of this consciousness through a freedom secured in the way described is necessary to its real existence, just as language of some sort is necessary to the real existence of thought, and bodily movement to that of the soul.

115. The demand, again, for a justification of what one is called on by authority to do presupposes some standard of right, recognised as equally valid for and by the person making the demand and others who form a society with him, and such a recognised standard in turn implies institutions for the regulation of men's dealings with each other, institutions of which the relation to the consciousness of right may be compared, as above, to that of language to thought. It cannot be said that the most elementary consciousness of right is prior to them, or they to it. They are the expressions in which it becomes real. As conflicting with the momentary inclinations of the individual, these institutions are a power which he obeys unwillingly ; which he has to, or is made to, obey. But it is only through them that the consciousness takes shape and form which expresses itself in the question, ' Why should I thus be constrained ? By what right is my natural right to do as I like overborne ? '

116. The doctrine that the rights of government are founded on the consent of the governed is a confused way of stating the truth, that the institutions by which man is moralised, by which he comes to do what he sees that he

must, as distinct from what he would like, express a conception of a common good; that through them that conception takes form and reality; and that it is in turn through its presence in the individual that they have a constraining power over him, a power which is not that of mere fear, still less a physical compulsion, but which leads him to do what he is not inclined to because there is a law that he should.

Rousseau, it will be remembered, speaks of the 'social pact' not merely as the foundation of sovereignty or civil government, but as the foundation of morality. Through it man becomes a moral agent; for the slavery to appetite he substitutes the freedom of subjection to a self-imposed law. If he had seen at the same time that rights do not begin till duties begin, and that if there was no morality prior to the pact there could not be rights, he might have been saved from the error which the notion of there being natural rights introduces into his theory. But though he does not seem himself to have been aware of the full bearing of his own conception, the conception itself is essentially true. Setting aside the fictitious representation of an original covenant as having given birth to that common 'ego' or general will, without which no such covenant would have been possible, and of obligations arising out of it, as out of a bargain made between one man and another, it remains true that only through a recognition by certain men of a common interest, and through the expression of that recognition in certain regulations of their dealings with each other, could morality originate, or any meaning be gained for such terms as 'ought' and 'right' and their equivalents.

117. Morality, in the first instance, is the observance of such regulations, and though a higher morality, the morality of the character governed by 'disinterested motives,' i.e. by interest in some form of human perfection, comes to differentiate itself from this primitive morality consisting in the observance of rules established for a common good, yet this outward morality is the presupposition of the higher morality. Morality and political subjection thus have a common source, '*political* subjection' being distinguished from that of a slave, as a subjection which secures rights to the subject. That common source is the rational recognition by certain human beings—it may be merely by children of the same parent—of a common well-being which is their well-being,

and which they conceive as their well-being whether at any moment any one of them is inclined to it or no, and the embodiment of that recognition in rules by which the inclinations of the individuals are restrained, and a corresponding freedom of action for the attainment of well-being on the whole is secured.

118. From this common source morality and political subjection in all its forms always retain two elements in common, one consisting in antagonism to some inclination, the other consisting in the consciousness that the antagonism to inclination is founded on reason or on the conception of some adequate good.   It is the antagonism to inclination involved in the moral life, as alone we know it, that makes it proper to speak analogically of moral 'laws' and 'imperatives.'   It must be remembered, however, that such language *is* analogical, and that there is an essential difference between laws in the strictest sense (laws which are indeed not adequately described as general commands of a political superior, sanctioned by liability to pains which that superior can inflict, but in which a command so sanctioned is an essential element), and the laws of conscience, of which it is the peculiar dignity that they have no external imponent and no sanction consisting in fear of bodily evil. The relation of constraint, in the one case between the man and the externally imposed law, in the other between some particular desire of the man and his consciousness of something absolutely desirable, we naturally represent in English, when we reflect on it, by the common term 'must.'   'I *must* connect with the main drainage,' says the householder to himself, reflecting on an edict of the Local Board.   'I *must* try to get A.B. to leave off drinking,' he says to himself, reflecting on a troublesome moral duty of benevolence to his neighbour.   And if the 'must' in the former case represents in part the knowledge that compulsion may be put on the man who neglects to do what he must, which is no part of its meaning in the second, on the other hand the consciousness that the constraint is for a common good, which wholly constitutes the power over inclination in the second case, must always be an element in that obedience which is properly called obedience to law, or civil or political obedience.   Simple fear can never constitute such obedience. To represent it as the basis of civil subjection is to confound

the citizen with the slave, and to represent the motive which
is needed for the restraint of those in whom the civil sense
is lacking, and for the occasional reinforcements of the law-
abiding principle in others, as if it were the normal influence
in habits of life of which the essential value lies in their
being independent of it. How far in any particular act of
conformity to law the fear of penalties may be operative, it
is impossible to say. What is certain is, that a habit of
subjection founded upon such fear could not be a basis of
political or free society; for to this it is necessary, not
indeed that everyone subject to the laws should take part in
voting them, still less that he should consent to their
application to himself, but that it should represent an idea
of common good, which each member of the society can
make his own so far as he is rational, i.e. capable of the
conception of a common good, however much particular
passions may lead him to ignore it and thus necessitate the
use of force to prevent him from doing that which, so far
as influenced by the conception of a common good, he would
willingly abstain from.

119. Whether the legislative and administrative agencies
of society can be kept in the main free from bias by private
interests, and true to the idea of common good, without
popular control; whether again, if they can, that 'civil
sense,' that appreciation of common good on the part of the
subjects, which is as necessary to a free or political society
as the direction of law to the maintenance of a common good,
can be kept alive without active participation of the people in
legislative functions; these are questions of circumstances
which perhaps do not admit of unqualified answers. The views
of those who looked mainly to the highest development of
political life in a single small society, have to be modified if
the object sought for is the extension of political life to the
largest number of people. The size of modern states renders
necessary the substitution of a representative system for one
in which the citizens shared directly in legislation, and this so
far tends to weaken the active interest of the citizens in the
common weal, though the evil may partly be counteracted
by giving increased importance to municipal or communal
administration. In some states, from the want of homo-
geneity or facilities of communication, a representative
legislature is scarcely possible. In others, where it exists, a

great amount of power, virtually exempt from popular control, has to be left with what Rousseau would have called the ' prince or magistrate.' In all this there is a lowering of civil vitality as compared with that of the ancient, and perhaps of some exceptionally developed modern, commonwealths. But perhaps this is a temporary loss that we have to bear as the price of having recognised the claim to citizenship as the claim of all men. Certainly all political ideals, which require active and direct participation by the citizens in the functions of the sovereign state, fail us as soon as we try to conceive their realisation on the wide area even of civilised mankind. It is easy to conceive a better system than that of the great states of modern Europe, with their national jealousies, rival armies, and hostile tariffs ; but the condition of any better state of things would seem to be the recognition of some single constraining power, which would be even more remote from the active co-operation of the individual citizen than is the sovereign power of the great states at present.

120. These considerations may remind us how far removed from any foundation in their own will the requirements of the modern state must seem to be to most of those who have to submit to them. It is true that the necessity which the state lays upon the individual is for the most part one to which he is so accustomed that he no longer kicks against it; but what is it, we may ask, but an external necessity, which he no more lays on himself than he does the weight of the atmosphere or the pressure of summer heat and winter frosts, that compels the ordinary citizen to pay rates and taxes, to serve in the army, to abstain from walking over the squire's fields, snaring his hares, or fishing in preserved streams, to pay rent, to respect those artificial rights of property which only the possessors of them have any obvious interest in maintaining, or even (if he is one of the ' proletariate ') to keep his hands off the superfluous wealth of his neighbour, when he has none of his own to lose ? Granted that there are good reasons of social expediency for maintaining institutions which thus compel the individual to actions and forbearances that are none of his willing, is it not abusing words to speak of them as founded on a conception of general good ? A conception does not float in the air. It must be somebody's conception. Whose

conception, then, of general good is it that these institutions
represent? Not that of most of the people who conform to
them, for they do so because they are made to, or have come
to do so habitually from having been long made to; (i.e. from
being frightened at the consequences of not conforming,
not consequences which follow from not conforming in the
ordinary course of nature, but consequences which the state
inflicts, artificial consequences.) But when a man is said
to obey an authority from interest in a common good, some
other good is meant than that which consists in escaping
the punishment which the authority would inflict on disobedience. Is then the conception of common good which is
alleged a conception of it on the part of those who founded
or who maintain the institutions in question? But is it not
certain that private interests have been the main agents in
establishing, and are still in maintaining, at any rate all the
more artificial rights of property? Have not our modern
states, again, in nearly every case been founded on conquest,
and are not the actual institutions of government in great
measure the direct result of such conquest, or, where revolutions have intervened, of violence which has been as little
governed by any conception of general good? Supposing
that philosophers can find exquisite reasons for considering
the institutions and requirements which have resulted from
all this self-seeking and violence to be contributory to the
common good of those who have to submit to them, is it not
trifling to speak of them as founded on or representing a
conception of this good, when no such conception has influenced those who established, maintain, or submit to them?
And is it not seriously misleading, when the requirements of
the state have so largely arisen out of force directed by
selfish motives, and when the motive to obedience to those
requirements is determined by fear, to speak of them as
having a common source with the morality of which it is
admitted that the essence is to be disinterested and spontaneous?

121. If we would meet these objections fairly, certain
admissions must be made. The idea of a common good
which the state fulfils has never been the sole influence
actuating those who have been agents in the historical process by which states have come to be formed; and even so
far as it has actuated them, it has been only as conceived in

some very imperfect form that it has done so. This is equally
true of those who contribute to the formation and maintenance of states rather as agents, and of those who do so
rather as patients. No one could pretend that even the
most thoughtful and dispassionate publicist is capable of the
idea of the good served by the state to which he belongs, in
all its fulness. He apprehends it only in some of its bearings; but it is as a common good that he apprehends it, i.e.
not as a good for himself or for this man or that more than
another, but for all members equally in virtue of their relation to each other and their common nature. The idea
which the ordinary citizen has of the common good served
by the state is much more limited in content. Very likely
he does not think of it at all in connection with anything
that the term 'state' represents to him. But he has a clear
understanding of certain interests and rights common to
himself with his neighbours, if only such as consist in getting
his wages paid at the end of the week, in getting his money's
worth at the shop, in the inviolability of his own person and
that of his wife. Habitually and instinctively, i.e. without
asking the reason why, he regards the claim which in these
respects he makes for himself as conditional upon his recognising a like claim in others, and thus as in the proper sense
a right,—a claim of which the essence lies in its being common to himself with others. Without this instinctive recognition he is one of the 'dangerous classes,' virtually outlawed
by himself. With it, though he have no reverence for the
'state' under that name, no sense of an interest shared with
others in maintaining it, he has the needful elementary conception of a common good maintained by law. It is the
fault of the state if this conception fails to make him a loyal
subject, if not an intelligent patriot. It is a sign that the
state is not a true state; that it is not fulfilling its primary
function of maintaining law equally in the interest of all,
but is being administered in the interest of classes; whence
it follows that the obedience which, if not rendered willingly,
the state compels the citizen to render, is not one that he
feels any spontaneous interest in rendering, because it does
not present itself to him as the condition of the maintenance
of those rights and interests, common to himself with his
neighbours, which he understands.

122. But if the law which regulates private relations and

its administration are so equally applied to all, that all who are capable of a common interest are prompted by that interest to conform to the law, the result is still only the loyal subject as distinct from the intelligent patriot, i.e. as distinct from the man who so appreciates the good which in common with others he derives from the state—from the nation organised in the form of a self-governing community to which he belongs—as to have a passion for serving it, whether in the way of defending it from external attack, or developing it from within. The citizens of the Roman empire were loyal subjects; the admirable maintenance of private rights made them that; but they were not intelligent patriots, and chiefly because they were not, the empire fell. That active interest in the service of the state, which makes patriotism in the better sense, can hardly arise while the individual's relation to the state is that of a passive recipient of protection in the exercise of his rights of person and property. While this is the case, he will give the state no thanks for the protection which he will come to take as a matter of course, and will only be conscious of it when it descends upon him with some unusual demand for service or payment, and then he will be conscious of it in the way of resentment. If he is to have a higher feeling of political duty, he must take part in the work of the state. He must have a share, direct or indirect, by himself acting as a member or by voting for the members of supreme or provincial assemblies, in making and maintaining the laws which he obeys. Only thus will he learn to regard the work of the state as a whole, and to transfer to the whole the interest which otherwise his particular experience would lead him to feel only in that part of its work that goes to the maintenance of his own and his neighbour's rights.

123. Even then his patriotism will hardly be the passion which it needs to be, unless his judgment of what he owes to the state is quickened by a feeling of which the 'patria,' the fatherland, the seat of one's home, is the natural object; and of this feeling the state becomes the object only so far as it is an organisation of a people to whom the individual feels himself bound by ties analogous to those which bind him to his family, ties derived from a common dwelling-place with its associations, from common memories, traditions and customs, and from the common ways of feeling and

thinking which a common language and still more a common literature embodies. Such an organisation of an homogeneous people the modern state in most cases is (the two Austrian states being the most conspicuous exceptions), and such the Roman state emphatically was not.

124. But, it will be said, we are here again falling back on our unproved assumption that the state is an institution for the promotion of a common good. This granted, it is not difficult to make out that in most men at any rate there is a sufficient interest in some form of social well-being, sufficient understanding of the community between their own well-being and that of their neighbours, to make them loyal to such ar institution. But the question is, whether the promotion of a common good, at any rate in any sense appreciable by the multitude, is any necessary characteristic of a state. It is admitted that the outward visible sign of a state is the presence of a supreme or independent coercive power, to which habitual obedience is rendered by a certain multitude of people, and that this power may often be exercised in a manner apparently detrimental to the general well-being. It may be the case, as we have tried to show that it is, that a power which is in the main so exercised, and is generally felt to be so, is not likely long to maintain its supremacy; but this does not show that a state cannot exist without the promotion of the common good of its subjects, or that (in any intelligible way) the promotion of such good belongs to the idea of a state. A short-lived state is not therefore not a state, and if it were, it is rather the active interference with the subject's well-being, than a failure to promote it, that is fatal to the long life of a state. How, finally, can the state be said to exist for the sake of an end, or to fulfil an idea, the contemplation of which, it is admitted, has had little to do with the actions which have had most to do with bringing states into existence?

125. The last question is a crucial one, which must be met at the outset. It must be noticed that the ordinary conception of organisation, as we apply it in the interpretation of nature, implies that agents may be instrumental in the attainment of an end or the fulfilment of an idea of which there is no consciousness on the part of the organic agents themselves. If it is true on the one hand that the interpretation of nature by the supposition of ends external

to it, with reference to which its processes are directed, has been discarded, and that its rejection has been the condition of growth in an exact knowledge of nature, on the other hand the recognition of ends immanent in nature, of ideas realised within it, is the basis of a scientific explanation of life. The phænomena of life are not ideal, in the sense in which the ideal is opposed to that which is sensibly verifiable, but they are related to the processes of material change which are their conditions, as ideas or ideal ends which those processes contribute to realise, because, while they determine the processes (while the processes would not be what they are but for relation to them), yet they are *not* those processes, *not* identical with any one or number of them, or all of them together. Life does not reside in any of the organs of life, or in any or all of the processes of material change through which these pass. Analyse or combine these as you will, you do not detect it as the result of the analysis or combination. It is a function or end which they realise according to a plan or idea which determines their existence before they exist and survives their disappearance. If it were held, then, that the state were an organised community in the same sense in which a living body is, of which the members at once contribute to the function called life, and are made what they are by that function, according to an idea of which there is no consciousness on their part, we should only be following the analogy of the established method of interpreting nature.

126. The objection to such a view would be that it represents the state as a purely natural, not at all as a moral, organism. Moral agency is not merely an agency by which an end is attained, or an idea realised, or a function fulfilled, but an agency determined by an idea on the part of the agent, by his conception of an end or function; and the state would be brought into being and sustained by merely natural, as opposed to moral, agency, unless there were a consciousness of ends—and of ends the same in principle with that served by the state itself—on the part of those by whom it is brought into being, and sustained. I say 'ends the same in principle with that served by the state itself,' because, if the state arose out of the action of men determined, indeed, by the consciousness of ends, but ends wholly heterogeneous to that realised by the state, it would not be

a moral institution, would not stand in any moral relation
to men. Now among the influences that have operated in
the formation of states, a large part, it must be admitted, are
simply natural. Such are the influences of climate, of distribution of mountain and plain, land and water, &c., of all
physical demarcations and means of communication. But
these, it is clear, are only organic to the formation of states
so far as, so to speak, they take a character, which does not
belong to them as merely natural, from agencies distinctively
human.

127. 'Human, if you like,' it may be replied, 'but not
moral, if a moral agency implies any reference to a social or
human good, to a good which the individual desires because
it is good for others, or for mankind, as well as himself. In
the earth-hunger of conquering hordes, in the passions of
military despots, in the pride or avarice or vindictiveness
which moved such men as Louis XI or Henry VIII to override the semi-anarchy of feudalism with a real sovereignty,
what is there of reference to such good? Yet if we suppose
the influence of such motives as these, together with the
natural influences just spoken of, to be erased from the
history of the formation of states, its distinguishing features
are gone.'

128. The selfish motives described must not, any more
than the natural influences, be regarded in abstraction, if
we would understand their true place in the formation of
states. The pure desire for social good does not indeed
operate in human affairs unalloyed by egotistic motives, but
on the other hand what we call egotistic motives do not act
without direction from an involuntary reference to social
good,—'involuntary' in the sense that it is so much a matter
of course that the individual does not distinguish it from
his ordinary state of mind. The most conspicuous modern
instance of a man who was instrumental in working great
and in some ways beneficial changes in the political order of
Europe, from what we should be apt to call the most purely
selfish motives, is Napoleon. Without pretending to analyse
these motives precisely, we may say that a leading one was
the passion for glory; but if there is to be truth in the statement that this passion governed Napoleon, it must be
qualified by the farther statement that the passion was itself
governed by social influences, operative on him, from which

it derived its particular direction. With all his egotism, his individuality was so far governed by the action of the national spirit in and upon him, that he could only glorify himself in the greatness of France; and though the national spirit expressed itself in an effort after greatness which was in many ways of a mischievous and delusive kind, yet it again had so much of what may be called the spirit of humanity in it, that it required satisfaction in the belief that it was serving mankind. Hence the aggrandisement of France, in which Napoleon's passion for glory satisfied itself, had to take at least the semblance of a deliverance of oppressed peoples, and in taking the semblance it to a great extent performed the reality; at any rate in western Germany and northern Italy, wherever the Code Napoléon was introduced.

129. It is thus that actions of men, whom in themselves we reckon bad, are 'overruled' for good. There is nothing mysterious or unintelligible in such 'overruling.' There is nothing in the effect which we ascribe to the 'overruling,' any more than in any effect belonging to the ordinary course of nature, which there was not in the cause as it really was and as we should see it to be if we fully understood it. The appearance to the contrary arises from our taking too partial and abstract a view of the cause. We look at the action e.g. of Napoleon with reference merely to the selfishness of his motives. We forget how far his motives, in respect of their concrete reality, in respect of the actual nature of the ends pursued as distinct from the particular relation in which those ends stood to his personality, were made for him by influences with which his selfishness had nothing to do. It was not his selfishness that made France a nation, or presented to him continuously an end consisting in the national aggrandisement of France, or at particular periods such ends as the expulsion of the Austrians from Italy, the establishment of a centralised political order in France on the basis of social equality, the promulgation of the civil code, the maintenance of the French system along the Rhine. His selfishness gave a particular character to his pursuit of these ends, and (so far as it did so) did so for evil. Finally it led him into a train of action altogether mischievous. But at each stage of his career, if we would understand what his particular agency really was, we must

take account of his ends in their full character, as determined by influences with which his passion for glory no doubt co-operated, but which did not originate with it or with him, and in some measure represented the struggle of mankind towards perfection.

130. And not only must we thus correct our too abstract views of the particular agency of such a man as Napoleon. If we would understand the apparent results of his action, we must bear in mind how much besides his particular agency has really gone to produce them, so far as they were good; how much of unnoticed effort on the part of men obscure because unselfish, how much of silent process in the general heart of man. Napoleon was called the 'armed soldier of revolution,' and it was in that character that he rendered what service he did to men ; but the revolution was not the making of him or his likes. Cæsar again we have learnt to regard as a benefactor of mankind, but it was not Cæsar that made the Roman law, through which chiefly or solely the Roman empire became a blessing. The idiosyncrasy, then, of the men who have been most conspicuous in the production of great changes in the condition of mankind, though it has been an essential element in their production, has been so only so far as it has been overborne by influences and directed to ends, which were indeed not external to the men in question—which on the contrary helped to make them inwardly and spiritually what they really were—but which formed no part of their distinguishing idiosyncrasy. If that idiosyncrasy was conspicuously selfish, it was still not through their selfishness that such men contributed to mould the institutions by which nations have been civilised and developed, but through their fitness to act as organs of impulses and ideas which had previously gained a hold on some society of men, and for the realisation of which the means and conditions had been preparing quite apart from the action of those who became the most noticeable instruments of their realisation.

131. The assertion, then, that an idea of social good is represented by, or realised in, the formation of states, is not to be met by pointing to the selfishness and bad passions of men who have been instrumental in forming them, if there is reason to think that the influences, under the direction of which these passions became thus instrumental, are due to

the action of such an idea. And when we speak thus we do
not refer to any action of the idea otherwise than in the consciousness of men. It may be legitimate, as we have seen,
to consider ideas as existing and acting otherwise, and perhaps, on thinking the matter out, we should find ourselves
compelled to regard the idea of social good as a communication to the human consciousness, a consciousness developing
itself in time, from an eternally complete consciousness.
But here we are considering it as a source of the moral
action of men, and therefore necessarily as having its seat
in their consciousness, and the proposition advanced is that
such an idea is a determining element in the consciousness
of the most selfish men who have been instrumental in the
formation or maintenance of states; that only through its
influence in directing and controlling their actions could
they be so instrumental; and that, though its active presence
in their consciousness is due to the institutions, the organisation of life, under which they are born and bred, the
existence of these institutions is in turn due to the action,
ander other conditions, of the same idea in the minds of men.

132. It is the necessity of a supreme coercive power to
the existence of a state that gives plausibility to the view
that the action of merely selfish passions may lead to the
formation of states. They have been motive causes, it would
seem, in the processes by which this 'imperium' has been
established; as, e.g., the acquisition of military power by a
tribal chieftain, the conquest of one tribe by another, the
supersession of the independent prerogatives of families by a
tyrant which was the antecedent condition of the formation
of states in the ancient world, the supersession of feudal
prerogatives by the royal authority which served the same
purpose in modern Europe. It is not, however, supreme
coercive power, simply as such, but supreme coercive power
exercised in a certain way and for certain ends, that makes
a state; viz. exercised according to law, written or customary, and for the maintenance of rights. The abstract consideration of sovereignty has led to these qualifications being
overlooked. Sovereignty = supreme coercive power, indeed,
but such power as exercised in and over a state, which
means with the qualifications specified; but the mischief of
beginning with an inquiry into sovereignty before the idea
of a state has been investigated, is that it leads us to adopt

this abstract notion of sovereignty, as merely supreme coercive power, and then, when we come to think of the state as distinguished by sovereignty, makes us suppose that supreme coercive power is all that is essential to a state, forgetting that it is rather the state that makes the sovereign, than the sovereign that makes the state.   Supposing one man had been master of all the slaves in one of the states of the American Union, there would have been a multitude of men under one supreme coercive power, but the slaves and the master would have formed no state, because there would have been no recognised rights of slave against slave enforced by the master, nor would dealings between master and slaves have been regulated by any law.   The fact that sovereign power, as implied in the fact of its supremacy, can alter any laws, is apt to make us overlook the necessity of conformity to law on the part of the sovereign, if he is to be the sovereign of a state.   A power that altered laws otherwise than according to law, according to a constitution, written or unwritten, would be incompatible with the existence of a state, which is a body of persons, recognised by each other as having rights, and possessing certain institutions for the maintenance of those rights.   The office of the sovereign, as an institution of such a society, is to protect those rights from invasion, either from without, from foreign nations, or from within, from members of the society who cease to behave as such.   Its supremacy is the society's independence of such attacks from without or within.   It is an agency of the society, or the society itself acting for this end.   If the power, existing for this end, is used on the whole otherwise than in conformity either with a formal constitution or with customs which virtually serve the purpose of a constitution, it is no longer an institution for the maintenance of rights and ceases to be the agent of a state.   We only count Russia a state by a sort of courtesy on the supposition that the power of the Czar, though subject to no constitutional control, is so far exercised in accordance with a recognised tradition of what the public good requires as to be on the whole a sustainer of rights.

It is true that, just as in a state, all law being derived from the sovereign, there is a sense in which the sovereign is not bound by any law, so there is a sense in which all rights are derived from the sovereign, and no power which

the sovereign refuses to allow can be a right; but it is only
in the sense that, the sovereign being the state acting in a
certain capacity, and the state being an institution for the
more complete and harmonious maintenance of the rights
of its members, a power, claimed as a right, but which the
state or sovereign refuses to allow, cannot be really compatible with the general system of rights. In other words,
it is true only on the supposition that a state is made a state
by the functions which it fulfils of maintaining the rights of
its members as a whole or a system, in such a way that none
gains at the expense of another (no one has any power
guaranteed to him through another's being deprived of that
power). Thus the state, or the sovereign as a characteristic
institution of the state, does not create rights, but gives
fuller reality to rights already existing. It secures and extends the exercise of powers, which men, influenced in dealing
with each other by an idea of common good, had recognised
in each other as being capable of direction to that common
good, and had already in a certain measure secured to each
other in consequence of that recognition. It is not a state
unless it does so.

133. It may be said that this is an arbitrary restriction
of the term 'state.' If any other word, indeed, can be found
to express the same thing, by all means let it be used instead.
But some word is wanted for the purpose, because as a matter
of fact societies of men, already possessing rights, and whose
dealings with each other have been regulated by customs
conformable to those rights, but not existing in the form to
which the term 'state' has just been applied (i.e. not having
a systematic law in which the rights recognised are harmonised, and which is enforced by a power strong enough
at once to protect a society against disturbance within and
aggression from without), have come to take on that form.
A word is needed to express that form of society, both
according to the idea of it which has been operative in the
minds of the members of the societies which have undergone
the change described (an idea only gradually taking shape
as the change proceeded), and according to the more explicit
and distinct idea of it which we form in reflecting on the
process. The word 'state' is the one naturally used for the
purpose. The exact degree to which the process must have
been carried before the term 'state' can be applied to the

people in which it has gone on, cannot be precisely determined, but as a matter of fact we never apply it except in
cases where it has gone some way, and we are justified in
speaking of the state according to its idea as the society in
which it is completed.

134. It is a mistake then to think of the state as an
aggregation of individuals under a sovereign ; equally so
whether we suppose the individuals as such, or apart from
what they derive from society, to possess natural rights, or
suppose them to depend on the sovereign for the possession
of rights. A state presupposes other forms of community,
with the rights that arise out of them, and only exists as
sustaining, securing, and completing them. In order to
make a state there must have been families of which the
members recognised rights in each other (recognised in each
other powers capable of direction by reference to a common
good); there must further have been intercourse between
families, or between tribes that have grown out of families,
of which each in the same sense recognised rights in the
other. The recognition of a right being very short of its
definition, the admission of a right in each other by two
parties, whether individuals, families, or tribes, being very
different from agreement as to what the right consists in,
what it is a right to do or acquire, the rights recognised
need definition and reconciliation in a general law. When
such a general law has been arrived at, regulating the
position of members of a family towards each other and the
dealings of families or tribes with each other; when it is
voluntarily recognised by a community of families or tribes,
and maintained by a power strong enough at once to enforce
it within the community and to defend the integrity of the
community against attacks from without, then the elementary
state has been formed.

135. That, however, is the beginning, not the end, of the
state. When once it has come into being, new rights arise
in it (1) through the claim for recognition on the part of
families and tribes living on the same territory with those
which in community form the state, but living at first in
some relation of subjection to them. A common humanity,
of which language is the expression, necessarily leads to
the recognition of some good as common to these families
with those which form the state. This is in principle the

recognition of rights on their part; and the consequent embodiment of this recognition in the laws of the state is their admission as members of it. (Instances of this process are found in the states of Greece and the early history of Rome.) (2) The same thing may happen in regard to external communities ('external' territorially), whether these have been already formed into states or no. It may happen through the conquest of one by another, through their submission to a common conqueror, as under the Roman empire, or through voluntary combination, as with the Swiss cantons and the United States of America. However the combination may arise, it results in new rights as between the combined communities within the system of a single state. (3) The extended intercourse between individuals, which the formation of the state renders possible, leads to new complications in their dealings with each other, and with it to new forms of right, especially in regard to property; rights as far removed from any obvious foundation on the *suum cuique* principle as the right of a college to the great tithes of a parish for which it does nothing. (4) The administration of the state gives rise to rights, to the establishment of powers necessary for its administration. (5) New situations of life may arise out of the extended dealings of man with man which the state renders possible (e.g. through the crowding of population in certain localities) which make new modes of protecting the people a matter virtually of right. And, as new rights arise in the state once formed, so further purposes are served. It leads to a development and moralisation of man beyond the stage which they must have reached before it could be possible.

136. On this I shall dwell more in my next course of lectures. What I am now concerned to point out is that, however necessary a factor force may have been in the process by which states have been formed and transformed, it has only been such a factor as co-operating with those ideas without which rights could not exist. I say ' could not *exist*,' not ' could not be recognised,' because rights are made by recognition. There is no right ' but thinking makes it so '; none that is not derived from some idea that men have about each other. Nothing is more real than a right, yet its existence is purely ideal, if by ' ideal ' is meant that which is not dependent on anything material but has its

being solely in consciousness. It is to these ideal realities that force is subordinate in the creation and development of states. The force of conquest from without, the force exercised within communities by such agents as the early Greek tyrants or the royal suppressors of feudalism in modern Europe, has only contributed to the formation of states in so far as its effects have taken a character which did not belong to them as effects of force; a character due to their operation in a moral world, in which rights already existed, resting on the recognition by men of each other as determined, or capable of being determined, by the conception of a common good. It is not indeed true that only a state can produce a state, though modern history might seem to favour that notion. As a matter of fact, the formation of modern states through feudalism out of an earlier tribal system has been dependent on ideas derived from the Roman state, if not on institutions actually handed down from it; and the improvement and development of the state-system which has taken place since the French Revolution has been through agencies which all presuppose and are determined by the previous existence of states. But the Greek states, so far as we know, were a first institution of the kind, not a result of propagation from previously existing states. But the action which brought them into being was only effectual for its purpose, because the idea of right, though only in the form of family or tribal right, was already in operation.

H. HAS THE CITIZEN RIGHTS AGAINST THE STATE ?

137. I PROPOSE to pursue the inquiry, begun in my last course, into the nature and functions of the state. In the last course we were chiefly occupied with criticism. We have seen that no true conception of the rights of individuals against each other or against the state, or of the rights of the state over individuals, can be arrived at, while we look upon the state merely as an aggregation of individuals under a sovereign power that is able to compel their obedience, and consider this power of compelling a general obedience to be the characteristic thing in a state. So long as this view is retained, no satisfactory answer can be given to the question, by what right the sovereign compels the obedience of individuals. It can only be met either by some device for representing the individuals as so consenting to the exercise of sovereign power over them that it is no violation of their individual rights, or by representing the rights of individuals as derived from the sovereign and thus as having no existence against it. But it is obviously very often against the will of individuals that the sovereign power is exercised over them ; indeed if it were not so, its character-istic as a power of compulsion would be lost; it would not be a sovereign power ; and the fact that the majority of a given multitude may consent to its exercise over an uncon-senting minority, is no justification for its exercise over that minority, if its justification is founded on consent ; the representation that the minority virtually consent to be bound by the will of the majority being an obvious fiction. On the other hand, the theory that all right is derived from a sovereign, that it is a power of which the sovereign secures the exercise to the individual, and that therefore there can

be no right against the sovereign, conflicts with the primary demands of human consciousness. It implies the identification of 'I ought' with 'I am forced to.' Reducing the 'right' of the sovereign simply to a power, it makes it unintelligible that this power should yet represent itself as a right, and claim obedience to itself as such. No such theory indeed admits of consistent statement. To say (with Hobbes) that a law may be inequitable or pernicious, though it cannot be unjust, is to admit a criticism of laws, a distinction between those enactments of the sovereign which are what they should be and those which are not. And this is to recognise the individual's demand for a justification of the laws which he obeys; to admit in effect that there is some rule of right, of which the individual is conscious, and to which law ought to conform.

138. It is equally impossible, then, to hold that the right of the sovereign power in a state over its members is dependent on their consent, and, on the other hand, that these members have no rights except such as are constituted and conferred upon them by the sovereign. The sovereign, and the state itself as distinguished by the existence of a sovereign power, presupposes rights and is an institution for their maintenance. But these rights do not belong to individuals as they might be in a state of nature, or as they might be if each acted irrespectively of the others. They belong to them as members of a society in which each recognises the other as an originator of action in the same sense in which he is conscious of being so himself (as an 'ego,' as himself the object which determines the action), and thus regards the free exercise of his own powers as dependent upon his allowing an equally free exercise of his powers to every other member of the society. There is no harm in saying that they belong to individuals as such, if we understand what we mean by 'individual,' and if we mean by it a self-determining subject, conscious of itself as one among other such subjects, and of its relation to them as making it what it is; for then there is no opposition between the attachment of rights to the individuals as such and their derivation from society. They attach to the individual, but only as a member of a society of free agents, as recognising himself and recognised by others to be such a member, as doing and done by accordingly. A right, then, to act unsocially,—to act otherwise than as

belonging to a society of which each member keeps the exercise of his powers within the limits necessary to the like exercise by all the other members,—is a contradiction. No one can say that, unless he has consented to such a limitation of his powers, he has a right to resist it. The fact of his not consenting would be an extinction of all right on his part.

139. The state then presupposes rights, and rights of individuals. It is a form which society takes in order to maintain them. But rights have no being except in a society of men recognising each other as ἴσοι καὶ ὅμοιοι. They are constituted by that mutual recognition. In analysing the nature of any right, we may conveniently look at it on two sides, and consider it as on the one hand a claim of the individual, arising out of his rational nature, to the free exercise of some faculty ; on the other, as a concession of that claim by society, a power given by it to the individual of putting the claim in force. But we must be on our guard against supposing that these distinguishable sides have any really separate existence. It is only a man's consciousness of having an object in common with others, a well-being which is consciously his in being theirs and theirs in being his,—only the fact that they are recognised by him and he by them as having this object,—that gives him the claim described. There can be no reciprocal claim on the part of a man and an animal each to exercise his powers unimpeded by the other, because there is no consciousness common to them. But a claim founded on such a common consciousness is already a claim conceded ; already a claim to which reality is given by social recognition, and thus implicitly a right.

140. It is in this sense that a slave has 'natural rights.' They are 'natural' in the sense of being independent of, and in conflict with, the laws of the state in which he lives, but they are not independent of social relations. They arise out of the fact that there is a consciousness of objects common to the slave with those among whom he lives,—whether other slaves or the family of his owner,—and that this consciousness constitutes at once a claim on the part of each of those who share it to exercise a free activity conditionally upon his allowing a like activity in the others, and a recognition of this claim by the others through which it is realised. The slave

thus derives from his social relations a real right which the law of the state refuses to admit. The law cannot prevent him from acting and being treated, within certain limits, as a member of a society of persons freely seeking a common good. Now that capability of living in a certain limited community with a certain limited number of human beings, which the slave cannot be prevented from exhibiting, is in principle a capability of living in community with any other human beings, supposing the necessary training to be allowed; and as every such capability constitutes a right, we are entitled to say that the slave has a right to citizenship, to a recognised equality of freedom with any and every one with whom he has to do, and that in refusing him not only citizenship but the means of training his capability of citizenship, the state is violating a right founded on that common human consciousness which is evinced both by the language which the slave speaks, and by actual social relations subsisting between him and others. And on the same principle upon which a state is violating natural rights in maintaining slavery, it does the same in using force, except under the necessity of self-defence, against members of another community. Membership of any community is so far, in principle, membership of all communities as to constitute a right to be treated as a freeman by all other men, to be exempt from subjection to force except for prevention of force.

141. A man may thus have rights as a member of a family or of human society in any other form, without being a member of a state at all,—rights which remain rights though any particular state or all states refuse to recognise them ; and a member of a state, on the ground of that capability of living as a freeman among freemen which is implied in his being a member of a state, has rights as against all other states and their members. These latter rights are in fact during peace recognised by all civilised states. It is the object of 'private international law' to reduce them to a system. But though it follows from this that the state does not create rights, it may be still true to say that the members of a state derive their rights from the state and have no rights against it. We have already seen that a right against society, as such, is an impossibility ; that every

right is derived from some social relation; that a right against any group of associated men depends on association, as ἴσος καὶ ὅμοιος, with them and with some other men. Now for the member of a state to say that his rights are derived from his social relations, and to say that they are derived from his position as member of a state, are the same thing. The state is for him the complex of those social relations out of which rights arise, so far as those rights have come to be regulated and harmonised according to a general law, which is recognised by a certain multitude of persons, and which there is sufficient power to secure against violation from without and from within. The other forms of community which precede and are independent of the formation of the state, do not continue to exist outside it, nor yet are they superseded by it. They are carried on into it. They become its organic members, supporting its life and in turn maintained by it in a new harmony with each other. Thus the citizen's rights, e.g. as a husband or head of a family or a holder of property, though such rights, arising out of other social relations than that of citizen to citizen, existed when as yet there was no state, are yet to the citizen derived from the state, from that more highly developed form of society in which the association of the family and that of possessors who respect each other's possessions are included as in a fuller whole; which secures to the citizen his family rights and his rights as a holder of property, but under conditions and limitations which the membership of the fuller whole— the reconciliation of rights arising out of one sort of social capability with those arising out of another—renders necessary. Nor can the citizen have any right against the state, in the sense of a right to act otherwise than as a member of some society, the state being for its members the society of societies, the society in which all their claims upon each other are mutually adjusted.

142. But what exactly is meant by the citizen's acting 'as a member of his state'? What does the assertion that he can have no right to act otherwise than as a member of his state amount to? Does it mean that he has no right to disobey the law of the state to which he belongs, whatever that law may be? that he is not entitled to exercise his powers in any way that the law forbids and to refuse to exercise them in any way that it commands? This question

was virtually dealt with before [1] in considering the justifiability of resistance to an ostensible sovereign. The only unqualified answer that can be given to it is one that may seem too general to be of much practical use, viz. that so far as the laws anywhere or at any time in force fulfil the idea of a state, there can be no right to disobey them; or, that there can be no right to disobey the law of the state except in the interest of the state ; i.e. for the purpose of making the state in respect of its actual laws more completely correspond to what it is in tendency or idea, viz. the reconciler and sustainer of the rights that arise out of the social relations of men. On this principle there can be no right to disobey or evade any particular law on the ground that it inter- feres with any freedom of action, any right of managing his children or ' doing what he will with his own,' which but for that law the individual would possess. Any power which has been allowed to the individual up to a certain time, he is apt to regard as permanently his right. It has, indeed, been so far his right, if the exercise of that power has been allowed with any reference to social good, but it does not, as he is apt to think, remain his right when a law has been enacted that interferes with it. A man e.g. has been allowed to drive at any pace he likes through the streets, to build houses without any reference to sanitary conditions, to keep his children at home or send them to work ' analphabetic,' to buy or sell alcoholic drinks at his pleasure. If laws are passed interfering with any or all of these powers, he says that his rights are being violated. But he only possessed these powers as rights through mem- bership of a society which secured them to him, and of which the only permanent bond consists in the reference to the well-being of its members as a whole. It has been the social recognition grounded on that reference that has rendered certain of his powers rights. If upon new con- ditions arising, or upon elements of social good being taken account of which had been overlooked before, or upon persons being taken into the reckoning as capable of participation in the social well-being who had previously been treated merely as means to its attainment,—if in any of these ways or otherwise the reference to social well-being suggest the necessity of some further regulation of the individual's

[1] [Above, sections 100, 101.]

liberty to do as he pleases, he can plead no right against this regulation, for every right that he has possessed has been dependent on that social judgment of its compatibility with general well-being which in respect to the liberties in question is now reversed.

143. 'Is then,' it may be asked, 'the general judgment as to the requirements of social well-being so absolutely authoritative that no individual right can exist against it? What if according to this judgment the institution of slavery is so necessary that citizens are prohibited by law from teaching slaves to read and from harbouring runaways? or if according to it the maintenance of a certain form of worship is so necessary that no other worship can be allowed and no opinion expressed antagonistic to it? Has the individual no rights against enactments founded on such accepted views of social well-being?' We may answer: A right against society as such, a right to act without reference to the needs or good of society, is an impossibility, since every right depends on some social relation, and a right against any group of associated men depends upon association on some footing of equality with them or with some other men. We saw how the right of the slave really rested on this basis, on a social capacity shown in the footing on which he actually lives with other men. On this principle it would follow, if we regard the state as the sustainer and harmoniser of social relations, that the individual can have no right against the state; that its law must be to him of absolute authority. But in fact, as actual states at best fulfil but partially their ideal function, we cannot apply this rule to practice. The general principle that the citizen must never act otherwise than as a citizen, does not carry with it an obligation under all conditions to conform to the law of his state, since those laws may be inconsistent with the true end of the state as the sustainer and harmoniser of social relations. The assertion, however, by the citizen of any right which the state does not recognise must be founded on a reference to an acknowledged social good. The fact that the individual would like to exercise the power claimed as a right does not render the exercise of it a right, nor does the fact that he has been hitherto allowed to exercise it render it a right, if social requirements have arisen under changed conditions. or have newly come to be recognised, with

which its exercise is incompatible. The reason that the assertion of an illegal right must be founded on reference to acknowledged social good is that, as we have seen, no exercise of a power, however abstractedly desirable for the promotion of human good it might be, can be claimed as a right unless there is some common consciousness of utility shared by the person making the claim and those on whom it is made. It is not a question whether or no it ought to be claimed as a right; it simply cannot be claimed except on this condition. It would have been impossible, e.g., in an ancient state, where the symbol of social union was some local worship, for a monotheistic reformer to claim a right to attempt the subversion of that worship. If a duty to do so had suggested itself, consciousness of the duty could never have expressed itself in the form of a claim of right, in the absence of any possible sense of a public interest in the religious revolution to which the claim could be addressed. Thus, just as it is not the exercise of every power, properly claimable as a right, that is a right in the full or explicit sense of being legally established, so it is not every power, of which the exercise would be desirable in an ideal state of things, that is properly claimable as a right. The condition of its being so claimable is that its exercise should be contributory to some social good which the public conscience is capable of appreciating, not necessarily one which in the existing prevalence of private interests can obtain due acknowledgment, but still one of which men in their actions and language show themselves to be aware.

144. Thus to the question, Has the individual no rights against enactments founded on imperfect views of social well-being? we may answer, He has no rights against them founded on any right to do as he likes. Whatever counter-rights he has must be founded on a relation to the social well-being, and that a relation of which his fellow-citizens are aware. He must be able to point to some public interest, generally recognised as such, which is involved in the exercise of the power claimed by him as a right; to show that it is not the general well-being, even as conceived by his fellow-citizens, but some special interest of a class that is concerned in preventing the exercise of the power claimed. In regard to the right of teaching or harbouring the slave, he must appeal to the actual capacity of the slave for community with other men as evinced in the manner described

above, to the recognition of this capacity as shown by the actual behaviour of the citizens in many respects towards the slave, to the addition to social well-being that results from the realisation of this capacity in all who possess it through rights being legally guaranteed to them. In this way he must show that the reference to social well-being, on which is founded the recognition of powers as rights, if fairly and thoroughly carried out, leads to the exercise of powers in favour of the slave, in the manner described, not to the prohibition of that exercise as the supposed law prohibits it. The response which in doing so he elicits from the conscience of fellow-citizens shows that in talking of the slave as 'a man and a brother,' he is exercising what is implicitly his right, though it is a right which has not become explicit through legal enactments. This response supplies the factor of social recognition which, as we have seen, is necessary in order to render the exercise of any power a right. To have an implicit right, however, to exercise a power which the law disallows is not the same thing as having a right to exercise that right. The right may be claimed without the power being actually exercised so long as the law prohibits its exercise. The question, therefore, would arise whether the citizen was doing his duty as such— acting as a member of the state—if he not merely did what he could for the repeal of the law prohibiting the instruction of a slave or the assistance of runaways, but himself in defiance of the law instructed and assisted them. As a general rule, no doubt, even bad laws, laws representing the interests of classes or individuals as opposed to those of the community, should be obeyed. There can be no right to disobey them, even while their repeal is urged on the ground that they violate rights, because the public interest, on which all rights are founded, is more concerned in the general obedience to law than in the exercise of those powers by individuals or classes which the objectionable laws unfairly withhold. The maintenance of a duty prohibiting the import of certain articles in the interest of certain manu-facturers would be no justification for smuggling these articles. The smuggler acts for his private gain, as does the man who buys of him; and no violation of the law for the private gain of the violator, however unfair the law violated, can justify itself by reference to a recognised public good, or consequently be vindicated as a right. On the other hand, there may be cases in which the public interest—not merely according to some remote philosopher's view of it, but according to conceptions which the people are able to assimilate—is best served by a violation of some actual law. It is so in regard to slavery when the public conscience has come to recognise a capacity for right (for exercising powers under the control of a reference to general well-being) in a body of men to whom legal rights have hitherto been refused, but when some powerful class in its own interest resists the alteration of the law. In such a case the violation of the law on behalf of the slave is not only not a violation in the interest of the violator; the general sense of right on which the general observance of law depends being represented by it, there is no danger of its making a breach in the law-abiding habits of the people.

145. 'But this,' it will be said, ' is to assume a condition of things in which the real difficulty of the question disappears. What is to be done when no recognition of the implicit rights of the slave can be elicited from the public conscience ; when the legal prohibitions described are supported by the only conceptions of general good of which the body of citizens is capable ? Has the citizen still a right to disregard these legal prohibitions ? Is the assertion of such a right compatible with the doctrine that social recognition of any mode of action as contributory to the common good is necessary to constitute a right so to act, and that no member of a state can have a right to act otherwise than according to that position ? ' The question, be it observed, is not as to the right of the slave, but as to the right of the citizen to treat the slave as having rights in a state of which the law forbids his being so treated. The claim of the slave to be free, his right implicit to have rights explicit, i.e. to membership of a society of which each member is treated by the rest as entitled to seek his own good in his own way, on the supposition that he so seeks it as not to interfere with the like freedom of quest on the part of others, rests, as we have seen, on the fact that the slave is determined by conceptions of a good common to himself with others, as shown by the actual social relations in which he lives. No state-law can neutralise this right. The state may refuse him

family rights and rights of property, but it cannot help his living as a member of a family, acting and being treated as a father, husband, son, or brother, and therefore cannot extinguish the rights which are necessarily involved in his so acting and being so treated.   Nor can it prevent him from appropriating things and from associating with others on the understanding that they respect each other's appropriations, and thus possessing and exercising rights of property.   He has thus rights which the state neither gives nor can take away, and they amount to or constitute a right to freedom in the sense explained.   The state, under which the slave is a slave, refusing to recognise this right, he is not limited in its exercise by membership of the state.   He has a right to assert his right to such membership in any way compatible with that susceptibility to the claims of human fellowship on which the right rests.   Other men have claims upon him, conditioning his rights, but the state, as such, which refuses to recognise his rights, has no claim on him.   The obligation to observe the law, because it is the law, does not exist for him.

146. It is otherwise with the citizen. The slave has a claim upon him to be treated in a certain way, the claim which is properly described as that of a common humanity.   But the state which forbids him so to treat the slave has also a claim upon him, a claim which embodies many of the claims that arise out of a common humanity in a form that reconciles them with each other.   Now it may be argued that the claim of the state is only absolutely paramount on the supposition that in its commands and prohibitions it takes account of all the claims that arise out of human fellowship; that its authority over the individual is in principle the authority of those claims, taken as a whole ; that if, as in the case supposed, its ordinances conflict with those claims as possessed by a certain class of persons, their authority, which is essentially a conditional or derived authority, disappears ; that a disregard of them in the interest of the claims which they disregard is really conformity to the requirements of the state according to its true end or idea, since it interferes with none of the claims or interests which the state has its value in maintaining or protecting, but, on the contrary, forces on the attention of members of the state claims which they hitherto disregarded; and that if the conscience of the

citizens is so far mastered by the special private interests which the institution of slavery breeds that it cannot be brought to recognise action on the slave's behalf as contributory to a common good, yet there is no ground under such conditions for considering a man's fellow-citizens to be the sole organs of the recognition which is needed to render his power of action a right; that the needful recognition is at any rate forthcoming from the slave, and from all those acquainted with the action in whom the idea of a good common to each man with others operates freely.

147. This may be truly urged, but it does not therefore follow that the duty of befriending the slave is necessarily paramount to the duty of obeying the law which forbids his being befriended: and if it is possible for the latter duty to be paramount, it will follow, on the principle that there is no right to violate a duty, that under certain conditions the right of helping the slave may be cancelled by the duty of obeying the prohibitory law. It would be so if the violation of law in the interest of the slave were liable to result in general anarchy, not merely in the sense of the dissolution of this or that form of civil combination, but of the disappearance of the conditions under which any civil combination is possible; for such a destruction of the state would mean a general loss of freedom, a general substitution of force for mutual good-will in men's dealings with each other, that would outweigh the evil of any slavery under such limitations and regulations as an organised state imposes on it.

I. *PRIVATE RIGHTS.*

THE RIGHT TO LIFE AND LIBERTY

148. RETURNING from this digression, we resume our consideration of the nature and functions of the state. In order to understand this nature, we must understand the nature of those rights which do not come into being with the state, but arise out of social relations that may exist where a state is not; it being the first though not the only office of the state to maintain those rights. They depend for their existence, indeed, on society, a society of men who recognise each other as ἴσοι καὶ ὅμοιοι, as capable of a common well-being, but not on society's having assumed the form of a state. They may therefore be treated as claims of the individual without reference to the form of the society which concedes or recognises them, and on whose recognition, as we have seen, their nature as rights depends. Only it must be borne in mind that the form in which these claims are admitted and acted on by men in their dealings with each other varies with the form of society; that the actual form, e.g., in which the individual's right of property is admitted under a patriarchal *régime* is very different from that in which it is admitted in a state; and that though the principle of each right is throughout the same, it is a principle which only comes to be fully recognised and acted on when the state has not only been formed, but fully developed according to its idea.

149. The rights which may be treated as independent of the state in the sense explained are of course those which are commonly distinguished as *private*, in opposition to *public* rights. 'If rights be analysed, they will be found to consist of several kinds. For, first, they are such as regard a man's own person; secondly, such as regard his dominion over the external and sensible things by which he is surrounded; thirdly, such as regard his private relations as a member of a family; fourthly, such as regard his social state or condition as a member of the community : the first of which classes may be designated as *personal rights* ; the second, as *rights of property* ; the third, as *rights in private relations* ; and the fourth, as *public rights*.' (Stephen, *Comm.*, I, p. 136.)

150. An objection might fairly be made to distinguishing one class of rights as 'personal,' on the ground that all rights are so; not merely in the legal sense of 'person,' according to which the proposition is a truism, since every right implies a person as its subject, but in the moral sense, since all rights depend on that capacity in the individual for being determined by a conception of well-being, as an object at once for himself and for others, which constitutes personality in the moral sense. By personal rights in the above classification are meant rights of life and liberty, i.e. of preserving one's body from the violence of other men, and of using it as an instrument only of one's own will; if of another's, still only through one's own. The reason why these come to be spoken of as 'personal' is probably the same with the reason why we talk of a man's 'person' in the sense simply of his body. They may, however, be reckoned in a special sense personal even by those who consider all rights personal, because the person's possession of a body and its exclusive determination by his own will is the condition of his exercising any other rights,—indeed, of all manifestation of personality. Prevent a man from possessing property (in the ordinary sense), and his personality may still remain. Prevent him (if it were possible) from using his body to express a will, and the will itself could not become a reality; he would not be really a person.

151. If there are such things as rights at all, then, there must be a right to life and liberty, or, to put it more properly, to free life. No distinction can be made between the right to life and the right to liberty, for there can be no right to mere life, no right to life on the part of a being that has not also the right to use the life according to the motions of its own will. What is the foundation of this right? The answer is, capacity on the part of the subject for membership of a society, for determination of the will, and through it of

the bodily organisation, by the conception of a well-being as common to self with others. This capacity is the foundation of the right, or the right potentially, which becomes actual through the recognition of the capacity by a society, and through the power which the society in consequence secures to the individual of acting according to the capacity. In principle, or intrinsically, or in respect of that which it has it in itself to become, the right is one that belongs to every man in virtue of his human nature (of the qualities that render him capable of any fellowship with any other men), and is a right as between him and any other men; because, as we have seen, the qualities which enable him to act as a member of any one society having the general well-being of its members for its object (as distinct from any special object requiring special talent for its accomplishment) form a capacity for membership of any other such society; but actually, or as recognised, it only gradually becomes a right of a man, as man, and against all men.

152. At first it is only a right of the man as a member of some one particular society, and a right as between him and the other members of that society, the society being naturally a family or tribe. Then, as several such societies come to recognise, in some limited way, a common well-being, and thus to associate on settled terms, it comes to be a right not merely between the members of any one of the societies, but between members of the several families or tribes in their dealings with each other, not, however, as men, but only as belonging to this or that particular family. This is the state of things in which, if one man is damaged or killed, compensation is made according to the terms of some customary law by the family or tribe of the offender to that of the man damaged or killed, the compensation varying according to the rank of the family. Upon this system, generally through some fusion of family demarcations and privileges, whether through pressure upward of a population hitherto inferior, or through a levelling effected by some external power, there supervenes one in which the relation between citizen and citizen, as such, is substituted for that between family and family as such. This substitution is one of the essential processes in the formation of the state. It is compatible, however, with the closest limitation of the privileges of citizenship, and implies no acknowledgment in

man as man of the right to free life ascribed to the citizen
as citizen. In the ancient world the companion of citizenship is everywhere slavery, and it was only actual citizenship,
not any such capacity for becoming a citizen as might
naturally be held to be implied in civil birth, that was
considered to give a right to live; for the exposure of
children was everywhere practised [1] (and with the approval
of the philosophers), a practice in strong contrast with the
principle of modern law that even a child in the womb has
a right to live.

153. The influences commonly pointed out as instrumental
in bringing about the recognition of rights in the man, as independent of particular citizenship, are these: (1) The adju-
dication by Roman prætors of questions at issue between
citizens and those who were not so, which led to the formation of the system of 'equity,' independent of the old civil
law and tending gradually to be substituted for it. The
existence of such a system, however, presupposes the
recognition of rights so far independent of citizenship in a
particular state as to obtain between citizens of different
states. (2) The doctrine of a 'law of nature,' applicable to
dealings of all men, popularised by the Stoics. (3) The
Christian conception of the universal redemption of a
brotherhood, of which all could become members through a
mental act within the power of all.

154. The admission of a right to free life on the part of
every man, as man, does in fact logically imply the conception of all men as forming one society in which each
individual has some service to render, one organism in
which each has a function to fulfil. There can be no claim
on society such as constitutes a right, except in respect of a
capacity freely (i.e. under determination by conception of
the good) to contribute to its good. If the claim is made
on behalf of any and every human being, it must be a claim
on human society as a whole, and there must be a possible

---

[1] Tacitus speaks of it as a peculiarity
of the Jews and Germans that they did
not allow the killing of younger children
(*Hist.*, V, 5; *Germ.* 19). Aristotle (Pol.
1335, b, 19) enjoins that μηδὲν πεπη-
ρωμένον shall be brought up, but seems
to condemn exposure, preferring that
the required limit of population should
be preserved by destruction of the
embryo, on the principle that τὸ ὅσιον
καὶ τὸ μὴ διωρισμένον τῇ αἰσθήσει καὶ
τῷ ζῆν ἔσται. Plato's rule is the same
as regards the defective children and
the procuring abortion, but he leaves it
in the dark whether he meant any
healthy children, actually born, to be
put out of the way (*Rep.* 460 C. and
461 C.).

common good of human society as a whole, conceivable as
independent of the special conditions of particular societies,
to render such a claim possible. We often find, however,
that men assimilate a practical idea in respect of one of
its implications without doing so in respect of the rest.
Thus the idea of the individual's right to free life has
been strongly laid hold of in Christendom in what may
be called an abstract or negative way, but little notice
has been taken of what it involves. Slavery is everywhere
condemned. It is established that no one has a right to
prevent the individual from determining the conditions of
his own life. We treat life as sacred even in the human
embryo, and even in hopeless idiots and lunatics recognise a
right to live, a recognition which can only be rationally
explained on either or both of two grounds : (1) that we do
not consider either their lives, or the society which a man
may freely serve, to be limited to this earth, and thus
ascribe to them a right to live on the strength of a social
capacity which under other conditions may become what it
is not here ; or (2) that the distinction between curable and
incurable, between complete and incomplete, social incapacity
is so indefinite that we cannot in any case safely assume it
to be such as to extinguish the right to live. Or perhaps it
may be argued that even in cases where the incapacity is ascer-
tainably incurable, the patient has still a social function (as
undoubtedly those who are incurably ill in other ways have),
a passive function as the object of affectionate ministrations
arising out of family instincts and memories ; and that the
right to have life protected corresponds to this passive social
function. The fact, however, that we have almost to cast
about in certain cases for an explanation of the established
belief in the sacredness of human life, shows how deeply
rooted that belief is unless where some counter-belief interferes with it.

155. On the other hand, it is equally noticeable that
there are counter-beliefs which, under conditions, do neutralise
it, and that certain other beliefs, which form its proper
complement, have very slight hold on the mind of modern
Christendom. It is taken for granted that the exigencies
of the state in war, whether the war be necessary or not for
saving the state from dissolution, absolutely neutralise the
right to live. We are little influenced by the idea of the

universal brotherhood of men, of mankind as forming one society with a common good, of which the conception may determine the action of its members. In international dealings we are apt to suppose that it can have no place at all. Yet, as has been pointed out, it is the proper correlative of the admission of a right to free life as belonging to man in virtue simply of his human nature. And though this right can only be grounded on the capacity, which belongs to the human nature, for freely fulfilling some function in the social organism, we do very little to give reality to the capacity or to enable it to realise itself. We content ourselves with enacting that no man shall be used by other men as a means against his will, but we leave it to be pretty much a matter of chance whether or no he shall be qualified to fulfil any social function, to contribute anything to the common good, and to do so freely (i.e. under the conception of a common good). The only reason why a man should not be used by other men simply as a means to their ends, is that he should use himself as a means to an end which is really his and theirs at once. But while we say that he shall not be used as a means, we often leave him without the chance of using himself for any social end at all.

156. Four questions then arise: (1) With what right do the necessities of war override the individual's right of life? (2) In what relation do the rights of states to act for their own interest stand to that right of human society, as such, of which the existence is implied in the possession of right by the individual as a member of that society, irrespectively of the laws of particular states? (3) On what principle is it to be assumed that the individual by a certain conduct of his own forfeits the right of free life, so that the state (at any rate for a time) is entitled to subject him to force, to treat him as an animal or a thing? Is this forfeiture ever so absolute and final that the state is justified in taking away his life? (4) What is the nature and extent of the individual's claim to be enabled to realise that capacity for contributing to a social good, which is the foundation of his right to free life?

K. *THE RIGHT OF THE STATE OVER THE INDIVIDUAL IN WAR*

157. (1) It may be admitted that to describe war as 'multitudinous murder' is a figure of speech. The essence of murder does not lie in the fact that one man takes away the life of another, but that he does this to 'gain his private ends' and with 'malice' against the person killed. I am not here speaking of the legal definition of murder, but of murder as a term of moral reprobation, in which sense it must be used by those who speak of war as 'multitudinous murder.' They cannot mean murder in the legal sense, because in that sense only 'unlawful killing,' which killing in war is not, is murder. When I speak of 'malice,' therefore, I am not using 'malice' in the legal sense. In that sense 'malice' is understood to be the attribute of every 'wrongful act done intentionally without just or lawful excuse,'[1] and is ascribed to acts (such as killing an officer of justice, knowing him to be such, while resisting him in a riot) in which there is no ill-will of the kind which we suppose in murder, when we apply the term in its natural sense as one of moral disapprobation. Of murder in the moral sense the characteristics are those stated, and these are not present in the case of a soldier who kills one on the other side in battle. He has no ill-will to that particular person or to any particular person. He incurs an equal risk with the person whom he kills, and incurs that risk not for the sake of killing him. His object in undergoing it is not private to himself, but a service (or what he supposes to be a service) to his country, a good which is his own no doubt (that is implied in his desiring it), but which he presents to himself as common to him with others. Indeed, those who might speak of war as 'multitudinous murder' would not look upon

---

[1] Markby, *Elements of Law*, sec. 226.

the soldier as a murderer. If reminded that there cannot be a murder without a murderer, and pressed to say who, when a bloody battle takes place, the murderer or murderers are, they would probably point to the authors of the war. It may be questioned, by the way, whether there has ever been a war of which the origination could be truly said to rest with a definite person or persons, in the same way in which the origination of an act which would be called murder in the ordinary sense rests with a particular person. No doubt there have been wars for which certain assignable individuals were specially blameable, wars which they specially helped to bring about or had special means of preventing (and the more the wickedness of such persons is kept in mind the better); but even in these cases the cause of the war can scarcely be held to be gathered up within the will of any individual, or the combined will of certain individuals, in the same way as is the cause of murder or other punishable acts. When A.B. is murdered, the sole cause lies in some definite volition of C.D. or others, however that volition may have been caused. But when a war ' breaks out,' though it is not to be considered, as we are too apt to consider it, a natural calamity which could not be prevented, it would be hard to maintain that the sole cause lies in some definite volition on the part of some assignable person or persons, even of those who are most to blame. Passing over this point, however, if the acts of killing in war are not murders (in the *moral* sense, the *legal* being out of the question) because they lack those characteristics on the part of the agent's state of mind which are necessary to constitute a murder, the persons who cause those acts to be committed, if such persons can be pointed out, are not the authors of murder, multitudinous or other. They would only be so if the characteristic of ' malice,' which is absent on the part of the immediate agent of the act, were present on their part as its ultimate agents. But this is not the case. However selfish their motives, they cannot fairly be construed into ill-will towards the persons who happened to be killed in the war; and therefore, whatever wickedness the persons responsible for the war are guilty of, they are not guilty of ' murder ' in any natural sense of the term, nor is there any murder in the case at all.

158. It does not follow from this, however, that war is

ever other than a great wrong, as a violation on a multi-tudinous scale of the individual's right to life. Whether it is so or not must be discussed on other grounds. If there is such a thing as a right to life on the part of the individual man as such, is there any reason to doubt that this right is violated in the case of every man killed in war? It is not to the purpose to allege that in order to a violation of right there must be not only a suffering of some kind on the part of the subject of a right, but an intentional act causing it on the part of a human agent. There is of course no viola-tion of right when a man is killed by a wild beast or a stroke of lightning, because there is no right as between a man and a beast or between a man and a natural force. But the deaths in a battle are caused distinctly by human agency and in-tentional agency. The individual soldier may not have any very distinct intention when he fires his rifle except to obey orders, but the commanders of the army and the statesmen who send it into the field intend the death of as many men as may be necessary for their purpose. It is true they do not intend the death of this or that particular person, but no more did the Irishman who fired into a body of police guarding the Fenian prisoners. It might fairly be held that this circum-stance exempted the Irishman from the special moral guilt of murder, though according to our law it did not exempt him from the legal guilt expressed by that term; but no one would argue that it made the act other than a violation of the right to life on the part of the policeman killed. No more can the absence of an intention to kill this or that spe-cific person on the part of those who cause men to be killed in battle save their act from being a violation of the right to life.

159. Is there then any condition on the part of the persons killed that saves the act from having this character? It may be urged that when the war is conducted according to usages that obtain between civilised nations, (not when it is a village-burning war like that between the English and Af-ghans), the persons killed are voluntary combatants, and οὐδεὶς ἀδικεῖται ἑκών. Soldiers, it may be said, are in the position of men who voluntarily undertake a dangerous employment. If some of them are killed, this is not more a violation of the human right to life than is the death of men who have engaged to work in a dangerous coal-pit. To this it must be

answered that if soldiers did in fact voluntarily incur the special risk of death incidental to their calling, it would not follow that the right to life was not violated in their being killed. It is not a right which it rests with a man to retain or give up at his pleasure. It is not the less a wrong that a man should be a slave because he has sold himself into slavery. The individual's right to live is but the other side of the right which society has in his living. The individual can no more voluntarily rid himself of it than he can of the social capacity, the human nature, on which it is founded. Thus, however ready men may be for high wages to work in a dangerous pit, a wrong is held to be done if they are killed in it. If provisions which might have made it safe have been neglected, some-one is held responsible. If nothing could make it safe, the working of the pit would not be allowed. The reason for not more generally applying the power of the state to prevent voluntary noxious employments, is not that there is no wrong in the death of the individual through the incidents of an employment which he has voluntarily undertaken, but that the wrong is more effectually prevented by training and trusting individuals to protect themselves than by the state protecting them. Thus the waste of life in war would not be the less a wrong,—not the less a violation of the right, which subsists between all members of society, and which none can alienate, that each should have his life respected by society,—if it were the fact that those whose lives are wasted voluntarily incurred the risk of losing them. But it can scarcely be held to be the fact. Not only is it impossible, even when war is conducted on the most civilised methods, to prevent great incidental loss of life (to say nothing of other injury) among non-combatants; the waste of the life of the combatants is one which the power of the state compels. This is equally true whether the army is raised by voluntary enlistment or by conscription. It is obviously so in the case of conscription; but under a system of voluntary enlistment, though the individual soldier cannot say that he in particular has been compelled by the government to risk his life, it is still the case that the state compels the risk of a certain number of lives. It decrees that an army of such a size shall be raised, though if it can get the men by voluntary hiring it does not exercise com-pulsion on the men of a particular age, and it sends the

army into the field.   Its compulsive agency causes the
death of the soldiers killed, not any voluntary action on the
part of the soldiers themselves.   The action of the soldiers
no doubt contributes to the result, for if they all refused to
fight there would be no killing, but it is an action put in
motion and directed by the power of the state, which is
compulsive in the sense that it operates on the individual
in the last resort through fear of death.

160. We have then in war a destruction of human life
inflicted on the sufferers intentionally by voluntary human
agency.   It is true, as we saw, that it is not easy to say in
any case by whose agency in particular.   We may say indeed
that it is by the agency of the state, but what exactly does
that mean?   The state here must = the sovereign power in
the state; but it is always difficult to say by whom that
power is wielded, and if we could in any case specify its
present holders, the further question will arise whether
their course of action has not been shaped for them
by previous holders of power.   But however widely distributed the agency may be which causes the destruction of
life in war, it is still intentional human agency.   The
destruction is not the work of accident or of nature.   If then
it is to be other than a wrong, because a violation of the
right to mutual protection of life involved in the membership of human society, it can only be because there is
exercised in war some right that is paramount to this.   It
may be argued that this is the case; that there is no right
to the preservation of life at the cost of losing the necessary
conditions of 'living well'; that war is in some cases the only
means of maintaining these conditions, and that where this
is so, the wrong of causing the destruction of physical life
disappears in the paramount right of preserving the conditions under which alone moral life is possible.

161. This argument, however, seems to be only available
for shifting the quarter in which we might be at first
disposed to lay the blame of the wrong involved in war, not
for changing the character of that wrong.   It goes to show
that the wrong involved in the death of certain soldiers does
not necessarily lie with the government which sends those
soldiers into the field, because this may be the only means
by which the government can prevent more serious wrong;
it does not show that there is no wrong in their death.   If

the integrity of any state can only be maintained at the cost of war, and if that state is more than what many so-called states have been,—more than an aggregation of individuals or communities under one ruling power,—if it so far fulfils the idea of a state, that its maintenance is necessary to the free development of the people belonging to it; then by the authorities or people of that state no wrong is done by the destruction of life which war involves, except so far as they are responsible for the state of things which renders the maintenance of the integrity of the state impossible by other means. But how does it come about that the integrity of such a state is endangered? Not by accident or by the forces of nature, but by intentional human agency in some form or other, however complicated; and with that agency lies the wrong-doing. To determine it (as we might be able to do if a horde of barbarians broke in on a civilised state, compelling it to resort to war for its defence) is a matter of small importance : what *is* important to bear in mind (being one of those obvious truths out of which we may allow ourselves to be sophisticated), is that the destruction of life in war is always wrong-doing, whoever be the wrong-doer, and that in the wars most strictly defensive of political freedom the wrong-doing is only removed from the defenders of political freedom to be transferred elsewhere. If it is difficult in any case to say precisely where, that is only a reason for more general self-reproach, for a more humbling sense (as the preachers would say) of complicity in that radical (but conquerable, because moral) evil of mankind which renders such a means of maintaining political freedom necessary. The language, indeed, which we hear from the pulpit about war being a punishment for the sins of mankind, is perfectly true, but it needs to be accompanied by the reminder that this punishment of sin is simply a consequence of the sin and itself a further sin, brought about by the action of the sinner, not an external infliction brought about by agencies to which man is not a party.

162. In fact, however, if most wars had been wars for the maintenance or acquisition of political freedom, the difficulty of fixing the blame of them, or at any rate of freeing one of the parties in each case from blame, would be much less than it really is.   Of the European wars of the last four

hundred years, how many could be fairly said to have been wars in which either or any of the parties were fighting for this end? Perhaps the wars in which the Dutch Republics defended themselves against Spain and against Louis XIV, and that in which Germany shook off the dominion of Napoleon. Perhaps the more recent struggles of Italy and Hungary against the Austrian Government. Perhaps in the first outset of the war of 1792 the French may be fairly held to have been defending institutions necessary for the development of social freedom and equality. In this war, however, the issue very soon ceased to be one between the defenders of such institutions on the one side, and their assailants on the other, and in most modern wars the issue has not been of this kind at all. The wars have arisen primarily out of the rival ambition of kings and dynasties for territorial aggrandisement, with national antipathies and ecclesiastical ambitions, and the passions arising out of religious partisanship, as complicating influences. As nations have come more and more to distinguish and solidify themselves, and a national consciousness has come definitely to be formed in each, the rival ambitions of nations have tended more and more first to support, then perhaps to supersede, the ambitions of dynasties as causes of war. The delusion has been practically dominant that the gain of one nation must mean the loss of another. Hence national jealousies in regard to colonial extension, hostile tariffs and the effort of each nation to exclude others from its markets. The explosion of this idea in the region of political economy has had little effect in weakening its hold on men's minds. The people of one nation still hear with jealousy of another nation's advance in commerce, as if it meant some decay of their own. And if the commercial jealousy of nations is very slow in disappearing, their vanity, their desire apart from trade each to become or to seem stronger than the other, has very much increased. A hundred and fifty years ago national vanity could scarcely be said to be an influence in politics. The people under one ruler were not homogeneous enough, had not enough of a corporate consciousness, to develope a national vanity. Now (under the name of patriotism) it has become a more serious disturber of peace than dynastic ambition. Where the latter is dangerous, it is because it has national vanity to work upon.

163. Our conclusion then is that the destruction of life in war (to say nothing of other evils incidental to it with which we are not here concerned) is always wrong-doing, with whomsoever the guilt of the wrong-doing may lie; that only those parties to a war are exempt from a share in the guilt who can truly plead that to them war is the only means of maintaining the social conditions of the moral development of man, and that there have been very few cases in which this plea could be truly made. In saying this it is not forgotten, either that many virtues are called into exercise by war, or that wars have been a means by which the movement of mankind, which there is reason for considering a progress to higher good, has been carried on. These facts do not make the wrong-doing involved in war any less so. If nothing is to be accounted wrong-doing through which final good is wrought, we must give up either the idea of there being such a thing as wrong-doing, or the idea of there being such a thing as final good. If final good results from the world of our experience, it results from processes in which wrong-doing is an inseparable element. Wrong-doing is voluntary action, either (in the deeper moral sense) proceeding from a will uninfluenced by the desire to be good on the part of the agent (which may be taken to include action tending to produce such action), or (in the sense contemplated by the ' jus naturæ ') it is action that interferes with the conditions necessary to the free-play and development of a good-will on the part of others. It may be that, according to the divine scheme of the world, such wrong-doing is an element in a process by which men gradually approximate more nearly to good (in the sense of a good will). We cannot think of God as a moral being without supposing this to be the case. But this makes no difference to wrong-doing in those relations in which it *is* wrong-doing, and with which alone we are concerned, viz. in relation to the will of human agents and to the results which those agents can foresee and intend to produce. If an action, so far as any results go which the agent can have in view or over which he has control, interferes with conditions necessary to the free-play and development of a good-will on the part of others, it is not the less wrong-doing because, through some agency which is not his, the effects which he intended, and which rendered it wrong-doing, come to contribute to an

ulterior good. Nor, if it issues from bad will (in the sense
explained), is it less wrong (in the moral sense) because this
will is itself, in the view of some higher being, contributory
to a moral good which is not, in whole or part, within the
view of the agent. If then war is wrong-doing in both the
above senses (as it is always, at any rate on the part of those
with whom the ultimate responsibility for it lies), it does not
cease to be so on account of any good resulting from it in a
scheme of providence.

164. 'But,' it may be asked, 'are we justified in saying
that it is always wrong-doing on the part of those with
whom the ultimate responsibility lies? It is admitted that
certain virtues may be evoked by war; that it may have results contributory to the moral progress of mankind; may
not the eliciting of these virtues, the production of these
results, be contemplated by the originators of war, and does
not the origination of war, so far as influenced by such
motives, cease to be wrong-doing? It must be admitted that
Cæsar's wars in Gaul were unprovoked wars of conquest, but
their effect was the establishment of Roman civilisation with
its equal law over a great part of western Europe, in such a
way that it was never wholly swept away, and that a permanent influence in the progress of the European polity
can be traced to it. May he not be credited with having
had, however indefinitely, such an effect as this in view?
Even if his wish to extend Roman civilisation was secondary to a plan for raising an army by which he might
master the Republic, is he to have no credit for the beneficent results which are admitted to have ensued from the
success of that plan? May not a similar justification be urged
for English wars in India? If, again, the establishment of
the civil unity of Germany and the liberation of Christian
populations in Turkey are admitted to have been gains to
mankind, is not that a justification of the persons concerned
in the origination of the wars that brought about those
results, so far as they can be supposed to have been influenced
by a desire for them?'

165. These objections might be to the purpose if we were
attempting the task (generally, if not always, an impossible
one) of determining the moral desert, good or ill, of those
who have been concerned in bringing this or that war about.
Their tendency merely is to distribute the blame of the

wrong-doing involved in war, to show how widely ramified
is the agency in that wrong-doing, not to affect its character
as wrong-doing. If the only way of civilising Gaul was to
kill all the people whom Cæsar's wars caused to be killed,
and if the desire for civilising it was a prevailing motive in
Cæsar's mind, so much the better for Cæsar, but so much the
worse for the other unassignable and innumerable human
agents who brought it about that such an object could only
be attained in such a way. We are not, indeed, entitled to
say that it could have been brought about in any other way.
It is true to say (if we know what we are about in saying it)
that nothing which happens in the world could have happened
otherwise than it has. The question for us is, whether that
condition of things which rendered e.g. Cæsar's Gallic wars,
with the violation of human rights which they involved, the
interference in the case of innumerable persons with the
conditions under which man can be helpful to man (physical
life being the first of these), the *sine qua non* in the promotion of ulterior human welfare, was or was not the work
of human agency. If it was (and there is no doubt that it
was, for to what merely natural agency could the necessity
be ascribed?), then in that ordinary sense of the word ' could '
in which it expresses our responsibility for our actions, men
could have brought about the good result without the evil
means. They could have done so if they had been better.
It was owing to human wickedness—if less on Cæsar's
part, then so much the more on the part of innumerable
others—that the wrong-doing of those wars was the appropriate means to this ulterior good. So in regard to
the other cases instanced. It is idle to speculate on
other means by which the permanent pacification of India,
or the unification of Germany, or the liberation of Chris-
tians in European Turkey might have been brought
about; but it is important to bear in mind that the innumerable wrong acts involved in achieving them—acts
wrong, because violations of the rights of those directly
affected by them—did not cease to be wrong acts because
under the given condition of things the results specified
would not have been obtained without them. This given
condition of things was not like that (e.g.) which compels
the castaways from a shipwreck, so many days from shore,
and with only so much provision in their boat, to draw lots

which shall be thrown overboard. It was a condition of
things which human wickedness, through traceable and un-
traceable channels, brought about. If the individual pro-
moters of wars, which through the medium of multitudinous
wrong-doing have yielded good to mankind, have been really
influenced by a desire for any such good,—and much scepti-
cism is justified in regard to such a supposition,—then so
much less of the guilt of the wrong-doing has been theirs.
No nation, at any rate, that has taken part in such wars can
fairly take credit for having been governed by such a motive.
It has been either a passive instrument in the hands of its
rulers, or has been animated by less worthy motives, very
mixed, but of which perhaps a diffused desire for excitement
has been the most innocent. On what reasonable ground
can Englishmen or Germans or Russians claim that their
several nations took part in the wars by which India was
pacified, Germany unified, Bulgaria liberated, under the
dominant influence of a desire for human good? Rather,
if the action of a national conscience in such matters is
possible at all, they should take shame for their share in
that general human selfishness which rendered certain conditions of human development only attainable by such means.

166. (2) Reverting then to the questions which arose[1] out
of the assertion of a right to free life on the part of the individual man as such, it appears that the first must be answered
in the negative. No state of war can make the destruction
of man's life by man other than a wrong, though the wrong
is not always chargeable upon all the parties to a war. The
second question is virtually answered by what has been said
about the first. In regard to the state according to its
idea the question could not arise, for according to its idea
the state is an institution in which all rights are harmoniously maintained, in which all the capacities that give rise
to rights have free-play given to them. No action in its
own interest of a state that fulfilled this idea could conflict
with any true interest or right of general society, of the men
not subject to its law taken as a whole. There is no such
thing as an inevitable conflict between states. There is
nothing in the nature of the state that, given a multiplicity
of states, should make the gain of the one the loss of the
other. The more perfectly each one of them attains its

[1] [Above, sec. 156.]

proper object of giving free scope to the capacities of all persons living on a certain range of territory, the easier it is for others to do so; and in proportion as they all do so the danger of conflict disappears.

167. On the other hand, the imperfect realisation of civil equality in the full sense of the term in certain states, is in greater or less degree a source of danger to all. The presence in states either of a prerogatived class or of a body of people who, whether by open denial of civil rights or by restrictive laws, are thwarted in the free development of their capacities, or of an ecclesiastical organisation which disputes the authority of the state on matters of right and thus prevents the perfect civil fusion of its members with other citizens, always breeds an imagination of there being some competition of interests between states. The privileged class involuntarily believes and spreads the belief that the interest of the state lies in some extension without, not in an improvement of organisation within. A suffering class attracts sympathy from without and invites interference with the state which contains it; and that state responds, not by healing the sore, but by defending against aggression what it conceives to be its special interests, but which are only special on account of its bad organisation. Or perhaps the suffering population overflows into another state, as the Irish into America, and there becomes a source not only of internal difficulty but of hostile feeling between it and the state where the suffering population still survives. People, again, who, in matters which the state treats as belonging to itself, take their direction from an ecclesiastical power external to the state under which they live, are necessarily in certain relations alien to that state, and may at any time prove a source of apparently conflicting interests between it and some other state, which under the influence of the hostile ecclesiastical power espouses their cause. Remove from European states, as they are and have been during the last hundred years, the occasions of conflict, the sources of apparently competing interests, which arise in one or other of the ways mentioned, —either from the mistaken view of state-interests which a privileged class inevitably takes, or from the presence in them of oppressed populations, or from what we improperly call the antagonism of religious confessions,—and there would not be or have been anything to disturb the peace

between them. And this is to say that the source of war
between states lies in their incomplete fulfilment of their
function; in the fact that there is some defect in the maintenance or reconciliation of rights among their subjects.

168. This is equally true in regard to those causes of
conflict which are loosely called 'religious.' These do not
arise out of any differences between the convictions of
different people in regard to the nature of God or their relations to Him, or the right way of worshipping Him. They
arise either out of some aggression upon the religious freedom of certain people, made or allowed by the powers of the
state, which thus puts these people in the position of an
alien or unenfranchised class, or else out of an aggression on
the rights of the state by some corporation calling itself
spiritual but really claiming sovereignty over men's actions
in the same relations in which the state claims to determine
them. There would be nothing tending to international disturbance in the fact that bodies of people who worship God
in the Catholic manner live in a state where the majority
worship in the Greek or Protestant manner, and alongside
of another state where the majority is Catholic, but for one
or other or both of these circumstances, viz. that the
Catholic worship and teaching is interfered with by the
Protestant or Greek state, and that Catholics are liable to a
direction by a power which claims to regulate men's transactions with each other by a law of its own, and which may
see fit (e.g.) to prohibit the Catholic subjects in the Greek or
Protestant state from being married, or having their parents
buried, or their children taught the necessary arts, in the
manner which the state directs. This reciprocal invasion of
right, the invasion of the rights of the state by the church
on the one side, and on the other the restriction placed by
the sovereign upon the subject's freedom, not of conscience,
(for that is impossible), but of expressing his conscience in
word and act, has sometimes caused a state of things in
which certain of the subjects of a state have been better
affected to another state than to their own, and in such a
case there is an element of natural hostility between the
states. An obvious instance to give of this relation between
states would have been that between Russia and Turkey, if
Turkey could be considered to have been constituted as a
state at all. Perhaps a better instance would be the position

of Ireland in the past; its disaffection to England and gravitation, first to France, then to the United States, caused chiefly by Protestant penal laws which in turn were at least provoked by the aggressive attitude of the church towards the English state. Whenever a like invasion of rights still takes place, e.g. in the treatment of the Catholic subjects of Russia in Poland, in the ultramontane movement of resistance to certain requirements of the state among the Catholic subjects of Germany, it tends to international conflict. And what is now a somewhat remote tendency has in the past been a formidable stimulant to war.

169. It is nothing then in the necessary organisation of the state, but rather some defect of that organisation in relation to its proper function of maintaining and reconciling rights, of giving scope to capacities, that leads to a conflict of apparent interests between one state and another. The wrong, therefore, which results to human society from conflicts between states cannot be condoned on the ground that it is a necessary incident of the existence of states. The wrong cannot be held to be lost in a higher right, which attaches to the maintenance of the state as the institution through which alone the freedom of man is realised. It is not the state, as such, but this or that particular state, which by no means fulfils its purpose, and might perhaps be swept away and superseded by another with advantage to the ends for which the true state exists, that needs to defend its interests by action injurious to those outside it. Hence there is no ground for holding that a state is justified in doing whatever its interests seem to require, irrespectively of effects on other men. If those effects are bad, as involving either a direct violation of personal rights or obstruction to the moral development of society anywhere in the world, then there is no ultimate justification for the political action that gives rise to them. The question can only be (as we have seen generally in regard to the wrong-doing of war), where in particular the blame lies. Whether there is any justification for a particular state, which in defence of its interests inflicts an injury on some portion of mankind; whether, e.g., the Germans are justified in holding Metz, on the supposition that their tenure of such a thoroughly French town necessarily thwarts in many ways the healthy activity of the

inhabitants, or the English in carrying fire and sword into
Afghanistan for the sake of acquiring a scientific frontier;
this must depend (1) on the nature of the interests thus
defended, (2) on the impossibility of otherwise defending
them, (3) on the question how they came to be endangered.
If they are interests of which the maintenance is essential
to those ends as a means to which the state has its value, if
the state which defends them has not itself been a joint-
cause of their being endangered, and if they cannot be
defended except at the cost of injury to some portion of
mankind, then the state which defends them is clear of the
guilt of that injury.   But the guilt is removed from it only
to be somewhere else, however wide its distribution may be.
It may be doubted, however, whether the second question
could ever be answered altogether in favour of a state which
finds it necessary to protect its interests at the cost of inflicting an injury on mankind.

170. It will be said, perhaps, that these formal argu-
ments in proof of the wrong-doing involved in war, and of
the unjustifiability of the policy which nations constantly
adopt in defence of their apparent interests, carry very
little conviction; that a state is not an abstract complex of
institutions for the maintenance of rights, but a nation, a
people, possessing such institutions; that the nation has its
passions which inevitably lead it to judge all questions of
international right from its own point of view, and to consider its apparent national interests as justifying anything;
that if it were otherwise, if the cosmopolitan point of view
could be adopted by nations, patriotism would be at an end;
that whether this be desirable or no, such an extinction of
national passions is impossible; that while they continue,
wars are as inevitable between nations as they would be
between individuals, if individuals were living in what
philosophers have imagined to be the state of nature, without recognition of a common superior; that nations in short
are in the position of men judging their own causes, which
it is admitted that no one can do impartially; and that this
state of things cannot be altered without the establishment
of a common constraining power, which would mean the
extinction of the life of independent states,—a result as undesirable as it is unattainable.   Projects of perpetual peace,
to be logical, must be projects of all-embracing empire.

171. There is some cogency in language of this kind. It is true that when we speak of a state as a living agency, we mean, not an institution or complex of institutions, but a nation organised in a certain way; and that members of the nation in their corporate or associated action are animated by certain passions, arising out of their association, which, though not egoistic relatively to the individual subjects of them (for they are motives to self-sacrifice), may, in their influence on the dealings of one nation with another, have an effect analogous to that which egoistic passions, properly so called, have upon the dealings of individuals with each other. On the other hand, it must be remembered that the national passion, which in any good sense is simply the public spirit of the good citizen, may take, and every day is taking, directions which lead to no collision between one nation and another; (or, to say the same thing negatively, that it is utterly false to speak as if the desire for one's own nation to show more military strength than others were the only or the right form of patriotism); and that though a nation, with national feeling of its own, must everywhere underlie a state, properly so called, yet still, just so far as the perfect organisation of rights within each nation, which entitles it to be called a state, is attained, the occasions of conflict between nations disappear; and again, that by the same process, just so far as it is satisfactorily carried out, an organ of expression and action is established for each nation in dealing with other nations, which is not really liable to be influenced by the same egoistic passions in dealing with the government of another nation as embroil individuals with each other. The love of mankind, no doubt, needs to be particularised in order to have any power over life and action. Just as there can be no true friendship except towards this or that individual, so there can be no true public spirit which is not localised in some way. The man whose desire to serve his kind is not centred primarily in some home, radiating from it to a commune, a municipality, and a nation, presumably has no effectual desire to serve his kind at all. But there is no reason why this localised or nationalised philanthropy should take the form of a jealousy of other nations or a desire to fight them, personally or by proxy. Those in whom it is strongest are every day expressing it in good works which benefit

their fellow-citizens without interfering with the men of
other nations. Those who from time to time talk of the
need of a great war to bring unselfish impulses into play,
give us reason to suspect that they are too selfish themselves
to recognise the unselfish activity that is going on all round
them. Till all the methods have been exhausted by which
nature can be brought into the service of man, till society
is so organised that everyone's capacities have free scope for
their development, there is no need to resort to war for a
field in which patriotism may display itself.

172. In fact, just so far as states are thoroughly formed,
the diversion of patriotism into the military channel tends
to come to an end. It is a survival from a condition of
things in which, as yet, the state, in the full sense, was not;
in the sense, namely, that in each territory controlled by a
single independent government, the rights of all persons, as
founded on their capacities for contributing to a common
good, are equally established by one system of law. If each
separately governed territory were inhabited by a people so
organised within itself, there would be nothing to lead to the
association of the public spirit of the good citizen with military aggressiveness,—an association which belongs properly
not to the πολιτεία, but to the δυναστεία. The Greek states,
however complete might be the equality of their citizens
among themselves, were all δυναστείαι in relation to some
subject populations, and, as such, jealous of each other. The
Peloponnesian war was eminently a war of rival δυναστείαι.
And those habits and institutions and modes of feeling in
Europe of the present day, which tend to international
conflict, are either survivals from the δυναστείαι of the past,
or arise out of the very incomplete manner in which, as
yet, over most of Europe the πολιτεία has superseded the
δυναστεία. Patriotism, in that special military sense in
which it is distinguished from public spirit, is not the temper
of the citizen dealing with fellow-citizens, or with men who
are themselves citizens of their several states, but that of the
follower of the feudal chief, or of the member of a privileged
class conscious of a power, resting ultimately on force, over
an inferior population, or of a nation holding empire over
other nations.

173. Standing armies, again, though existing on a larger

scale now than ever before, are not products of the civilisation of Europe, but of the predominance over that civilisation
of the old δυναστείαι. The influences which have given rise
to and keep up those armies essentially belong to a state of
things in which mankind—even European mankind—is not
yet thoroughly organised into political life. Roughly sum-
marised, they are these: (1). The temporary confiscation by
Napoleon to his own account of the products of the French
Revolution, which thus, though founded on a true idea of
a citizenship in which not the few only, but all men, should
partake, for the time issued in a δυναστεία over the countries
which most directly felt the effects of the revolution.
(2). The consequent revival in dynastic forms, under the influence of antagonism to France, of national life in Germany.
(3). The aspiration after national unity elsewhere in Europe,
—a movement which must precede the organisation of states
on a sound basis, and for the time readily yields itself to
direction by a δυναστεία. (4). The existence, over all the
Slavonic side of Europe, of populations which are only just
beginning to make any approach to political life—the life
of the πολιτεία, or 'civitas'—and still offer a tempting field
to the ambition of rival δυναστείαι, Austrian, Russian, and
Turkish (which, indeed, are by no means to be put on a
level, but are alike as not resting on a basis of citizenship).
(5). The tenure of a great Indian empire by England, which
not only gives it a military character which would not belong to it simply as a state, but brings it into outward
relations with the δυναστείαι just spoken of. This is no
doubt a very incomplete account of the influences which
have combined to ' turn Europe into a great camp' (a very
exaggerated expression); but it may serve to show what a
fuller account would show more clearly, that the military
system of Europe is no necessary incident of the relations
between independent states, but arises from the fact that the
organisation of state-life, even with those peoples that have
been brought under its influence at all, is still so incomplete.

174. The more complete that organisation becomes, the
more the motives and occasions of international conflict
tend to disappear, while the bonds of unity become stronger.
The latter is the case, if for no other reason, yet for this;
that the better organisation of the state means freer scope
to the individual (not necessarily to do as he likes, e.g. in

the buying and selling of alcohol, but in such development of activity as is good on the whole). This again means free intercourse between members of one state and those of another, and in particular more freedom of trade. All restrictions on freedom of wholesome trade are really based on special class-interests, and must disappear with the realisation of that idea of individual right, founded on the capacity of every man for free contribution to social good, which is the true idea of the state. And as trade between members of different states becomes freer and more full, the sense of common interests between them, which war would infringe, becomes stronger. The bond of peace thus established is sometimes depreciated as a selfish one, but it need be no more selfish than that which keeps the peace between members of the same state, who have no acquaintance with each other. In one case as in the other it may be said that the individual tries to prevent a breach of the peace because he knows that he has more to gain than to lose by it. In the latter case, however, this account of the matter would be, to say the least, insufficient. The good citizen observes the law in letter and in spirit, not from any fear of consequences to himself if he did not, but from an idea of the mutual respect by men for each other's rights as that which should be an idea which has become habitual with him, and regulates his conduct without his asking any questions about it. There was a time, however, when this idea only thus acted spontaneously in regulating a man's action towards his family or immediate neighbours or friends. Considerations of interest were the medium through which a wider range of persons came to be brought within its range. And thus, although considerations of an identity of interests, arising out of trade, may be the occasion of men's recognising in men of other nations those rights which war violates, there is no reason why, upon that occasion and through the familiarity which trade brings about, an idea of justice, as a relation which should subsist between all mankind as well as between members of the same state, may not come to act on men's minds as independently of all calculation of their several interests as does the idea which regulates the conduct of the good citizen.

175. If the necessary or impelling power of the idea of what is due from members of different nations to each other

is weak, it must be observed on the other hand that the individual members of a nation have no such apparent interest in their government's dealing unfairly with another nation as one individual may have in getting the advantage of another. Thus, so far as this idea comes to form part of the habit of men's minds, there ceases to be anything in the passions of the people which a government represents to stimulate the government to that unfairness in dealing with another government, to which an individual might be moved by self-seeking passions in dealing with another individual, in the absence of an impartial authority having power over both. If at the same time the several governments are purely representative of the several peoples, as they should become with the due organisation of the state, and thus have no dynastic interests of their own in embroiling one nation with another, there seems to be no reason why they should not arrive at a passionless impartiality in dealing with each other, which would be beyond the reach of the individual in defending his own cause against another. At any rate, if no government can ever get rid of some bias in its own favour, there remains the possibility of mediation in cases of dispute by disinterested governments. With the abatement of national jealousies and the removal of those deeply-seated causes of war which, as we have seen, are connected with the deficient organisation of states, the dream of an international court with authority resting on the consent of independent states may come to be realised. Such a result may be very remote, but it is important to bear in mind that there is nothing in the intrinsic nature of a system of independent states incompatible with it, but that on the contrary every advance in the organisation of mankind into states in the sense explained is a step towards it.

L. *THE RIGHT OF THE STATE TO PUNISH*

176. (3) WE come now to the third of the questions
raised[1] in regard to the individual's right to free life, the
question under what conditions that right may be forfeited;
the question, in other words, of the state's right of punishment. The right (i.e. the power secured by social recognition) of free life in every man rests on the assumed
capacity in every man of free action contributory to social
good ('free' in the sense of determined by the idea of a
common good. Animals may and do contribute to the good
of man, but not thus 'freely'). This right on the part of
associated men implies the right on their part to prevent
such actions as interfere with the possibility of free action
contributory to social good. This constitutes the right of
punishment, the right so far to use force upon a person
(to treat him as an animal or a thing) as may be necessary
to save others from this interference.

177. Under what conditions a person needs to be thus
dealt with, what particular actions on his part constitute
such an interference, is a question which can only be
answered when we have considered what powers in particular
need to be secured to individuals or to officials in order to
the possibility of free action of the kind described. Every
such power is a right of which the violation, if intended as
a violation of a right, requires a punishment, of which the
kind and amount must depend on the relative importance of
the right and of the extent to which its general exercise is
threatened. Thus every theory of rights in detail must be
followed by, or indeed implies, a corresponding theory of
punishment in detail, a theory which considers what particular acts are punishable, and how they should be punished.
The latter cannot precede the former: all that can be done

[1] [Above, sec. 156.]

here is further to consider what general rules of punishment are implied in the principle on which we hold all right
of punishment to rest, and how far in the actual practice of
punishment that principle has been realised.

178. It is commonly asked whether punishment according
to its proper nature is retributive or preventive or reformatory. The true answer is that it is and should be all three.
The statement, however, that the punishment of the criminal
by the state is retributive, though true in a sense that will
be explained directly, yet so readily lends itself to a mis-
understanding, that it is perhaps best avoided. It is not true
in the sense that in legal punishment as it should be there
survives any element of private vengeance, of the desire on
the part of the individual who has received a hurt from
another to inflict an equivalent hurt in return. It is true
that the beginning of punishment by the state first appears
in the form of a regulation of private vengeance, but it is
not therefore to be supposed that punishment by the state
is in any way a continuation of private vengeance. It is the
essence of the former to suppress and supersede the latter,
but it only does so gradually, just as rights in actuality are
only formed gradually. Private vengeance belongs to the
state of things in which rights are not as yet actualised; in
the sense that the powers which it is for the social good that
a man should be allowed to exercise, are not yet secured to
him by society. In proportion as they are actualised, the
exercise of private vengeance must cease. A *right* of private vengeance is an impossibility; for, just so far as the
vengeance is private, the individual in executing it is
exercising a power not derived from society nor regulated
by reference to social good, and such a power is not a
right. Hence the view commonly taken by writers of the
seventeenth and eighteenth centuries implies an entire misconception of the nature of a right; the view, viz., that there
first existed rights of self-defence and self-vindication on the
part of individuals in a state of nature, and that these came
to be devolved on a power representing all individuals, so
that the state's right of using force against those men who
use or threaten force against other men, is merely the sum
or equivalent of the private rights which individuals would
severally possess if there were no public equivalent for them.
This is to suppose that to have been a right which in truth,

under the supposed conditions, would merely have been
animal impulse and power, and public right (which is a
pleonasm, for all right is public) to have resulted from the
combination of these animal impulses and powers; it is to
suppose that from a state of things in which 'homo homini
lupus,' by mere combination of wolfish impulses, there could
result the state of things in which 'homo homini deus.'

179. In a state of things in which private vengeance for
hurt inflicted was the universal practice, there could be no rights
at all. In the most primitive society in which rights can exist,
it must at least within the limits of the family be suppressed
by that authority of the family or its head which first constitutes rights. In such a society it is only on the members
of another family that a man may retaliate at pleasure a
wrong done to him, and then the vengeance is not, strictly
speaking, taken by individual upon individual, though individuals may be severally the agent and patient of it, but by
family upon family. Just because there is as yet no idea of
a state independent of ties of birth, much less of a universal
society from relation to which a man derives rights, there is
no idea of rights attaching to him as a citizen or as a man,
but only as a member of a family. That social right, which
is at once a right of society over the individual, and a right
which society communicates and secures to the individual,
appears, so far, only as a control exercised by the family
over its members in their dealings with each other, as an
authorisation which it gives them in prosecuting their quar-
rels with members of another family, and at the same time
to a certain extent as a limitation on the manner in which
feuds between families may be carried on, a limitation
generally dependent on some religious authority equally
recognised by the families at feud.

180. From this state of things it is a long step to the
régime of law in a duly constituted state. Under it the arm
of the state alone is the organ through which force may be
exercised on the individual; the individual is prohibited
from averting violence by violence, except so far as is necessary for the immediate protection of life, and altogether
from avenging wrong done to him, on the understanding that
the society, of which he is an organ and from which he
derives his rights, being injured in every injury to him, duly
protects him against injury, and when it fails to prevent

such injury from being done, inflicts such punishment on
the offender as is necessary for future protection.   But the
process from the one state of things to the other, though a
long one, consists in the further development of that social
right [1] which properly speaking was the only right the
individual ever had, and from the first, or ever since a
permanent family tie existed, was present as a qualifying
and restraining element in the exercise of private vengeance
so far as that exercise partook at all in the nature of a right.
The process is not a continuance of private vengeance under
altered forms, but a gradual suppression of it by the fuller
realisation of the higher principle which all along controlled it.

181. But it will be asked, how upon this view of the
nature of punishment as inflicted by the state it can be considered retributory.   If no private vengeance, no vengeance
of the injured individual, is involved in punishment, there
can be no vengeance in it at all.   The conception of vengeance is quite inappropriate to the action of society or the
state on the criminal.   The state cannot be supposed capable
of vindictive passion.   Nor, if the essence of crime is a wrong
done to society, does it admit of retaliation upon the person
committing it.   A hurt done to an individual can be requited
by the infliction of a like hurt upon the person who has done
it ; but no equivalent of wrong done to society can be paid
back to the doer of it.

182. It is true that there is such a thing as a national
desire for revenge [2] (France and Germany) : and, if a state =
a nation organised in a certain way, why should it not be
' capable of vindictive passion ' ?   No doubt there is a unity
of feeling among the members of a nation which makes
them feel any loss of strength, real or apparent, sustained by
the nation in its corporate character, as a hurt or disgrace to
themselves, which they instinctively desire to revenge.   The

---

[1] ' Social right,' i.e. right belonging
to a society of persons recognising a
common good, and belonging through
membership of the society to the several
persons constituting it.   The society to
which the right belongs, is in principle
or possibility a society of all men as
rendered capable of free intercourse
with each other by the organisation of
the state.   Actually at first it is only
this or that family ; then some association of families ; finally the state, as
including all other forms of association,
reconciling the rights which arise out
of them, and thus the most perfect
medium through which the individual
can contribute to the good of mankind
and mankind to his.

[2] ' Happy shall he be that rewardeth
thee as thou hast served us.'

corporate feeling is so strong that individuals feel themselves
severally hurt in the supposed hurt of the nation. But when
it is said that a crime is an offence against the state, it is not
meant that the body of persons forming the nation feel any
hurt in the sense in which the person robbed or wounded
does, such a hurt as excites a natural desire for revenge.
What is meant is that there is a violation of a system of
rights which the nation has, no doubt, an interest in maintaining, but a purely social interest, quite different from
the egoistic interest of the individual of which the desire
for vengeance is a form. A nation is capable of vindictive
feeling, but not so a nation as acting through the medium
of a settled, impartial, general law for the maintenance of
rights, and that is what we mean when we talk of the state
as that against which crimes are committed and which
punishes them.

183. It is true that when a crime of a certain sort, e.g. a
cold-blooded murder, has been committed, a popular sympathy with the sufferer is excited, which expresses itself in
the wish to 'serve out' the murderer. This has some re-
semblance to the desire for personal revenge, but is really
quite different, because not egoistic. Indignation against
wrong done to another has nothing in common with a desire
to revenge a wrong done to oneself. It borrows the language
of private revenge, just as the love of God borrows the
language of sensuous affection. Such indignation is inseparable from the interest in social well-being, and along
with it is the chief agent in the establishment and maintenance of legal punishment. Law indeed is necessarily general,
while indignation is particular in its reference; and accordingly the treatment of any particular crime, so far as
determined by law, cannot correspond with the indignation
which the crime excites; but the law merely determines the
general category under which the crime falls, and fixes
certain limits to the punishment that may be inflicted under
that category. Within those limits discretion is left to the
judge as to the sentence that he passes, and his sentence is
in part influenced by the sort of indignation which in the
given state of public sentiment the crime is calculated to
excite; though generally much more by his opinion as to the
amount of terror required for the prevention of prevalent
crime. Now what is it in punishment that this indignation

demands ? If not the sole foundation of public punishment,
it is yet inseparable from that public interest, on which the
system of rights, with the corresponding system of punishments protective of rights, depends. In whatever sense
then this indignation demands retribution in punishment,
in that sense retribution would seem to be a necessary
element in punishment. It demands retribution in the sense
of demanding that the criminal should have his due, should
be dealt with according to his deserts, should be punished
justly.

184. This is quite a different thing from an equivalence
between the amount of suffering inflicted by the criminal and
that which he sustains in punishment. The amount of
suffering which is caused by any crime is really as incalcu-
lable as that which the criminal endures in punishment,
whatever the punishment. It is only in the case of death
for murder that there is any appearance of equivalence
between the two sufferings, and in this case the appearance
is quite superficial. The suffering involved in death depends
almost entirely on the circumstances, which are absolutely
different in the case of the murdered man and in that of the
man executed for murder. When a man is imprisoned with
hard labour for robbery, there is not even an appearance of
equivalence of suffering between the crime and the punishment. In what then does the justice of a punishment, or its
correspondence with the criminal's deserts consist ? It will
not do to say that these terms merely represent the result
of an association of ideas between a crime and the penalty
which we are accustomed to see inflicted on it; that society
has come to attach certain penalties to certain actions as a
result of the experience (1) of suffering and loss caused by
those acts, and (2) of the kind of suffering of which the expectation will deter men from doing them; and that these
penalties having become customary, the onlookers and the
criminal himself, when one of them is inflicted, feel that he
has got what was to be expected, and call it his due or desert
or a just punishment. If this were the true account of the
matter, there would be nothing to explain the difference
between the emotion excited by the spectacle of a just
punishment inflicted, or the demand that it should be inflicted, on the one side, and on the other that excited by the
sight of physical suffering following according to the usual

course of things upon a physical combination of circumstances, or the expectation that such suffering will follow.
If it is said that the difference is explained by the fact that
in the one case both the antecedent (the criminal act) and
the consequent represent voluntary human agency, while in
the other they do not, we reply, Just so, but for that reason
the conception of a punishment as just differs wholly from
any conception of it that could result either from its being
customary, or from the infliction of such punishment having
been commonly found a means for protecting us against hurt.

185. The idea of punishment implies on the side of the
person punished at once a capacity for determination by the
conception of a common or public good, or in other words a
practical understanding of the nature of rights as founded
on relations to such public good, and an actual violation of a
right or omission to fulfil an obligation, the right or obligation being one of which the agent might have been aware
and the violation or omission one which he might have
prevented. On the side of the authority punishing, it implies
equally a conception of right founded on relation to public
good, and one which, unlike that on the part of the criminal,
is realised in act; a conception of which the punitive act, as
founded on a consideration of what is necessary for the maintenance of rights, is the logical expression. A punishment
is unjust if either element is absent; if either the act
punished is not a violation of known rights or an omission
to fulfil known obligations of a kind which the agent might
have prevented, or the punishment is one that is not required for the maintenance of rights, or (which comes to
the same thing), if the ostensible rights for the maintenance
of which the punishment is required are not real rights, are
not liberties of action or acquisition which there is any real
public interest in maintaining.

186. When the specified conditions of just punishment
are fulfilled, the person punished himself recognises it as
just, as his due or desert, and it is so recognised by the
onlooker who thinks himself into the situation. The criminal,
being susceptible to the idea of public good, and through it
to the idea of rights, though this idea has not been strong
enough to regulate his actions, sees in the punishment its
natural expression. He sees that the punishment is his own
act returning on himself, in the sense that it is the necessary

outcome of his act in a society governed by the conception of rights, a conception which he appreciates and to which he does involuntary reverence.

It is the outcome of his act, or his act returning upon himself, in a different way from that in which a man's act returns on himself when, having misused his body, he is visited according to physical necessity by painful consequences. The cause of the suffering which the act entails in the one case is the relation of the act to a society governed by the conception of rights; in the other it is not. For that reason, the painful consequence of the act to the doer in the one case is, in the other is not, properly a punishment. We do indeed commonly speak of the painful consequences of imprudent or immoral acts ('immoral' as distinct from 'illegal') as a punishment of them, but this is either metaphorically or because we think of the course of the world as regulated by a divine sovereign, whom we conceive as a maintainer of rights like the sovereign of a state. We may think of it as divinely regulated, and so regulated with a view to the realisation of moral good, but we shall still not be warranted in speaking of the sufferings which follow in the course of nature upon certain kinds of conduct as punishments, according to the distinctive sense in which crime is punished, unless we suppose the maintenance of rights to be the object of the moral government of the world,—which is to put the cart before the horse; for, as we have seen, rights are relative to morality, not morality to rights (the ground on which certain liberties of action and acquisition should be guaranteed as rights being that they are conditions of the moral perfection of society).

While there would be reason, then, as against those who say that the punishment of crime is merely preventive, in saying that it is also retributive, if the needed correction of the 'merely preventive' doctrine could not be more accurately stated, it would seem that the truth can be more accurately stated by the proposition that punishment is not justified unless it is just, and that it is not just unless the act punished is an intentional violation of real right or neglect of real obligation which the agent could have avoided (i.e. unless the agent knowingly and by intentional act interferes with some freedom of action or acquisition which there is a public interest in maintaining), and unless the future maintenance of rights requires that the criminal be dealt with as he is in the punishment.[1]

187. It is clear, however, that this requirement, that punishment of crime should be just, may be covered by the statement that in its proper nature it is preventive, if the nature of that which is to be prevented by it is sufficiently defined. Its proper function is, in the interest of rights that are genuine (in the sense explained), to prevent actions of the kind described by associating in the mind of every possible doer of them a certain terror with the contemplation of the act,—such terror as is necessary on the whole to protect the rights threatened by such action. The whipping of an ill-behaved dog is preventive, but not preventive in the sense in which the punishment of crime is so, because (1) the dog's ill conduct is not an intentional violation of a right or neglect of a known obligation, the dog having no conception of right or obligation, and (2) for the same reason the whipping does not lead to the association of terror in the minds of other dogs with the violation of rights and neglect of obligations. To shoot men down who resist a successful *coup d'état* may be effectually preventive of further resistance to the government established by the *coup d'état*, but it does not satisfy the true idea of punishment, because the terror produced by the massacre is not necessary for the protection of genuine rights, rights founded on public interest. To hang men for sheep-stealing, again, does not satisfy the idea; because, though it is a genuine right that sheep-stealing violates, in a society where there was any decent reconciliation of rights no such terror as is caused by the punishment of death would be required for the protection of the right. It is because the theory that punishment is 'merely preventive' favours the notion that the repetition of any action which any sufficient body of men find inconvenient may justifiably be prevented by any sort of terror that may be convenient for the purpose, that it requires to be guarded by substituting for the qualifying

---

[1] The conceptions of the just and of justice implied in this statement of the conditions of just punishment may be expressed briefly as follows. 'The just' = that complex of social conditions which for each individual is necessary to enable him to realise his capacity of contributing to social good. 'Justice' is the habit of mind which leads us to respect those conditions in dealing with others,—not to interfere with them so far as they already exist, and to bring them into existence so far as they are not found in existence.

'merely' a statement of what it is which the justifiable
punishment prevents and why it prevents it.

188. But does our theory, after all has been said about
the wrongness of punishment that is not just, afford any
standard for the apportionment of just punishment, any
criterion of the amount of interference with a criminal's
personal rights that is appropriate to his crime, except such
as is afforded by a prevalent impression among men as to
what is necessary for their security? Can we construe it
so as to afford such a criterion, without at the same time
condemning a great deal of punishment which yet society
could be never brought to dispense with? Does it really
admit of being applied at all in the presence of the admitted
impossibility of ascertaining the degree of moral guilt of
criminals, as depending on their state of character or habitual motives? How, according to it, can we justify punishments inflicted in the case of 'culpable negligence,' e.g.
when an engine-driver, by careless driving, for which we
think very little the worse of him, is the occasion of a bad
accident, and is heavily punished in consequence?

189. It is true that there can be no *a priori* criterion of
just punishment, except of an abstract and negative kind.
We may say that no punishment is just, unless the rights
which it serves to protect are powers on the part of individuals or corporations of which the general maintenance is
necessary to the well-being of society on the whole, and
unless the terror which the punishment is calculated to inspire is necessary for their maintenance. For a positive and
detailed criterion of just punishment, we must wait till a
system of rights has been established in which the claims
of all men, as founded on their capacities for contributing
to social well-being, are perfectly harmonised, and till experience has shown the degree and kind of terror with which
men must be affected in order to the suppression of the anti-
social tendencies which might lead to the violation of such
a system of rights. And this is perhaps equivalent to saying
that no complete criterion of just punishment can be arrived
at till punishment is no longer necessary; for the state of
things supposed could scarcely be realised without bringing
with it an extinction of the tendencies which state-punishment is needed to suppress. Meanwhile there is no method
of approximation to justice in punishment but that which
consists in gradually making the system of established rights

just, i.e. in harmonising the true claims of all men, and in discovering by experience the really efficient means of restraining tendencies to violation of rights. An intentional violation of a right must be punished, whether the right violated is one that should be a right or no, on the principle that social well-being suffers more from violation of any established right, whatever the nature of the right, than from the establishment as a right of a power which should not be so established; and it can only be punished in the way which for the time is thought most efficient by the maintainers of law for protecting the right in question by associating terror with its violation. This, however, does not alter the moral duty, on the part of the society authorising the punishment, to make its punishments just by making the system of rights which it maintains just. The justice of the punishment depends on the justice of the general system of rights; not merely on the propriety with reference to social well-being of maintaining this or that particular right which the crime punished violates, but on the question whether the social organisation in which a criminal has lived and acted is one that has given him a fair chance of not being a criminal.

190. We are apt to think that the justice of a punishment depends on some sort of equality between its magnitude and that of the crime punished, but this notion arises from a confusion of punishment as inflicted by the state for a wrong done to society with compensation to the individual for damage done him. Neither a crime nor its punishment admits of strictly quantitative measurement. It may be said, indeed, that the greater the crime the heavier should be its punishment, but this is only true if by the 'heavier punishment' is understood that with which most terror is associated in the popular imagination, and if the conception of the 'greater crime' is taken on the one hand to exclude any estimation of the degree of moral guilt, and, on the other hand, to be determined by an estimate not only of the importance in the social system of the right violated by the crime, but of the amount of terror that needs to be associated with the crime in the general apprehension in order to its prevention. But when its terms are thus understood, the statement that the greater the crime the heavier should be its punishment, becomes an identical proposition. It amounts

to this, that the crime which requires most terror to be associated with it in order to its prevention should have most terror thus associated with it.

191. But why do the terms 'heavier punishment' and 'greater crime' need to be thus understood? Why should not the 'greater crime' be understood to mean the crime implying most moral wickedness, or partly this, partly the crime which violates the more important kind of right? Why should a consideration of the amount of terror that needs to be associated with it in order to its prevention enter into the determination of the 'greater crime' at all? Why again should not the 'heavier punishment' mean simply that in which the person punished actually suffers most pain? Why should it be taken to mean that with which most terror is associated upon the contemplation? In short, is not the proposition in question at once true and significant in the sense that the crime which implies the most moral depravity, or violates the most important right (such as the right to life), or which does both, should be visited with the punishment that involves most pain to the sufferer?

192. The answer is : As regards heaviness of punishment, it is not in the power of the state to regulate the amount of pain which it causes to the person whom it punishes. If it could only punish justly by making this pain proportionate in each case to the depravity implied in the crime, it could not punish justly at all. The amount of pain which any kind of punishment causes to the particular person depends on his temperament and circumstances, which neither the state nor its agent, the judge, can ascertain. But if it could be ascertained, and if (which is equally impossible) the amount of depravity implied in each particular crime could be ascertained likewise in order to make the pain of the punishment proportionate to the depravity, a different punishment would have to be inflicted in each case according to the temperament and circumstances of the criminal. There would be an end to all general rules of punishment.

193. In truth, however, the state in its capacity as the sustainer of rights (and it is in this capacity that it punishes) has nothing to do with the amount of moral depravity in the criminal, and the primary reference in punishment, as inflicted by the state, is not to the effect of

the punishment on the person punished but to its effect on others. The considerations determining its amount should be prospective rather than retrospective. In the crime a right has been violated. No punishment can undo what has been done, or make good the wrong to the person who has suffered. What it can do is to make less likely the doing of a similar wrong in other cases. Its object, therefore, is not to cause pain to the criminal for the sake of causing it, nor chiefly for the sake of preventing him, individually, from committing the crime again, but to associate terror with the contemplation of the crime in the mind of others who might be tempted to commit it. And this object, unlike that of making the pain of the punishment commensurate with the guilt of the criminal, is in the main attainable. The effect of the spectacle of punishment on the onlooker is independent of any minute inquiry into the degree to which it affects the particular criminal. The attachment of equal penalties to offences that are alike in respect of the importance of the rights which they violate, and in respect of the ordinary temptations to them, will, on the whole, lead to the association of an equal amount of terror with the prospect of committing like offences in the public mind. When the circumstances, indeed, of two criminals guilty of offences alike in both the above respects are very greatly and obviously different, so different as to make the operation of the same penalty upon them very conspicuously different, then the penalty may be varied without interfering with its terrifying effect on the public mind. We will suppose e.g. that a fraud on the part of a respectable banker is equivalent, both in respect of the rights which it violates and of the terror needed to prevent the recurrence of like offences, to a burglary. It will not follow because the burglary is punished by imprisonment with hard labour that hard labour should be inflicted on the fraudulent banker likewise. The infliction of hard labour is in everyone's apprehension so different to the banker from what it is to the burglar, that its infliction is not needed in order to equalise the terror which the popular imagination associates with the punishment in the two cases.

194. On the same principle may be justified the consideration of extenuating circumstances in the infliction of punishment. In fact, whether under that name or another, they are taken account of in the administration of criminal law

among all civilised nations. 'Extenuating circumstances' is not a phrase in use among our lawyers, but in fact the consideration of them does constantly, with the approval of the judge, convert what would otherwise have been conviction for murder into conviction for manslaughter, and when there has been conviction for murder, leads to the commutation of the sentence. This fact is often taken to show that the degree of moral depravity on the part of the criminal, the question of his character and motive, is and must be considered in determining the punishment due to him. In truth, however, 'extenuating circumstances' may very well make a difference in the kind of terror which needs to be associated with a crime in order to the future protection of rights, and under certain conditions the consideration of them may be sufficiently justified on this ground. Suppose a theft by a starving man, or a hare shot by an angry farmer whose corn it is devouring. These are crimes, but crimes under such extenuating circumstances that there is no need to associate very serious terror with them in order to the protection of the essential rights of property. In the latter case the right which the farmer violates is one which perhaps might be disallowed altogether without interference with any right which society is interested in maintaining. In the former case the right violated is a primary and essential one ; one which, where there are many starving people, is in fact pretty sure to be protected by the most stringent penalties. And it might be argued that on the principle stated this is as it should be ; that, so far from the hunger of the thief being a reason for lightening his punishment, it is a reason for increasing it, in order that the special temptation to steal when far gone in hunger may, if possible, be neutralised by a special terror associated with the commission of the crime under those conditions. But this would be a one-sided application of the principle. It is not the business of the state to protect one order of rights specially, but all rights equally. It ought not therefore to protect a certain order of rights by associating special terror with the violation of them, when the special temptation to their violation itself implies a violation of right in the persons of those who are so tempted, as is the case when a general danger to property arises from the fact that many people are on the edge of starvation. The attempt to do so is at once ineffectual and diverts attention from the true way of protecting the endangered right, which is to pre-vent people from falling into a state of starvation. In any tolerably organised society the condition of a man, ordi-narily honest and industrious, who is driven to theft by hunger, will be so abnormal that very little terror needs to be asso-ciated with the crime as so committed in order to main-tain the sanctity of property in the general imagination. Suppose again a man to be killed in a quarrel arising out of his having tampered with the fidelity of his neighbour's wife. In such a case 'extenuating circumstances' may fairly be pleaded against the infliction of the extremest penalty, because the extremest terror does not need to be associated with homicide, as committed under such con-ditions, in order to the general protection of human life, and because the attempt so to associate it would tend, so far as successful, to weaken the general sense of the wrong—the breach of family right—involved in the act which, in the case supposed, provokes the homicide.

195. 'After all,' it may be said, 'this is a far-fetched way of explaining the admission of extenuating circum-stances as modifying the punishment of crime. Why so strenuously avoid the simpler explanation, that extenuating circumstances are taken into account because they are held to modify the moral guilt of the crime? Is not their recognition a practical proof that the punishment of a crime by the state represents the moral disapproval of the community? Does it not show that, however imperfectly the amount of punishment inflicted on a crime may in fact correspond to its moral wickedness, it is generally felt that it ought to do so?'

196. The answer is that there are two reasons for hold-ing that the state neither can nor should attempt to adjust the amount of punishment which it inflicts on a crime to the degree of moral depravity which the crime implies. (1) That the degree of moral depravity implied in any crime is unascertainable. It depends on the motive of the crime, and on this as part of the general character of the agent; on the relation in which the habitual set of his character stands to the character habitually set on the pursuit of goodness. No one can ascertain this in regard to himself. He may know that he is always far from being what he

ought to be; that one particular action of his represents on the whole, with much admixture of inferior motives, the better tendency; another, with some admixture of better motives, the worse. But any question in regard to the degree of moral goodness or badness in any action of his own or of his most intimate friend is quite unanswerable. Much less can a judge or jury answer such a question in regard to an unknown criminal. We may be sure indeed that any ordinary crime—nay, perhaps even that of the 'disinterested rebel'—implies the operation of some motive which is morally bad, for though it is not necessarily the worst men who come into conflict with established rights, it probably never can be the best; but the degree of badness implied in such a conflict in any particular case is quite beyond our ken, and it is this degree that must be ascertained if the amount of punishment which the state inflicts is to be proportionate to the moral badness implied in the crime. (2) The notion that the state should, if it could, adjust the amount of punishment which it inflicts on a crime to the moral wickedness of the crime, rests on a false view of the relation of the state to morality. It implies that it is the business of the state to punish wickedness, as such. But it has no such business. It cannot undertake to punish wickedness, as such, without vitiating the disinterestedness of the effort to escape wickedness, and thus checking the growth of a true goodness of the heart in the attempt to promote a goodness which is merely on the surface. This, however, is not to be understood as meaning that the punishment of crime serves no moral purpose. It does serve such a purpose, and has its value in doing so, but only in the sense that the protection of rights, and the association of terror with their violation, is the condition antecedent of any general advance in moral well-being.

197. The punishment of crime, then, neither is, nor can, nor should be adjusted to the degree of moral depravity, properly so called, which is implied in the crime. But it does not therefore follow that it does not represent the disapproval which the community feels for the crime. On the whole, making allowance for the fact that law and judicial custom vary more slowly than popular feeling, it does represent such disapproval. And the disapproval may fitly be called moral, so far as that merely means that it is

a disapproval relating to voluntary action. But it is a disapproval founded on a sense of what is necessary for the protection of rights, not on a judgment of good and evil of that kind which we call conscience when it is applied to our own actions, and which is founded on an ideal of moral goodness with which we compare our inward conduct ('inward,' as representing motives and character). It is founded essentially on the outward aspect of a man's conduct, on the view of it as related to the security and freedom in action and acquisition of other members of society. It is true that this distinction between the outward and inward aspects of conduct is not present to the popular mind. It has not been recognised by those who have been the agents in establishing the existing law of crimes in civilised nations. As the state came to control the individual or family in revenging hurts, and to substitute its penalties for private vengeance, rules of punishment came to be enacted expressive of general disapproval, without any clear consciousness of what was the ground of the disapproval. But in fact it was by what have been just described as the outward consequences of conduct that a general disapproval of it was ordinarily excited. Its morality in the stricter or inward sense was not matter of general social consideration. Thus in the main it has been on the ground of its interference with the general security and freedom in action and acquisition, and in proportion to the apprehension excited by it in this respect, that conduct has been punished by the state. Thus the actual practice of criminal law has on the whole corresponded to its true principle. So far as this principle has been departed from, it has not been because the moral badness of conduct, in the true or inward sense, has been taken account of in its treatment as a crime, for this has not been generally contemplated at all, but because 'religious' considerations have interfered. Conduct which did not call for punishment by the state as interfering with any true rights (rights that should be rights) has been punished as 'irreligious.' This, however, did not mean that it was punished on the ground of moral badness, properly so called. It meant that its consequences were feared either as likely to weaken the belief in some divine authority on which the established system of rights was supposed to rest, or as likely to bring evil on the community through provoking the wrath of some unseen power.

198. This account of the considerations which have regulated the punishment of crimes explains the severity with which 'criminal negligence' is in some cases punished, and that severity is justified by the account given of the true principle of criminal law, the principle, viz., that crime should be punished according to the importance of the right which it violates, and to the degree of terror which in a well-organised society needs to be associated with the crime in order to the protection of the right. It cannot be held that the carelessness of an engine-driver who overlooks a signal and causes a fatal accident, implies more moral depravity than is implied in such negligence as all of us are constantly guilty of. Considered with reference to the state of mind of the agent, it is on a level with multitudes of actions and omissions which are not punished at all. Yet the engine-driver would be found guilty of manslaughter and sentenced to penal servitude. The justification is not to be found in distinctions between different kinds of negligence on the part of different agents, but in the effect of the negligence in different cases upon the rights of others. In the case supposed, the most important of all rights, the right to life, on the part of railway passengers depends for its maintenance on the vigilance of the drivers. Any preventible failure in such vigilance requires to have sufficient terror associated with it in the mind of other engine-drivers to prevent the recurrence of a like failure in vigilance. Such punishment is just, however generally virtuous the victim of it is, because it is necessary to the protection of rights of which the protection is necessary to social well-being; and the victim of it, in proportion to his sense of justice, which means his habit of practically recognising true rights, will recognise it as just.

199. On this principle crimes committed in drunkenness must be dealt with. Not only is all depravity of motive specially inapplicable to them, since the motives actuating a drunken man often seem to have little connection with his habitual character; it is not always the case that a crime committed in drunkenness is even intentional. When a man in a drunken rage kills another, he no doubt intends to kill him, or at any rate to do him 'grievous bodily harm,' and perhaps the association of great penal terror with such an offence may tend to restrain men from committing it even when drunk; but when a drunken mother lies on her child and smothers it, the hurt is not intentional but accidental. The drunkenness, however, is not accidental, but preventible by the influence of adequate motives. It is therefore proper to treat such a violation of right, though committed unknowingly, as a crime, and to associate terror with it in the popular imagination, in order to the protection of rights by making people more careful about getting drunk, about allowing or promoting drunkenness, and about looking after drunken people. It is unreasonable, however, to do this and at the same time to associate so little terror, as in practice we do, with the promotion of dangerous drunkenness. The case of a crime committed by a drunkard is plainly distinguishable from that of a crime committed by a lunatic, for the association of penal terror with the latter would tend neither to prevent a lunatic from committing a crime nor people from becoming lunatics.

200. The principle above stated, as that according to which punishment by the state should be inflicted and regulated, also justifies a distinction between crimes and civil injuries, i.e. between breaches of right for which the state inflicts punishment without redress to the person injured, and those for which it procures or seeks to procure redress to the person injured without punishment of the person causing the injury. We are not here concerned with the history of this distinction (for which see Maine, *Ancient Law*, chap. x, and W. E. Hearn, *The Aryan Household*, chap. xix), nor with the question whether many breaches of right now among us treated as civil injuries ought not to be treated as crimes, but with the justification that exists for treating certain kinds of breach of right as cases in which the state should interfere to procure redress for the person injured, but not in the way of inflicting punishment on the injurer until he wilfully resists the order to make redress. The principle of the distinction as ordinarily laid down, viz. that civil injuries 'are violations of rights when considered in reference to the injury sustained by the individual,' while crimes are 'violations of rights when considered in reference to their evil tendency as regards the community at large' (Stephen, Book V, chap. i), is misleading; for if the well-being of the community did not suffer in the hurt done to the individual, that hurt would not be a violation of a right

in the true sense at all, nor would the community have any
ground for insisting that the hurt shall be redressed, and for
determining the mode in which it shall be redressed. A
violation of right cannot in truth be considered merely in
relation to injury sustained by an individual, for, thus considered, it would not be a violation of right. It may be said
that the state is only concerned in procuring redress for civil
injuries, because, if it left an individual to procure redress in
his own way, there would be no public peace. But there are
other and easier ways of preventing fighting than by procuring redress of wrong. We prevent our dogs from fighting,
not by redressing wrongs which they sustain from each
other (of wrongs as of rights they are in the proper sense
incapable), but by beating them or tying them up. The
community would not keep the peace by procuring redress
for hurt or damage sustained by individuals, unless it conceived itself as having interest in the security of individuals
from hurt and damage, unless it considered the hurt done to
individuals as done to itself. The true justification for
treating some breaches of right as cases merely for redress,
others as cases for punishment, is that, in order to the general
protection of rights, with some it is necessary to associate a
certain terror, with others it is not.

201. What then is the general ground of distinction
between those with which terror does, and those with which
it does not, need to be associated? Clearly it is purposeless
to associate terror with breaches of right in the case where
the breaker does not know that he is violating a right, and
is not responsible for not knowing it. No association of terror
with such a breach of right can prevent men from similar
breaches under like conditions. In any case, therefore, in
which it is, to begin with, open to dispute whether a breach
of right has been committed at all, e.g. when it is a question
whether a contract has been really broken, owing to some
doubt as to the interpretation of the contract or its application to a particular set of circumstances, or whether a
commodity of which someone is in possession properly belongs to another,—in such a case, though the judge finally
decides that there has been a breach of right, there is no
ground for treating it as a crime or punishing it. If, in the
course of judicial inquiry, it turns out that there has been
fraud by one or other of the parties to the litigation, a

criminal prosecution, having punishment, not redress, for its
object, should properly supervene upon the civil suit, unless
the consequences of the civil suit are incidentally such as to
amount to a sufficient punishment of the fraudulent party.
Again, it is purposeless to associate terror with a breach of
obligation which the person committing it knows to be a
breach, but of an obligation which he has no means of fulfilling, e.g. non-payment of an acknowledged debt by a man
who, through no fault of his own, is without means of
paying it. It is only in cases of one or other of the above
kinds,—cases in which the breach of right, supposing it to
have been committed, has presumably arisen either from
inability to prevent it or from ignorance of the existence of
the right,—that it can be held as an absolute rule to be no
business of the state to interfere penally but only in the way
of restoring, so far as possible, the broken right.

202. But there are many cases of breach of right which
can neither be definitely reduced to one of the above kinds,
nor distinguished from them by any broad demarcation;
cases in which the breaker of a right has been ignorant of it,
because he has not cared to know, or in which his inability
to fulfil it is the result of negligence or extravagance.
Whether these should be treated penally or no, will depend
partly on the seriousness of the wrong done through avoid-
able ignorance or negligence, partly on the sufficiency of the
deterrent effect incidentally involved in the civil remedy. In
the case e.g. of inability to pay a debt through extravagance
or recklessness, it may be unnecessary and inadvisable to
treat the breach of right penally, in consideration that it is
indirectly punished by poverty and the loss of reputation
incidental to bankruptcy, and the creditors should not look
to the state to protect them from the consequences of lending
on bad security. The negligence of a trustee, again, may be
indirectly punished by his being obliged to make good the
property lost through his neglect to the utmost of his means.
This may serve as a sufficiently deterrent example without
the negligence being proceeded against criminally. Again,
damage done to property by negligence is in England dealt
with civilly, not criminally; and it may be held that in this
case the liability to civil action is a sufficient deterrent. On
the other hand, negligence which, as negligence, is not really
distinguishable from the above, is rightly treated criminally
when its consequences are more serious; e.g. that of the

railway-servant whose negligence results in a fatal accident, that of the bank-director who allows a misleading statement of accounts to be published, fraudulently perhaps in the eye of the law, but in fact negligently. As a matter of principle, no doubt, if intentional violation of the right of property is treated as penal equally with the violation of the right of life, the negligent violation should be treated as penal in the one case as much as in the other. But as the consequences of an action for damages may be virtually though not ostensibly penal to the person proceeded against, it may be convenient to leave those negligences which do not, like the negligence of a railway-servant, affect the most important rights, or do not affect rights on a very large scale as does that of a bank-director, to be dealt with by the civil process.

203. The actual distinction between crimes and civil injuries in English law is no doubt largely accidental. As the historians of law point out, the civil process, having compensation, not punishment, for its object, is the form which the interference of the community for the maintenance of rights originally takes. The community, restraining private vengeance, helps the injured person to redress, and regulates the way in which redress shall be obtained. This procedure no doubt implies the conviction that the community is concerned in the injury done to an individual, but it is only by degrees that this conviction becomes explicit, and that the community comes to treat all preventible breaches of right as offences against itself or its sovereign representative, i.e. as crimes or penal; in the language of English law, as 'breaches of the king's peace.' Those offences are first so treated which happen to excite most public alarm, most fear for general safety (hence, among others, anything thought sacrilegious). In a country like England, where no code has been drawn up on general principles, the class of injuries that are treated penally is gradually enlarged as public alarm happens to be excited in particular directions, but it is largely a matter of accident how the classification of crimes on one side and civil injuries on the other happens to stand at any particular time.[1]

[1] See Markby, *Elements of Law*, chap. xi, especially note 1, p. 243; and Austin, Lecture XXVII. Between crimes and civil injuries the distinction, as it actually exists, is merely one of procedure (as stated by Austin, p. 518). The violation of right in one case is proceeded against by the method of indictment, in the other by an 'action.' The distinction that in one case punishment is

204. According to the view here taken, then, there is no direct reference in punishment by the state, either retrospective or prospective, to moral good or evil. The state in its judicial action does not look to the moral guilt of the criminal whom it punishes, or to the promotion of moral good by means of his punishment in him or others. It looks not to virtue and vice but to rights and wrongs. It looks back to the wrong done in the crime which it punishes; not, however, in order to avenge it, but in order to the consideration of the sort of terror which needs to be associated with such wrong-doing in order to the future maintenance of rights. If the character of the criminal comes into account at all, it can only be properly as an incident of this consideration. Thus punishment of crime is preventive in its object; not, however, preventive of any or every evil and by any and every means, but (according to its idea or as it should be) *justly* preventive of *injustice*; preventive of interference with those powers of action and acquisition which it is for the general well-being that individuals should possess, and according to laws which allow those powers equally to all men. But in order effectually to attain its preventive object and to attain it justly, it should be reformatory. When the reformatory office of punishment is insisted on, the reference may be, and from the judicial point of view must be, not to the moral good of the criminal as an ultimate end, but to his recovery from criminal habits as a means to that which is the proper and direct object of state-punishment, viz. the general protection of rights. The reformatory function of punishment is from this point of view an incident of its preventive function, as regulated by the consideration of what is just to the criminal as well as to others. For the

the object of the process, in the other redress, is introduced in order to explain the difference of procedure; and to justify this distinction resort is had to the further distinction, that civil injury is considered to affect the individual merely, crime to affect the state. But in fact the action for civil injury may incidentally have a penal result (Austin, p. 521), and if it had not, many violations of right now treated as civil injuries would have to be treated as crimes. As an explanation therefore of the distinction between crimes and injuries as it stands, it is not correct to say that for the former punishment is sought, for the latter merely redress. Nor for reasons already given is it true of any civil injury to say that it affects, or should be considered as affecting, injured individuals *merely*. The only distinction of principle is that between violations of right which call for punishment and those which do not; and those only do not call for punishment in some form or other which arise either from uncertainty as to the right violated, or from inability to prevent the violation.

fulfilment of this latter function, the great thing, as we have seen, is by the punishment of an actual criminal to deter other possible criminals; but for the same purpose, unless the actual criminal is to be put out of the way or locked up for life, it must be desirable to reform him so that he may not be dangerous in future. Now when it is asked why he should not be put out of the way, it must not be forgotten that among the rights which the state has to maintain are included rights of the criminal himself. These indeed are for the time suspended by his action in violation of rights, but founded as they are on the capacity for contributing to social good, they could only be held to be finally forfeited on the ground that this capacity was absolutely extinct.

205. This consideration limits the kind of punishment which the state may justly inflict. It ought not in punishing to sacrifice unnecessarily to the maintenance of rights in general what might be called the reversionary rights of the criminal, rights which, if properly treated, he might ultimately become capable of exercising for the general good. Punishment therefore either by death or by perpetual imprisonment is justifiable only on one of two grounds; either that association of the extremest terror with certain actions is under certain conditions necessary to preserve the possibility of a social life based on the observance of rights, or that the crime punished affords a presumption of a permanent incapacity for rights on the part of the criminal. The first justification may be pleaded for the executions of men concerned in treasonable outbreaks, or guilty of certain breaches of discipline in war (on the supposition that the war is necessary for the safety of the state and that such punishments are a necessary incident of war). Whether the capital punishment is really just in such cases must depend, not only on its necessity as an incident in the defence of a certain state, but on the question whether that state itself is fulfilling its function as a sustainer of true rights. For the penalty of death for murder both justifications may be urged. It cannot be defended on any other ground, but it may be doubted whether the presumption of permanent incapacity for rights is one which in our ignorance we can ever be entitled to make. As to the other plea, the question is whether, with a proper police system and sufficient certainty of detection and conviction, the

association of this extremest terror with the murderer is
necessary to the security of life. Where the death-penalty,
however, is unjustifiable, so must be that of really permanent
imprisonment; one as much as the other is an absolute
deprivation of free social life, and of the possibilities of moral
development which that life affords. The only justification
for a sentence of permanent imprisonment in a case where
there would be none for capital punishment would be that,
though inflicted as permanent, the imprisonment might be
brought to an end in the event of any sufficient proof appear-
ing of the criminal's amendment. But such proof could only
be afforded if the imprisonment were so modified as to allow
the prisoner a certain amount of liberty.

206. If punishment then is to be just, in the sense that
in its infliction due account is taken of all rights, including
the suspended rights of the criminal himself, it must be, so
far as public safety allows, reformatory. It must tend to
qualify the criminal for the resumption of rights. As reformatory, however, punishment has for its direct object the
qualification for the exercise of rights, and is only concerned
with the moralisation of the criminal indirectly so far as it
may result from the exercise of rights. But even where it
cannot be reformatory in this sense, and over and above its
reformatory function in cases where it has one, it has a
moral end. Just because punishment by the state has for
its direct object the maintenance of rights, it has, like every
other function of the state, indirectly a moral object, because
true rights, according to our definition, are powers which it
is for the general well-being that the individual (or association) should possess, and that well-being is essentially a
moral well-being. Ultimately, therefore, the just punishment of crime is for the moral good of the community. It
is also for the moral good of the criminal himself, unless—
and this is a supposition which we ought not to make—he is
beyond the reach of moral influences. Though not inflicted
for that purpose, and though it would not the less have to
be inflicted if no moral effect on the criminal could be dis-
cerned, it is morally the best thing that can happen to him.
It is so, even if a true social necessity requires that he be
punished with death. The fact that society is obliged so to
deal with him affords the best chance of bringing home to
him the anti-social nature of his act. It is true that the

last utterances of murderers generally convey the impression that they consider themselves interesting persons, quite sure of going to heaven; but these are probably conventional. At any rate if the solemn infliction of punishment on behalf of human society, and without any sign of vindictiveness, will not breed the shame which is the moral new birth, presumably nothing else within human reach will.

M. THE RIGHT OF THE STATE TO PROMOTE MORALITY

207. THE right of the individual man as such to free life is constantly gaining on its negative side more general recognition. It is the basis of the growing scrupulosity in regard to punishments which are not reformatory, which put rights finally out of the reach of a criminal instead of qualifying him for their renewed exercise. But the only rational foundation for the ascription of this right is the ascription of capacity for free contribution to social good. We treat this capacity in the man whose crime has given proof of its having been overcome by anti-social tendencies, as yet giving him a title to a further chance of its development; on the other hand, we act as if it conferred no title on its possessors, before a crime has been committed, to be placed under conditions in which its realisation would be possible. Is this reasonable? Yet are not all modern states so acting? Are they not allowing their ostensible members to grow up under conditions which render the development of social capacity practically impossible? Was it not more reasonable, as in the ancient states, to deny the right to life in the human subject as such, than to admit it under conditions which prevent the realisation of the capacity that forms the ground of its admission? This brings us to the fourth of the questions that arose [1] out of the assertion of the individual's right to free life. What is the nature and extent of the individual's claim to be enabled positively to realise that capacity for freely contributing to social good which is the foundation of his right to free life?

208. In dealing with this question, it is important to bear in mind that the capacity we are considering is essentially a free or (what is the same) a moral capacity. It is

[1] [Above, sec. 156.]

a capacity, not for action determined by relation to a certain end, but for action determined by a conception of the end to which it is relative. Only thus is it a foundation of rights. The action of an animal or plant may be made contributory to social good, but it is not therefore a foundation of rights on the part of an animal or plant, because they are not affected by the conception of the good to which they contribute. A right is a power of acting for his own ends,—for what he conceives to be his good,—secured to an individual by the community, on the supposition that its exercise contributes to the good of the community. But the exercise of such a power cannot be so contributory, unless the individual, in acting for his own ends, is at least affected by the conception of a good as common to himself with others. The condition of making the animal contributory to human good is that we do not leave him free to determine the exercise of his powers; that we determine them for him; that we use him merely as an instrument; and this means that we do not, because we cannot, endow him with rights. We cannot endow him with rights because there is no conception of a good common to him with us which we can treat as a motive to him to do to us as he would have us do to him. It is not indeed necessary to a capacity for rights, as it is to true moral goodness, that interest in a good conceived as common to himself with others should be a man's dominant motive. It is enough if that which he presents to himself from time to time as his good, and which accordingly determines his action, is so far affected by consideration of the position in which he stands to others,—of the way in which this or that possible action of his would affect them, and of what he would have to expect from them in return,—as to result habitually, without force or fear of force, in action not incompatible with conditions necessary to the pursuit of a common good on the part of others. In other words, it is the presumption that a man in his general course of conduct will of his own motion have respect to the common good, which entitles him to rights at the hands of the community. The question of the moral value of the motive which may induce this respect—whether an unselfish interest in common good or the wish for personal pleasure and fear of personal pain—does not come into the account at all. An agent, indeed, who could only be induced by fear of death or bodily harm to behave conformably to the requirements of the community, would not be a subject of rights, because this influence could never be brought to bear on him so constantly, if he were free to regulate his own life, as to secure the public safety. But a man's desire for pleasure to himself and aversion from pain to himself, though dissociated from any desire for a higher object, for any object that is desired because good for others, may constitute a capacity for rights, if his imagination of pleasure and pain is so far affected by sympathy with the feeling of others about him as to make him, independently of force or fear of punishment, observant of established rights. In such a case the fear of punishment may be needed to neutralise anti-social impulses under circumstances of special temptation, but by itself it could never be a sufficiently uniform motive to qualify a man, in the absence of more spontaneously social feelings, for the life of a free citizen. The qualification for such a life is a spontaneous habit of acting with reference to a common good, whether that habit be founded on an imagination of pleasures and pains or on a conception of what ought to be. In either case the habit implies at least an understanding that there is such a thing as a common good, and a regulation of egoistic hopes and fears, if not an inducing of more 'disinterested' motives, in consequence of that understanding.

209. The capacity for rights, then, being a capacity for spontaneous action regulated by a conception of a common good, either so regulated through an interest which flows directly from that conception, or through hopes and fears which are affected by it through more complex channels of habit and association, is a capacity which cannot be generated —which on the contrary is neutralised—by any influences that interfere with the spontaneous action of social interests. Now any direct enforcement of the outward conduct, which ought to flow from social interests, by means of threatened penalties—and a law requiring such conduct necessarily implies penalties for disobedience to it—does interfere with the spontaneous action of those interests, and consequently checks the growth of the capacity which is the condition of the beneficial exercise of rights. For this reason the effectual action of the state, i.e. tne community as acting through law, for the promotion of habits of true citizenship, seems neces-

sarily to be confined to the removal of obstacles. Under this head, however, there may and should be included much that most states have hitherto neglected, and much that at first sight may have the appearance of an enforcement of moral duties, e.g. the requirement that parents have their children taught the elementary arts. To educate one's children is no doubt a moral duty, and it is not one of those duties, like that of paying debts, of which the neglect directly interferes with the rights of someone else. It might seem, therefore, to be a duty with which positive law should have nothing to do, any more than with the duty of striving after a noble life. On the other hand, the neglect of it does tend to prevent the growth of the capacity for beneficially exer- cising rights on the part of those whose education is neg- lected, and it is on this account, not as a purely moral duty on the part of a parent, but as the prevention of a hindrance to the capacity for rights on the part of children, that edu- cation should be enforced by the state. It may be objected, indeed, that in enforcing it we are departing in regard to the parents from the principle above laid down; that we are in- terfering with the spontaneous action of social interests, though we are doing so with a view to promoting this spon- taneous action in another generation. But the answer to this objection is, that a law of compulsory education, if the preferences, ecclesiastical or otherwise, of those parents who show any pratical sense of their responsibility are duly respected, is from the beginning only felt as compulsion by those in whom, so far as this social function is concerned, there is no spontaneity to be interfered with; and that in the second generation, though the law with its penal sanctions still continues, it is not felt as a law, as an enforcement of action by penalties, at all.

210. On the same principle the freedom of contract ought probably to be more restricted in certain directions than is at present the case. The freedom to do as they like on the part of one set of men may involve the ultimate dis- qualification of many others, or of a succeeding generation, for the exercise of rights. This applies most obviously to such kinds of contract or traffic as affect the health and housing of the people, the growth of population relatively to the means of subsistence, and the accumulation or distri- bution of landed property. In the hurry of removing those

restraints on free dealing between man and man, which have arisen partly perhaps from some confused idea of maintaining morality, but much more from the power of class-interests, we have been apt to take too narrow a view of the range of persons—not one generation merely, but succeeding generations—whose freedom ought to be taken into account, and of the conditions necessary to their freedom ('freedom' here meaning their qualification for the exercise of rights). Hence the massing of population without regard to conditions of health; unrestrained traffic in deleterious commodities; unlimited upgrowth of the class of hired labourers in particular industries which circumstances have suddenly stimulated, without any provision against the danger of an impoverished proletariate in following generations. Meanwhile, under pretence of allowing freedom of bequest and settlement, a system has grown up which prevents the landlords of each generation from being free either in the government of their families or in the disposal of their land, and aggravates the tendency to crowd into towns, as well as the difficulties of providing healthy house-room, by keeping land in a few hands. It would be out of place here to consider in detail the remedies for these evils, or to discuss the question how far it is well to trust to the initiative of the state or of individuals in dealing with them. It is enough to point out the directions in which the state may remove obstacles to the realisation of the capacity for beneficial exercise of rights, without defeating its own object by vitiating the spontaneous character of that capacity.

N. THE RIGHT OF THE STATE IN REGARD TO PROPERTY

211. WE have now considered the ground of the right to free life, and what is the justification, if any, for the apparent disregard of that right, (*a*) in war, (*b*) in the infliction of punishment. We have also dealt with the question of the general office of the state in regard to the development of that capacity in individuals which is the foundation of the right, pointing out on the one hand the necessary limitation of its office in this respect, on the other hand the directions in which it may remove obstacles to that development. We have next to consider the rationale of the rights of property.

In discussions on the 'origin of property' two questions are apt to be mixed up which, though connected, ought to be kept distinct. One is the question how men have come to appropriate; the other the question how the idea of right has come to be associated with their appropriations. As the term 'property' not only implies a permanent possession of something, or a possession which can only be given up with the good will of the possessor, but also a possession recognised as a right, an inquiry into the origin of property must involve both these questions, but it is not the less important that the distinction between them should be observed. Each of them again has both its analytical and its historical side. In regard to the first question it is important to learn all that can be learnt as to the kind of things that were first, and afterwards at successive periods, appropriated; as to the mode in which, and the sort of persons or societies by whom, they were appropriated. This is an historical inquiry. But it cannot take the place of a metaphysical or psychological analysis of the conditions on the part of the appropriating subject implied in the fact that he does such a thing as appropriate. So, too, in regard to the second question, it is important to investigate historically the forms in which the right of men in their appropriations has been recognised; the parties, whether individuals or societies, to whom the right has been allowed ; and the sort of objects, capable of appropriation, to which it has been considered to extend. But neither can these inquiries help us to understand, in the absence of a metaphysical or moral analysis, either what is implied in the ascription of a right to certain appropriations, or why there should be a right to them.

212. We have then two questions, as above stated, each requiring two different methods of treatment. But neither have the questions themselves, nor the different methods of dealing with them, been duly distinguished.

It is owing to confusion between them that the right of property in things has been supposed to originate in the first occupancy of them. This supposition, in truth, merely disguises the identical proposition that in order to property there must to begin with have been some appropriation. The truism that there could be no property in anything which had not been at some time and in some manner appropriated, tells us nothing as to how or why the property in it, as a right, came to be recognised, or why that right should be recognised. But owing to the confusion between the origin of appropriation and the origin of property as a right, an identical proposition as to the beginning of appropriation seemed to be an instructive statement as to the basis of the rights of property. Of late, in a revulsion from theories founded on identical propositions, ' historical' inquiries into the ' origin of property ' have come into vogue. The right method of dealing with the question has been taken to lie in an investigation of the earliest forms in which property has existed. But such investigation, however valuable in itself, leaves untouched the questions, (1) what it is in the nature of men that makes it possible for them, and moves them, to appropriate; (2) why it is that they conceive of themselves and each other as having a right in their appropriations; (3) on what ground this conception is treated as a moral authority,—as one that should be acted on.

213. (1) Appropriation is an expression of will; of the individual's effort to give reality to a conception of his own

good; of his consciousness of a possible self-satisfaction as an object to be attained. It is different from mere provision to supply a future want. Such provision appears to be made by certain animals, e.g. ants. It can scarcely be made under the influence of the imagination of pain incidental to future want derived from previous experience, for the ant lays up for the winter though it has not previously lived through the winter. It may be suggested that it does so from inherited habit, but that this habit has originally arisen from an experience of pain on the part of ants in the past. Whether this is the true account of the matter we have not, I think, —perhaps from the nature of the case we cannot have—the means of deciding. We conceal our ignorance by saying that the ant acts instinctively, which is in effect a merely negative statement, that the ant is not moved to make provision for winter either by imagination of the pain which will be felt in winter if it does not, or by knowledge (conception of the fact) that such pain will be felt. In fact, we know nothing of the action of the ant from the inside, or as an expression of consciousness. If we are not entitled to deny dogmatically that it expresses consciousness at all, neither are we entitled to say that it does express consciousness, still less what consciousness it expresses. On the other hand we are able to interpret the acts of ourselves, and of those with whom we can communicate by means of signs to which we and they attach the same meaning, as expressions of consciousness of a certain kind, and thus by reflective analysis to assure ourselves that acts of appropriation in particular express a will of the kind stated; that they are not merely a passing employment of such materials as can be laid hands on to satisfy this or that want, present or future, felt or imagined, but reflect the consciousness of a subject which distinguishes itself from its wants; which presents itself to itself as still there and demanding satisfaction when this or that want, or any number of wants, have been satisfied; which thus not merely uses a thing to fill a want, and in so doing at once destroys the thing and for the time removes the want, but says to itself, ' This shall be mine to do as I like with, to satisfy my wants and express my emotions as they arise.'

214. One condition of the existence of property, then, is appropriation, and that implies the conception of himself on

the part of the appropriator as a permanent subject for whose use, as instruments of satisfaction and expression, he takes and fashions certain external things, certain things external to his bodily members. These things, so taken and fashioned, cease to be external as they were before. They become a sort of extension of the man's organs, the constant apparatus through which he gives reality to his ideas and wishes. But another condition must be fulfilled in order to constitute property, even of the most simple and primitive sort. This is the recognition by others of a man's appropriations as something which they will treat as his, not theirs, and the guarantee to him of his appropriations by means of that recognition. What then is the ground of the recognition? The writers of the seventeenth and eighteenth centuries, who discussed the basis of the rights of property, took it for granted, and in so doing begged the question. Grotius makes the right of property rest on contract, but clearly until there is a recognised ' meum ' and ' tuum ' there can be no contract. Contract presupposes property. The property in a particular thing may be derived from a contract through which it has been obtained in exchange for another thing or for some service rendered, but that implies that it was previously the property of another, and that the person obtaining it had a property in something else, if only in the labour of his hands, which he could exchange for it. [1] Hobbes is so far more logical that he does

[1] Grotius, *De Jure, etc.* Book II, chap. ii. § 5. 'Simul discimus quomodo res in proprietatem iverint . . . pacto quodam aut expresso, ut per divisionem, aut tacito, ut per occupationem : simul atque enim communio displicuit, nec .nstituta est divisio, censeri debet inter omnes convenisse ut, quod quisque occupasset, id proprium haberet.' But he supposes a previous process by which things had been appropriated (§ 4), owing to the necessity of spending labour on them in order to satisfy desire for a more refined kind of living than could be supplied by spontaneous products of the earth. 'Hinc discimus quæ fuerit causa, ob quam a primævâ communione rerum primo mobilium, deinde et immobilium discessum est : nimirum quod non contenti homines vesci sponte natis, antra habitare . . . vitæ genus exquisitius delegissent, industria opus fuit, quam singuli rebus

singulis adhiberent.' . . . The 'communio rerum,' thus departed from when labour came to be expended on things, Grotius had previously described (§ 1) as a state of things in which everyone had a right to whatever he could lay hands on. 'Erant omnia communia ef indivisa omnibus, veluti unum cunctis patrimonium esset. Hinc factum ut statim quisque hominum ad suos usus arripere posset quod vellet, et quæ consumi poterant consumere, ac talis usus universalis juris erat tum vice proprietatis. Nam quod quisque sic arripuerat, id ei eripere alter nisi per injuriam non poterat.' Here then a virtual right of property, though not so called, seems to be supposed in two forms previous to the establishment of what Grotius calls the right of property by contract. There is (1) a right of property in what each can 'take to his use and consume' out of the

not derive property from contract, but treats property and
'the validity of covenants' as co-ordinately dependent on
the existence of a sovereign power of compulsion.[1] But his
account of this, as of all other forms of right, is open to the
objection (before dwelt on) that if the sovereign power is
merely a strongest force it cannot be a source of rights; and
that if it is other than this, if it is a representative and
maintainer of rights, its existence presupposes rights, which
remain to be accounted for. As previously shown, Hobbes,
while professing to make all rights dependent on the sovereign power, presupposes rights in his account of the institution of this power. The validity of contracts 'begins not
but with its institution,' yet its own right is derived from an
irrevocable contract of all with all in which each devolves his
' persona,' the body of his rights, upon it. Without pressing
his particular forms of expression unfairly against him, it is
clear that he could not really succeed in thinking of rights
as derived simply from supreme force; that he could not
associate the idea of absolute right with the sovereign without supposing prior rights which it was made the business
of the sovereign to enforce, and in particular such a recognised distinction between 'meum' and 'tuum' as is necessary to a covenant. Nor when we have dropped Hobbes'
notion of government or law-making power, as having originated in a covenant of all with all, shall we succeed any
better in deriving rights of property, any more than other
rights, from law or a sovereign which makes law, unless we
regard the law or sovereign as the organ or sustainer of a

raw material supplied by nature; (2)
a further right of each man in that on
which he has expended labour. Grotius
does not indeed expressly call this a
right, but if there is a right, as he says
there is, on the part of each man to
that which he is able ' ad suos arripere
usus,' much more must there be a right
to that which he has not only taken
but fashioned by his labour. On the
nature and rationale of this right
Grotius throws no light, but it is
clearly presupposed by that right of
property which he supposes to be
derived from contract, and must be recognised before any such contract could
be possible.

[1] 'There is annexed to the sovereignty the whole power of prescribing
the rules whereby every man may know
what goods he may enjoy and what actions he may do without being molested
by any of his fellow-subjects: and this
is it men call propriety. For before
constitution of sovereign power all men
had right to all things, which necessarily causeth war; and therefore this
propriety, being necessary to peace,
and depending on sovereign power, is
the act of that power in order to the
public peace.' (*Leviathan*, pt. II, chap.
xviii.) ' The nature of justice consisteth
in keeping of valid covenants, but the
validity of covenants begins not but
with the constitution of a civil power,
sufficient to compel men to keep them;
and then it is also that propriety begins.'
(*Ibid.* chap. xv.)

general social recognition of certain powers, as powers which should be exercised.

215. Locke[1] treats property—fairly enough so long as only its simplest forms are in question—as derived from labour. By the same law of nature and reason by which a man has 'a property in his own person,' 'the labour of his body and the work of his hand are properly his' too. Now that the right to free life, which we have already dwelt on, carries with it a certain right to property, to a certain permanent apparatus beyond the bodily organs, for the maintenance and expression of that life, is quite true. But apart from the difficulty of tracing some kinds of property, in which men are in fact held to have a right, to the labour of anyone, even of someone from whom it has been derived by inheritance or bequest (a difficulty to be considered presently), to say that it is a 'law of nature and reason' that a man should have a property in the work of his hands is no more than saying that that on which a man has impressed his labour is recognised by others as something which should be his, just as he himself is recognised by them as one that should be his own master. The ground of the recognition is the same in both cases, and it is Locke's merit to have pointed this out; but what the ground is he does not consider, shelving the question by appealing to a law of nature and reason.

216. The ground of the right to free life, the reason why a man is secured in the free exercise of his powers through recognition of that exercise by others as something that should be, lay, as we saw, in the conception on the part of everyone who concedes the right to others and to whom it is conceded, of an identity of good for himself and others. It is only as within a society, as a relation between its members, though the society be that of all men, that there can be such a thing as a right; and the right to free life rests on the common will of the society, in the sense that each member of the society within which the right subsists contributes to satisfy the others in seeking to satisfy himself, and that each is aware that the other does so; whence there results a common interest in the free play of the powers of all. And just as the recognised interest of a society con-

[1] *Civil Government*, chap. v. The most important passages are quoted in   Fox Bourne's *Life of Locke*, vol. ii. pp. 171 and 172.

stitutes for each member of it the right to free life, just as it makes each conceive of such life on the part of himself and his neighbour as what should be, and thus forms the basis of a restraining custom which secures it for each, so it constitutes the right to the instruments of such life, making each regard the possession of them by the other as for the common good, and thus through the medium first of custom, then of law, securing them to each.

217. Thus the doctrine that the foundation of the right of property lies in the will, that property is 'realised will,' is true enough if we attach a certain meaning to ' will '; if we understand by it, not the momentary spring of any and every spontaneous action, but a constant principle, operative in all men qualified for any form of society, however frequently overborne by passing impulses, in virtue of which each seeks to give reality to the conception of a well-being which he necessarily regards as common to himself with others. A will of this kind explains at once the effort to appropriate, and the restraint placed on each in his appropriations by a customary recognition of the interest which each has in the success of the like effort on the part of the other members of a society with which he shares a common well-being. This customary recognition, founded on a moral or rational will, requires indeed to be represented by some adequate force before it can result in a real maintenance of the rights of property. The wild beast in man will not otherwise yield obedience to the rational will. And from the operation of this compulsive force, very imperfectly controlled by the moral tendencies which need its co-operation,—in other words from the historical incidents of conquest and government,—there result many characteristics of the institution of property, as it actually exists, which cannot be derived from the spiritual principle which we have assigned as its foundation. Still, without that principle it could not have come into existence, nor would it have any moral justification at all.

218. It accords with the account given of this principle that the right of property, like every other form of right, should first appear within societies founded on kinship, these being naturally the societies within which the restraining conception of a common well-being is first operative. We are apt indeed to think of the state of things in which

the members of a family or clan hold land and stock in common, as the antithesis of one in which rights of property exist. In truth it is the earliest stage of their existence, because the most primitive form of society in which the fruit of his labour is secured to the individual by the society, under the influence of the conception of a common well-being. The characteristic of primitive communities is not the absence of distinction between 'meum' and 'tuum,' without which no society of intelligent as opposed to in-stinctive agents would be possible at all, but the common possession of certain materials, in particular land, on which labour may be expended. It is the same common interest which prevents the separate appropriation of these materials, and which secures the individual in the enjoyment and use of that which his labour can extract from them.

219. From the moral point of view, however, the clan-system is defective, because under it the restraint imposed upon the individual by his membership of a society is not, and has not the opportunity of becoming, a self-imposed restraint, a free obedience, to which, though the alternative course is left open to him, the individual submits, because he conceives it as his true good. The area within which he can shape his own circumstances is not sufficient to allow of the opposite possibilities of right and wrong being presented to him, and thus of his learning to love right for its own sake. And the other side of this moral tutelage of the individual, this withholding from him of the opportunity of being freely determined by recognition of his moral relations, is the confinement of those relations themselves, which under the clan-system have no actual existence except as between members of the same clan. A necessary condition at once of the growth of a free morality, i.e. a certain behaviour of men determined by an understanding of moral relations and by the value which they set on them as understood, and of the conception of those relations as relations between all men, is that free play should be given to every man's powers of appropriation. Moral freedom is not the same thing as a control over the outward circumstances and appliances of life. It is the end to which such control is a generally necessary means, and which gives it its value. In order to obtain this control, men must cease to be limited in their activities by the customs of the clan. The range of their appropriations

must be extended; they must include more of the permanent
material on which labour may be expended, and not merely
the passing products of labour spent on unappropriated
material; and they must be at once secured and controlled
in it by the good-will, by the sense of common interest, of a
wider society, of a society to which any and every one may
belong who will observe its conditions, and not merely those
of a particular parentage; in other words by the law, written
or unwritten, of a free state.

220. It is too long a business here to attempt an account
of the process by which the organisation of rights in the
state has superseded that of the clan, and at the same time
the restriction of the powers of appropriation implied in the
latter has been removed. It is important to observe, however, that this process has by no means contributed un-
mixedly to the end to which, from the moral point of view,
it should have contributed.   That end is at once the
emancipation of the individual from all restrictions upon the
free moral life, and his provision with means for it.   But
the actual result of the development of rights of property
in Europe, as part of its general political development, has
so far been a state of things in which all indeed *may* have
property, but great numbers in fact cannot have it in that
sense in which alone it is of value, viz. as a permanent
apparatus for carrying out a plan of life, for expressing ideas
of what is beautiful, or giving effect to benevolent wishes.
In the eye of the law they have rights of appropriation, but
in fact they have not the chance of providing means for a
free moral life, of developing and giving reality or expression to a good will, an interest in social well-being.   A man
who possesses nothing but his powers of labour and who
has to sell these to a capitalist for bare daily maintenance,
might as well, in respect of the ethical purposes which the
possession of property should serve, be denied rights of
property altogether.   Is the existence of so many men in
this position, and the apparent liability of many more to be
brought to it by a general fall of wages, if increase of population goes along with decrease in the productiveness of the
earth, a necessary result of the emancipation of the individual and the free play given to powers of appropriation? or
is it an evil incident, which may yet be remedied, of that
historical process by which the development of the rights of

property has been brought about, but in which the agents
have for the most part had no moral objects in view at all ?

221. Let us first be clear about the points in which the
conditions of property, as it actually exists, are at variance
with property according to its idea or as it should be. The
rationale of property, as we have seen, is that everyone
should be secured by society in the power of getting and
keeping the means of realising a will, which in possibility
is a will directed to social good. Whether anyone's will is
actually and positively so directed, does not affect his claim
to the power. This power should be secured to the individual irrespectively of the use which he actually makes of it,
so long as he does not use it in a way that interferes with
the exercise of like power by another, on the ground that its
uncontrolled exercise is the condition of attainment by man
of that free morality which is his highest good. It is not
then a valid objection to the manner in which property is
possessed among us, that its holders constantly use it in a
way demoralising to themselves and others, any more than
such misuse of any other liberties is an objection to securing
men in their possession. Only then is property held in a
way inconsistent with its idea, and which should, if possible,
be got rid of, when the possession of property by one man
interferes with the possession of property by another; when
one set of men are secured in the power of getting and
keeping the means of realising their will, in such a way that
others are practically denied the power. In that case it
may truly be said that ' property is theft.' The rationale
of property, in short, requires that everyone who will conform to the positive condition of possessing it, viz. labour,
and the negative condition, viz. respect for it as possessed
by others, should, so far as social arrangements can make him
so, be a possessor of property himself, and of such property
as will at least enable him to develope a sense of responsibility, as distinct from mere property in the immediate
necessaries of life.

222. But then the question arises, whether the rationale
of property, as thus stated, is not inconsistent with the
unchecked freedom of appropriation, or freedom of appropriation checked only by the requirement that the thing
appropriated shall not have previously been appropriated by
another. Is the requirement that every honest man should

be a proprietor to the extent stated, compatible with any great inequalities of possession ? In order to give effect to it, must we not remove those two great sources of the inequality of fortunes, (1) freedom of bequest, and the other arrangements by which the profits of the labour of several generations are accumulated on persons who do not labour at all ; (2) freedom of trade, of buying in the cheapest market and selling in the dearest, by which accumulated profits of labour become suddenly multiplied in the hands of a particular proprietor? Now clearly, if an inequality of fortunes, of the kind which naturally arises from the admission of these two forms of freedom, necessarily results in the existence of a proletariate, practically excluded from such ownership as is needed to moralise a man, there would be a contradiction between our theory of the right of property and the actual consequence of admitting the right according to the theory ; for the theory logically necessitates freedom both in trading and in the disposition of his property by the owner, so long as he does not interfere with the like freedom on the part of others ; and in other ways as well its realisation implies inequality.

223. Once admit as the idea of property that nature should be progressively adapted to the service of man by a process in which each, while working freely or for himself, i.e. as determined by a conception of his own good, at the same time contributes to the social good, and it will follow that property must be unequal. If we leave a man free to realise the conception of a possible well-being, it is impossible to limit the effect upon him of his desire to provide for his future well-being, as including that of the persons in whom he is interested, or the success with which at the prompting of that desire he turns resources of nature to account. Considered as representing the conquest of nature by the effort of free and variously gifted individuals, property must be unequal ; and no less must it be so if considered as a means by which individuals fulfil social functions. As we may learn from Aristotle, those functions are various and the means required for their fulfilment are various. The artist and man of letters require different equipment and apparatus from the tiller of land and the smith. Either then the various apparatus needed for various functions must be provided for individuals by society, which would

imply a complete regulation of life incompatible with that highest object of human attainment, a free morality; or we must trust for its provision to individual effort, which will imply inequality between the property of different persons.

224. The admission of freedom of trade follows from the same principle. It is a condition of the more complete adaptation of nature to the service of man by the free effort of individuals. 'To buy in the cheapest and sell in the dearest market' is a phrase which may no doubt be used to cover objectionable transactions, in which advantage is taken of the position of sellers who from circumstances are not properly free to make a bargain. It is so employed when the cheapness of buying arises from the presence of labourers who have no alternative but to work for 'starvation wages.' But in itself it merely describes transactions in which commodities are bought where they are of least use and sold where they are of most use. The trader who profits by the transaction is profiting by what is at the same time a contribution to social well-being.

In regard to the freedom which a man should be allowed in disposing of his property by will or gift, the question is not so simple. The same principle which forbids us to limit the degree to which a man may provide for his future, forbids us to limit the degree to which he may provide for his children, these being included in his forecast of his future. It follows that the amount which children may inherit may not rightly be limited; and in this way inequalities of property, and accumulations of it to which possessors have contributed nothing by their own labour, must arise. Of course the possessor of an estate, who has contributed nothing by his own labour to its acquisition, may yet by his labour contribute largely to the social good, and a well-organised state will in various ways elicit such labour from possessors of inherited wealth. Nor will it trust merely to encouraging the voluntary fulfilment of social functions, but will by taxation make sure of some positive return for the security which it gives to inherited wealth. But while the mere permission of inheritance, which seems implied in the permission to a man to provide unlimitedly for his future, will lead to accumulations of wealth, on the other hand, if the inheritance is to be equal among all children, and, failing children, is to pass to the next of kin, the accumulation will be checked. It is not therefore the right of inheritance, but the right of bequest, that is most likely to lead to accumulation of wealth, and that has most seriously been questioned by those who hold that universal ownership is a condition of moral well-being. Is a proprietor to be allowed to dispose of his property as he likes among his children (or, if he has none, among others), making one very rich as compared with the others, or is he to be checked by a law requiring approximately equal inheritance?

225. As to this, consider that on the same principle on which we hold that a man should be allowed to accumulate as he best can for his children, he should have discretion in distributing among his children. He should be allowed to accumulate, because in so doing he at once expresses and developes the sense of family responsibility, which naturally breeds a recognition of duties in many other directions. But if the sense of family responsibility is to have free play, the man must have due control over his family, and this he can scarcely have if all his children as a matter of necessity inherit equally, however undutiful or idle or extravagant they may be. For this reason the true theory of property would seem to favour freedom of bequest, at any rate in regard to wealth generally. There may be special reasons, to be considered presently, for limiting it in regard to land. But as a general rule, the father of a family, if left to himself and not biassed by any special institutions of his country, is most likely to make that distribution among his children which is most for the public good. If family pride moves him to endow one son more largely than the rest, in order to maintain the honour of his name, family affection will keep this tendency within limits in the interest of the other children, unless the institutions of his country favour the one tendency as against the other. And this they will do if they maintain great dignities, e.g. peerages, of which the possession of large hereditary wealth is virtually the condition, and if they make it easy, when the other sons have been impoverished for the sake of endowing the eldest, to maintain the former at the public expense by means of appointments in the church or state.

It must be borne in mind, further, that the freedom of bequest which is to be justified on the above principles must not be one which limits that freedom in a subsequent generation. It must therefore be distinguished from the power of settlement allowed by English law and constantly exercised in dealing with landed estate; for this power, as exercised by the landowning head of a family in one generation, prevents the succeeding head of the family from being free to make what disposition he thinks best among his children and ties up the succession to the estate to his eldest son. The practice of settlement in England, in short, as applied to landed estate, cancels the freedom of bequest in the case of most landowners and neutralises all the dispersive tendency of family affection, while it maintains in full force all the accumulative tendency of family pride. This, however, is no essential incident of a system in which the rights of individual ownership are fully developed, but just the contrary.

226. The question then remains, whether the full development of those rights, as including that of unlimited accumulation of wealth by the individual and of complete freedom of bequest on his part, necessarily carries with it the existence of a proletariate, nominal owners of their powers of labour, but in fact obliged to sell these on such terms that they are owners of nothing beyond what is necessary from day to day for the support of life, and may at any time lose even that, so that, as regards the moral functions of property, they may be held to be not proprietors at all; or whether the existence of such a class is due to causes only accidentally connected with the development of rights of individual property.

We must bear in mind (1) that the increased wealth of one man does not naturally mean the diminished wealth of another. We must not think of wealth as a given stock of commodities of which a larger share cannot fall to one without taking from the share that falls to another. The wealth of the world is constantly increasing in proportion as the constant production of new wealth by labour exceeds the constant consumption of what is already produced. There is no natural limit to its increase except such as arises from the fact that the supply of the food necessary to sustain labour becomes more difficult as more comes to be required owing to the increase in the number of labourers, and from the possible ultimate exhaustion of the raw materials of labour in the world. Therefore in the accumulation of wealth, so far as it arises from the saving by anyone of the products

of his labour, from his bequest of this capital to another who
farther adds to it by saving some of the profit which the
capital yields, as employed in the payment for labour or in
trade either by the capitalist himself or someone to whom he
lends it, and from the continuation of this process through
generations, there is nothing which tends to lessen for anyone else the possibilities of ownership. On the contrary,
supposing trade and labour to be free, wealth must be constantly distributed throughout the process in the shape of
wages to labourers and of profits to those who mediate in the
business of exchange.

227. It is true that the accumulation of capital naturally
leads to the employment of large masses of hired labourers.
But there is nothing in the nature of the case to keep these
labourers in the condition of living from hand to mouth, to
exclude them from that education of the sense of responsibility which depends on the possibility of permanent ownership. There is nothing in the fact that their labour is
hired in great masses by great capitalists to prevent them
from being on a small scale capitalists themselves. In their
position they have not indeed the same stimulus to saving,
or the same constant opening for the investment of savings,
as a man who is αὐτουργός; but their combination in
work gives them every opportunity, if they have the needful
education and self-discipline, for forming societies for the
investment of savings. In fact, as we know, in the well-paid
industries of England the better sort of labourers do become
capitalists, to the extent often of owning their houses and a
good deal of furniture, of having an interest in stores, and
of belonging to benefit-societies through which they make
provision for the future. It is not then to the accumulation
of capital, but to the condition, due to antecedent circumstances unconnected with that accumulation, of the men
with whom the capitalist deals and whose labour he buys
on the cheapest terms, that we must ascribe the multiplica-
tion in recent times of an impoverished and reckless proletariate.

228. It is difficult to summarise the influences to which
is due the fact that in all the chief seats of population in
Europe the labour-market is constantly thronged with men
who are too badly reared and fed to be efficient labourers;

who for this reason, and from the competition for employment with each other, have to sell their labour very cheap; who have thus seldom the means to save, and whose standard of living and social expectation is so low that, if they have the opportunity of saving, they do not use it, and keep bringing children into the world at a rate which perpetuates the evil. It is certain, however, that these influences have no necessary connection with the maintenance of the right of individual property and consequent unlimited accumulation of capital, though they no doubt are connected with that régime of force and conquest by which existing governments have been established,—governments which do not indeed create the rights of individual property, any more than other rights, but which serve to maintain them. It must always be borne in mind that the appropriation of land by individuals has in most countries—probably in all where it approaches completeness—been originally effected, not by the expenditure of labour or the results of labour on the land, but by force. The original landlords have been conquerors.

229. This has affected the condition of the industrial classes in at least two ways: (1) When the application of accumulated capital to any work in the way of mining or manufacture has created a demand for labour, the supply has been forthcoming from men whose ancestors, if not themselves, were trained in habits of serfdom; men whose life has been one of virtually forced labour, relieved by church-charities or the poor law (which in part took the place of these charities); who were thus in no condition to contract freely for the sale of their labour, and had nothing of that sense of family-responsibility which might have made them insist on having the chance of saving. Landless countrymen, whose ancestors were serfs, are the parents of the proletariate of great towns. (2) Rights have been allowed to landlords, incompatible with the true principle on which rights of property rest, and tending to interfere with the development of the proprietorial capacity in others. The right to freedom in unlimited acquisition of wealth, by means of labour and by means of the saving and successful application of the results of labour, does not imply the right of anyone to do as he likes with those gifts of nature, without which there would be nothing to spend labour upon.

The earth is just as much an original natural material necessary to productive industry, as are air, light, and water, but while the latter from the nature of the case cannot be appropriated. the earth can be and has been. The only justification for this appropriation, as for any other, is that it contributes on the whole to social well-being; that the earth as appropriated by individuals under certain conditions becomes more serviceable to society as a whole, including those who are not proprietors of the soil, than if it were held in common. The justification disappears if these conditions are not observed; and from government having been chiefly in the hands of appropriators of the soil, they have not been duly observed. Landlords have been allowed to ' do what they would with their own,' as if land were merely like so much capital, admitting of indefinite extension. The capital gained by one is not taken from another, but one man cannot acquire more land without others having less; and though a growing reduction in the number of landlords is not necessarily a social evil, if it is compensated by the acquisition of other wealth on the part of those extruded from the soil, it is only not an evil if the landlord is prevented from so using his land as to make it unserviceable to the wants of men (e.g. by turning fertile land into a forest), and from taking liberties with it incompatible with the conditions of general freedom and health; e.g. by clearing out a village and leaving the people to pick up houseroom as they can elsewhere (a practice common under the old poor-law, when the distinction between close and open villages grew up), or, on the other hand, by building houses in unhealthy places or of unhealthy structure, by stopping up means of communication, or forbidding the erection of dissenting chapels. In fact the restraints which the public interest requires to be placed on the use of land if individual property in it is to be allowed at all, have been pretty much ignored, while on the other hand, that full development of its resources, which individual ownership would naturally favour, has been interfered with by laws or customs which, in securing estates to certain families, have taken away the interest, and tied the hands, of the nominal owner—the tenant for life—in making the most of his property.

230. Thus the whole history of the ownership of land in Europe has been of a kind to lead to the agglomeration

of a proletariate, neither holding nor seeking property wherever a sudden demand has arisen for labour in mines or manufactures. This at any rate was the case down to the epoch of the French Revolution; and this, which brought to other countries deliverance from feudalism, left England, where feudalism had previously passed into unrestrained landlordism, almost untouched. And while those influences of feudalism and landlordism which tend to throw a shiftless population upon the centres of industry have been left unchecked, nothing till quite lately was done to give such a population a chance of bettering itself, when it had been brought together. Their health, housing, and schooling were unprovided for. They were left to be freely victimised by deleterious employments, foul air, and consequent craving for deleterious drinks. When we consider all this, we shall see the unfairness of laying on capitalism or the free development of individual wealth the blame which is really due to the arbitrary and violent manner in which rights over land have been acquired and exercised, and to the failure of the state to fulfil those functions which under a system of unlimited private ownership are necessary to maintain the conditions of a free life.

231. Whether, when those functions have been more fully recognised and executed, and when the needful control has been established in the public interest over the liberties which landlords may take in the use of their land, it would still be advisable to limit the right of bequest in regard to land, and establish a system of something like equal inheritance, is a question which cannot be answered on any absolute principle. It depends on circumstances. Probably the question should be answered differently in a country like France or Ireland, where the most important industries are connected directly with the soil, and in one like England where they are not so. The reasons must be cogent which could justify that interference with the control of the parent over his family, which seems to be implied in the limitation of the power of bequeathing land when the parent's wealth lies solely in land, and which arises, be it remembered, in a still more mischievous way from the present English practice of settling estates. But it is important to bear in mind that the question in regard to land stands on a different footing from that in regard to wealth generally, owing to the fact that

land is a particular commodity limited in extent, from which alone can be derived the materials necessary to any industry whatever, on which men must find house-room if they are to find it at all, and over which they must pass in communicating with each other, however much water or even air may be used for that purpose. These are indeed not reasons for preventing private property in land or even free bequest of land, but they necessitate a special control over the exercise of rights of property in land, and it remains to be seen whether that control can be sufficiently established in a country where the power of great estates has not first been broken, as in France, by a law of equal inheritance.

232. To the proposal that 'unearned increment' in the value of the soil, as distinct from value produced by expenditure of labour and capital, should be appropriated by the state, though fair enough in itself, the great objection is that the relation between earned and unearned increment is so complicated, that a system of appropriating the latter to the state could scarcely be established without lessening the stimulus to the individual to make the most of the land, and thus ultimately lessening its serviceableness to society.

O. *THE RIGHT OF THE STATE IN REGARD TO THE FAMILY*

233. In the consideration of those rights which do not arise out of the existence of the state, but which are antecedent to it (though of course implying society in some form), and which it is its office to enforce, we now come to family or household rights—also called, though not very distinctively, rights in private relations—of which the most important are the reciprocal rights of husband and wife, parent and child. The distinctive thing about these is that they are not merely rights of one person as against all or some other persons over some thing, or to the performance of or abstention from some action; they are rights of one person as against all other persons to require or prevent a certain behaviour on the part of another. Right to free life is a right on the part of any and every person to claim from all other persons that course of action or forbearance which is necessary to his free life. It is a right against all the world, but not a right over any particular thing or person. A right of property, on the other hand, is a right against all the world, and also over a particular thing; a right to claim from any and every one certain actions and forbearances in respect of a particular thing (hence called 'jus in rem'). A right arising from contract, unlike the right of property or the right of free life, is not a right as against all the world, but a right as against a particular person or persons contracted with to claim a certain performance or forbearance. It may or may not be a right over a particular thing, but as it is not necessarily so, while it is a right against a particular person or persons in distinction from all the world, it is called 'jus in personam' as distinct from 'in rem.' The right of husband over wife and that of parent over children (or *vice versa*) differs from

the right arising out of contract, inasmuch as it is not merely a right against the particular person contracted with, but a right against all the world. In this respect it corresponds to the right of property; but differs again from this, since it is not a right over a thing but over a person. It is a right to claim certain acts or forbearances from all other persons in respect of a particular person : or (more precisely) to claim a certain behaviour from a certain person, and at the same time to exclude all others from claiming it. Just because this kind of right is a right over a person, it is always reciprocal as between the person exercising it and the person over whom it is exercised. All rights are reciprocal as between the person exercising them and the person against whom they are exercised. My claim to the right of free life implies a like claim upon me on the part of those from whom I claim acts and forbearances necessary to my free life. My claim upon others in respect of the right of property, or upon a particular person in respect of an action which he has contracted to perform, implies the recognition of a corresponding claim upon me on the part of all persons or the particular party to the contract. But the right of a husband in regard to his wife not merely implies that all those as against whom he claims the right have a like claim against him, but that the wife over whom he asserts the right has a right, though not a precisely like right, over him. The same applies to the right of a father over a son, and of a master over a servant.

234. A German would express the peculiarity of the rights now under consideration by saying that, not only are persons the subjects of them, but persons are the objects of them. By the 'subject' of rights he would mean the person exercising them or to whom they belong; by 'object' that in respect of which the rights are exercised. The piece of land or goods which I own is the 'object' of the right of property, the particular action which one person contracts to perform for another is the 'object' of a right of contract; and in like manner the person from whom I have a right to claim certain behaviour, which excludes any right on the part of anyone else to claim such behaviour from him or her, is the 'object' of the right. But English writers commonly call that the subject of a right which the Germans would call the object. By the subject of a right of property they would not mean

the person to whom the right belongs, but the thing over which, or in respect of which, the right exists. And in like manner, when a right is exercised over, or in respect of a person, such as a wife or a child, they would call that person, and not the person exercising the right, the subject of it. By the object of a right, on the other hand, they mean the action or forbearance which someone has a right to claim. The object of a right arising out of contract would be the action which the person contracting agrees to perform. The object of a connubial right would not be, as according to German usage, the person in regard to, or over, whom the right is exercised—that person would be the subject of the right—but either the behaviour which the person possessing the right is entitled to claim from that person, or the forbearances in respect to that person, which he is entitled to claim from others. (Austin, I. 378 and II. 736.) Either usage is justifiable in itself. The only matter of importance is not to confuse them. There is a convenience in expressing the peculiarity of family rights by saying, according to the sense of the terms adopted by German writers, that not only are persons subjects of them but persons are objects of them. It is in this sense that I shall use these terms, if at all.

235. So much for the peculiarity of family rights, as distinct from other rights. The distinction is not merely a formal one. From the fact that these rights have persons for their objects, there follow important results, as will appear, in regard to the true nature of the right, to the manner in which it should be exercised. The analytical, as distinct from the historical, questions which have to be raised with reference to family rights correspond to those raised with reference to rights of property. As we asked what in the nature of man made appropriation possible for him, so now we ask (1) what it is in the nature of man that makes him capable of family life. As we asked next how appropriations came to be so sanctioned by social recognition as to give rise to rights of property, so now we have to ask (2) how certain powers exercised by a man, certain exemptions which he enjoys from the interference of others, in his family life, come to be recognised as rights. And as we inquired further how far the actual institutions of property correspond with the idea of property as a right which for social good should be exercised, so now we have to inquire (3) into the proper

adjustment of family rights, as determined by their idea ; in what form these rights should be maintained ; bearing in mind (a) that, like all rights, their value depends on their being conditions of which the general observance is neces- sary to a free morality, and (b) their distinctive character as rights of which, in the sense explained, persons are the objects.

236. (1) We saw that appropriation of that kind which, when secured by a social power, becomes property, supposes an effort on the part of the individual to give reality to a conception of his own good, as a whole or as something per- manent, in distinction from the mere effort to satisfy a want as it arises. The formation of family life supposes a like effort, but it also supposes that in the conception of his own good to which a man seeks to give reality there is included a conception of the well-being of others, connected with him by sexual relations or by relations which arise out of these. He must conceive of the well-being of these others as a per- manent object bound up with his own, and the interest in it as thus conceived must be a motive to him over and above any succession of passing desires to obtain pleasure from, or give pleasure to, the others ; otherwise there would be nothing to lead to the establishment of a household, in which the wants of the wife or wives are permanently provided for, in the management of which a more or less definite share is given to them (more definite, indeed, as approach is made to a monogamistic system, but not wholly absent anywhere where the wife is distinguished from the female), and upon which the children have a recognised claim for shelter and sustenance.

237. No doubt family life as we know it is an institution of gradual growth. It may be found in forms where it is easy to ignore the distinction between it and the life of beasts. It is possible that the human beings with whom it first began— beings 'human' because capable of it—may have been 'de- scended' from animals not capable of it, i.e. they may have been connected with such animals by certain processes of generation. But this makes no difference in the nature of the capacity itself, which is determined not by a past history but by its results, its functions, that of which it is a capacity. As the foundation of any family life, in the form in which we know it, implies that upon the mere sexual impulse there

has supervened on the part of the man a permanent interest
in a woman as a person with whom his own well-being is
united, and a consequent interest in the children born of her,
so in regard to every less perfect form out of which we can
be entitled to say that the family life, as we know it, has
developed, we must be also entitled to say that it expresses
some interest which is in principle identical with that described, however incompletely it has emerged from lower
influences.

238. (2) Such an interest being the basis of family relations,
it is quite intelligible that everyone actuated by the interest
should recognise, and be recognised by, everyone else to
whom he ascribes an interest like his own, as entitled to
behave towards the objects of the interest—towards his wife
and children—in a manner from which everyone else is excluded; that there should thus come to be rights in family
relations to a certain privacy in dealing with them; rights
to deal with them as his alone and not another's; claims,
ratified by the general sense of their admission being for the
common good, to exercise certain powers and demand certain
forbearances from others, in regard to wife and children. It
is only indeed at an advanced stage of reflection that men
learn to ascribe to other men, simply as men, the interests
which they experience themselves; and hence it is at first
only within narrow societies that men secure to each other
the due privileges and privacies of family life. In others of
the same kin or tribe they can habitually imagine an interest
like that of which each feels his own family life to be the
expression, and hence in them they spontaneously respect
family rights; but they cannot thus practically think themselves into the position of a stranger, and hence towards
him they do not observe the same restraints. They do not
regard the women of another nation as sacred to the hus-
bands and families of that nation. But that power of making
another's good one's own, which in the more intense and in-
dividualised form is the basis of family relations, must
always at the same time exist in that more diffused form in
which it serves as the basis of a society held together by the
recognition of a common good. Wherever, therefore, the
family relations exist, there is sure to exist also a wider
society which by its authority gives to the powers exercised
in those relations the character of rights. By what process

the relations of husband and wife and the institution of the household may have come to be formed among descendants of a single pair, it is impossible to conceive or to discover, but in fact we find no trace in primitive history of households except as constituents of a clan recognising a common origin; and it is by the customs of the clan, founded on the conception of a common good, that those forbearances on the part of members of one household in dealing with another, which are necessary to the privacy of the several households, are secured.

239. The history of the development of family life is the history of the process (a) by which family rights have come to be regarded as independent of the special custom of a clan and the special laws of a state, as rights which all men and women, as such, are entitled to. This, however, characterises the history of all rights alike. It is a history farther (b) of the process by which the true nature of these rights has come to be recognised, as rights over persons; rights of which persons are the objects, and which therefore imply reciprocal claims on the part of those over whom they are exercised and of those who exercise them. The establishment of monogamy, the abolition of ‘ patria potestas ’ in its various forms, the ‘ emancipation of women ’ (in the proper sense of the phrase), are involved in these two processes. The principles (1) that all men and all women are entitled to marry and form households, (2) that within the household the claims of the husband and wife are throughout reciprocal, cannot be realised without carrying with them not merely monogamy, but the removal of those faulty relations between men and women which survive in countries where monogamy is established by law.

240. Under a system of polygamy, just so far as it is carried out, there must be men who are debarred from marrying. It can only exist, indeed, alongside of a slavery, which excludes masses of men from the right of forming a family. Nor does the wife, under a polygamous system, though she ostensibly marries, form a household, or become the co-ordinate head of a family, at all. The husband alone is head of the family and has authority over the children. The wife, indeed, who for the time is the favourite, may practically share the authority, but even she has no equal and assured position. The ‘ consortium omnis vitæ,’ the ‘ individua vitæ consuetudo,’ which

according to the definition in the Digest is an essential element in marriage, is not hers.[1]

And further as the polygamous husband requires a self-restraint from his wife which he does not put on himself, he is treating her unequally. He demands a continence from her which, unless she is kept in the confinement of slavery, can only rest on the attachment of a person to a person and on a personal sense of duty, and at the same time is practically ignoring the demand, which this personal attachment on her part necessarily carries with it, that he should keep himself for her as she keeps herself for him. The recognition of children as having claims upon their parents reciprocal to those of the parents over them, equally involves the condemnation of polygamy. For these claims can only be duly satisfied, the responsibilities of father and mother towards the children (potentially persons) whom they have brought into the world can only be fulfilled, if father and mother jointly take part in the education of the children; if the children learn to love and obey father and mother as one authority. But if there is no permanent 'consortium vitæ' of one husband with one wife, this joint authority over the children becomes impossible. The child, when its physical dependence on the mother is over, ceases to stand in any special relation to her. She has no recognised duties to him, or he to her. These lie between him and his father only, and just because the father's interests are divided between the children of many wives, and because these render their filial offices to the father separately, not to father and mother jointly, the true domestic training is lost.

241. Monogamy, however, may be established, and an advance so far made towards the establishment of a due reciprocity between husband and wife, as well as towards a fulfilment of the responsibilities incurred in bringing children into the world, while yet the true claims of men in respect of women, and of women in respect of men, and of children upon their parents, are far from being generally realised. Wherever slavery exists alongside of monogamy, on the one side people of the slave class are prevented from

---

[1] 'Nuptiæ sunt conjunctio maris et feminæ, consortium omnis vitæ, divini et humani juris communicatio.' *Digest*, xxiii. 2, 1. 'Matrimonium est viri et mulieris conjunctio individuam vitæ consuetudinem continens.' *Inst.*, i. 9, 2. (Quoted by Trendelenburg, *Naturrecht*. p. 282.)

forming family ties, and on the other those people who are privileged to marry, though they are confined to one wife, are constantly tempted to be false to the true monogamistic idea by the opportunity of using women as chattels to minister to their pleasures. The wife is thus no more than an institution, invested with certain dignities and privileges. for the continuation of the family ; a continuation, which under pagan religions is considered necessary for the maintenance of certain ceremonies, and to which among ourselves an importance is attached wholly unconnected with the personal affection of the man for the wife.[1] When slavery is abolished, and the title of all men and women equally to form families is established by law, the conception of the position of the wife necessarily rises. The ἑταίρα and παλλακή cease at any rate to be recognised accompaniments of married life, and the claim of the wife upon the husband's fidelity, as reciprocal to his claim upon hers, becomes established by law.

242. Thus that marriage should only be lawful with one wife, that it should be for life, that it should be terminable by the infidelity of either husband or wife, are rules of right ; not of morality, as such, but of right. Without such rules the rights of the married persons are not maintained. Those outward conditions of family life would not be secured to them, which are necessary on the whole for the development of a free morality. Polygamy is a violation of the rights, (1) of those who through it are indirectly excluded from regular marriage, and thus from the moral education which results from this ; (2) of the wife, who is morally lowered by exclusion from her proper position in the household and by being used, more or less, as the mere instrument of the husband's pleasure ; (3) of the children, who lose the chance of that full moral training which depends on the connected action of father and mother. The terminability of marriage at the pleasure of one of the parties to it (of its terminability at the desire of both we will speak presently) is a violation of the rights at any rate of the unconsenting party, on the grounds (a) that liability to it tends to prevent marriage

---

[1] Her position among the Greeks is well illustrated by a passage from the speech of Demosthenes (?) against Neæra, § 122 (quoted by W. E. Hearn, *The Aryan Household*, p. 71). τὰς μὲν γὰρ ἑταίρας ἡδονῆς ἕνεκ' ἔχομεν, τὰς δὲ παλλακὰς τῆς καθ' ἡμέραν θεραπείας τοῦ σώματος, τὰς δὲ γυναῖκας τοῦ παιδοποιεῖσθαι γνησίως καὶ τῶν ἔνδον φύλακα πιστὴν ἔχειν.

from becoming that 'individua vitæ consuetudo' which gives
it its moral value, and (b) that, when the marriage is dissolved, the woman, just in proportion to her capacity for
self-devotion and the degree to which she has devoted
herself to her original husband, is debarred from forming
that 'individua vitæ consuetudo' again, and thus crippled
in her moral possibilities. It is a violation of the rights of
children for the same reason for which polygamy is so.

On the other hand, that the wife should be bound indis-
solubly by the marriage-tie to an unfaithful husband (or
vice versa), is a violation of the right of wife (or husband, as
the case may be), because on the one hand the restraint
which makes her liable to be used physically as the instrument of the husband's pleasures, when there is no longer
reciprocal devotion between them, is a restraint which
(except in peculiar cases) renders moral elevation impossible;
and on the other, she is prevented from forming such a true
marriage as would be, according to ordinary rules, the
condition of the realisation of her moral capacities. Though
the husband's right to divorce from an unfaithful wife has
been much more thoroughly recognised than the wife's to
divorce from an unfaithful husband, he would be in fact less
seriously wronged by the inability to obtain a divorce, for it
is only the second of the grounds just stated that fully
applies to him. The rights of the children do not seem so
plainly concerned in the dissolution of a marriage to which
husband or wife has been unfaithful. In some cases the
best chance for them might seem to lie in the infidelities
being condoned and an outward family peace re-established.
But that their rights are violated by the infidelity itself is
plain. In the most definite way it detracts from their
possibilities of goodness. Without any consent on their
part, quite independently of any action of their own will,
they are placed by it in a position which tends—though
special grace may counteract it—to put the higher kinds of
goodness beyond their reach.

243. These considerations suggest some further questions
which may be discussed under the following heads. (1) If
infidelity in marriage is a violation of rights in the manner
stated, and if (as it must be) it is a wilful and knowing
violation, why is it not treated as a crime, and, like other
such violations of rights, punished by the state in order to

the better maintenance of rights?   (2) Should any other reason but the infidelity of husband or wife be allowed for the legal dissolution of the marriage-tie?   (3) How are the rights connected with marriage related to the morality of marriage ?

(1) There is good reason why the state should not take upon itself to institute charges of adultery, but leave them to be instituted by the individuals whose rights the adultery violates. The reasons ordinarily alleged would be, (a) the analogy of ordinary breaches of contract, against which the state leaves it to the individual injured to set the law in motion; (b) the practical impossibility of preventing adultery through the action of the functionaries of the state. The analogy, however, from ordinary breaches of contract does not really hold. In the first place, though marriage involves contract, though without contract there can be no marriage, yet marriage at once gives rise to rights and obligations of a kind which cannot arise out of contract, in particular to obligations towards the children born of the marriage. These children, at any rate, are in no condition to seek redress—even if from the nature of the case redress could be had—for the injuries inflicted on them by a parent's adultery, as a person injured by a breach of contract can seek redress for it. Again, though the state leaves it to the individual injured by a breach of contract to institute proceedings for redress, if the breach involves fraud, it, at any rate in certain cases, treats the fraud as a crime and punishes. Now in every breach of the marriage-contract by adultery there is that which answers to fraud in the case of ordinary breach of contract. The marriage-contract is broken knowingly and intentionally. If there were no reason to the contrary, then, it would seem that the state, though it might leave to the injured individuals the institution of proceedings against adultery, should yet treat adultery as a crime and seek to prevent it by punishment in the interest of those whose virtual rights are violated by it, though not in the way of breach of contract. But there are reasons to the contrary—reasons that arise out of the moral purposes served by the marriage-tie—which make it desirable both that it should be at the discretion of the directly injured party whether a case of adultery should be judicially dealt with at all, and that in no case should penal terror be

associated with such a violation of the marriage-bond. Under ordinary conditions, it is a public injury that a violation of his rights should be condoned by the person suffering it. If the injured individual were likely to fail in the institution of proceedings for his own redress or defence, the public interest would require that the matter should be taken out of his hands. But if an injured wife or husband is willing to condone a breach of his or her rights through adultery, it is generally best that it should be condoned. That married life should be continued in spite of anything like dissoluteness on the part of husband or wife, is no doubt undesirable. The moral purposes which married life should serve cannot be served, either for the married persons themselves or for the children, under such conditions. On the other hand, the condonation of a single offence would generally be better for all concerned than an application for divorce. The line cannot be drawn at which, with a view to the higher ends which marriage should serve, divorce becomes desirable. It is therefore best that the state, while uniformly allowing the right of divorce where the marriage-bond has been broken by adultery (since otherwise the right of everyone to form a true marriage, a marriage which shall be the basis of family life, is neutralised,) and taking care that procedure for divorce be cheap and easy, should leave the enforcement of the right to the discretion of individuals.

244. On similar grounds, it is undesirable that adultery as such should be treated as a crime, that penal terror should be associated with it. Though rights, in the strict sense, undoubtedly arise out of marriage, though marriage has thus its strictly legal aspect, it is undesirable that this legal aspect should become prominent. It may suffer in respect of its higher moral purposes, if the element of force appears too strongly in the maintenance of the rights to which it gives rise. If a husband who would otherwise be false to the marriage-bond is kept outwardly faithful to it by fear of the punishment which might attend its breach, the right of the wife and children is indeed so far protected, but is anything gained for those moral ends, for the sake of which the maintenance of these rights is alone of value? The man in whom disloyal passion is neutralised by fear of punishment will contribute little in his family life to the moral development of himself, his wife, or his children. If he cannot be kept

true by family affection and sympathy with the social disapprobation attaching to matrimonial infidelity (and unless
it is a matter of social disapprobation no penalties will be
effectually enforced against it), he will not be kept true in a
way that is of any value to those concerned by fear of penalties.
In other words, the rights that arise out of marriage are not
of a kind which can in their essence be protected by associating penal terror with their violation, as the rights of life
and property can be.   They are not rights to claim mere
forbearances or to claim the performance of certain outward
actions, by which a right is satisfied irrespectively of the disposition with which the act is done.   They are claims which
cannot be met without a certain disposition on the part of
the person upon whom the claim rests, and that disposition
cannot be enforced.   The attempt to enforce the outward
behaviour in order to satisfy the claim, which is a claim not
to the outward behaviour merely but to this in connection
with a certain disposition, defeats its own end.

245. For the protection, therefore, of the rights of married persons and their children against infidelity, it does not
appear that the law can do more than secure facilities of
divorce in the case of adultery.   This indeed is not in itself
a protection against the wrong involved in adultery, but
rather a deliverance from the further wrong to the injured
husband or wife and to the children that would be involved
in the continuance of any legal claim over them on the part
of the injurer.   But indirectly it helps to prevent the wrong
being done by bringing social disapprobation to bear on cases
of infidelity, and thus helping to keep married persons faithful through sympathy with the disapprobation of which they
feel that they would be the objects when they imagine themselves unfaithful.   The only other effectual way in which the
state can guard against the injuries in question is by requiring
great precaution and solemnity in the contraction of mar-
riages.   This it can do by insisting on the consent of parents
to the marriage of all minors, exacting a long notice (perhaps
even a preliminary notice of betrothal), and, while not preventing civil marriage, by encouraging the celebration of
marriage in the presence of religious congregations and with
religious rites.

246. Question (2) is one that does not admit of being
answered on any absolute principle   We must bear in mind

that all rights—in idea or as they should be—are relative
to moral ends.   The ground for securing to individuals in
respect of the marriage-tie certain powers as rights, is that
in a general way they are necessary to the possibility of a
morally good life, either directly to the persons exercising
them or to their children.   The more completely marriage is a
' consortium omnis vitæ ' in the sense of a unity in all interests
and for the whole of a lifetime, the more likely are the external conditions of a moral life to be fulfilled in regard
both to married persons and their children.   Therefore the
general rule of the state in dealing with marriage should be
to secure such powers as are favourable and withhold such
as are not favourable to the ' consortium omnis vitæ.'   But
in the application of the principle great difficulties arise.
Lunacy may clearly render the ' consortium omnis vitæ '
finally impossible ; but what kind and degree of lunacy ?   If
the lunatic may possibly recover, though there is undoubtedly
reason for the separation from husband or wife during lunacy,
should permanent divorce be allowed ?   If it is allowed, and
the lunatic recovers, a wrong will have been done both to
him and to the children previously born of the marriage.   On
the other hand, to reserve the connubial rights of a lunatic of
whose recovery there is hope, and to restore them when he
recovers, may involve the wrong of bringing further children
into the world with the taint of lunacy upon them.   Is cruelty
to be a ground of divorce, and if so, what amount ?   There
is a degree of persistent cruelty which renders ' consortium
omnis vitæ' impossible, but unless it is certain that cruelty
has reached the point at which a restoration of any sort of
family life becomes impossible, a greater wrong both to wife
and children may be involved in allowing divorce than in refusing it.   A husband impatient for the time of the restraint
of marriage may be tempted to passing cruelty as a means of
ridding himself of it, while if no such escape were open to him
he might get the better of the temporary disturbing passion
and settle down into a decent husband.   The same consideration applies still more strongly to allowing incompatibility of temper as a ground of divorce.   It would be hard to
deny that it might be of a degree and kind in which it so
destroyed the possibility of ' consortium omnis vitæ,' that,
with a view to the interests of the children, who ought in such
a case to be chiefly considered. divorce implied less wrong

than the maintenance of the marriage-tie. But on the other hand, to hold out the possibility of divorce on the ground of incompatibility is just the way to generate that incompatibility. On the whole, the only conclusion seems to be that this last ground should not be allowed, and that in deciding on other grounds large discretion should be allowed to a well-constituted court.

P. RIGHTS AND VIRTUES

247. WE have now considered in a perfunctory way those rights which are antecedent to the state, which are not derived from it but may exist where a state is not, and which it is the office of the state to maintain. We have inquired what it is in the nature of man that renders him capable of these rights, what are the moral ends to which the rights are relative, and in what form the rights should be realised in order to the attainment of these ends. In order to make the inquiry into rights complete, we ought to go on to examine in the same way the rights which arise out of the establishment of a state, the rights connected with the several functions of government; how these functions come to be necessary, and how they may best be fulfilled with a view to those moral ends to which the functions of the state are ultimately relative. According to my project, I should then have proceeded to consider the social virtues, and the ‘moral sentiments’ which underlie our particular judgments as to what is good and evil in conduct. All virtues are really social; or, more properly, the distinction between social and self-regarding virtues is a false one. Every virtue is self-regarding in the sense that it is a disposition, or habit of will, directed to an end which the man presents to himself as his good; every virtue is social in the sense that unless the good to which the will is directed is one in which the well-being of society in some form or other is involved, the will is not virtuous at all.

248. The virtues are dispositions to exercise positively, in some way contributory to social good, those powers which, because admitting of being so exercised, society should secure to him; the powers which a man has a right to possess. which constitute his rights. It is therefore con-

venient to arrange the virtues according to the division of rights. E.g. in regard to the right of all men to free life, the obligations, strictly so called, correlative to that right having been considered (obligations which are all of a negative nature, obligations to forbear from meddling with one's neighbour), we should proceed to consider the activities by which a society of men really free is established, or by which some approach is made to its establishment ('really free,' in the sense of being enabled to make the most of their capabilities). These activities will take different forms under different social conditions, but in rough outline they are those by which men in mutual helpfulness conquer and adapt nature, and overcome the influences which would make them victims of chance and accident, of brute force and animal passion. The virtuous disposition displayed in these activities may have various names applied to it according to the particular direction in which it is exerted; 'industry,' 'courage,' 'public spirit.' A particular aspect of it was brought into relief among the Greeks under the name of ἀνδρεία. The Greek philosophers already gave an extension to the meaning of this term beyond that which belonged to it in popular usage, and we might be tempted further to extend it so as to cover all the forms in which the habit of will necessary to the maintenance and furtherance of free society shows itself. The name, however, does not much matter. It is enough that there are specific modes of human activity which contribute directly to maintain a shelter for man's worthier energies against disturbance by natural forces and by the consequences of human fear and lust. The state of mind which appears in them may properly be treated as a special kind of virtue. It is true that the principle and the end of all virtues is the same. They are all determined by relation to social well-being as their final cause, and they all rest on a dominant interest in some form or other of that well-being; but as that interest may take different directions in different persons, as it cannot be equally developed at once in everyone, it may be said roughly that a man has one kind of virtue and not others.

249. As the kind of moral duties (in distinction from those obligations which are correlative to rights) which relate to the maintenance of free society and the disposition to fulfil those duties should form a special object of inquiry,

so another special kind would be those which have to do with the management of property, with the acquisition and expenditure of wealth. To respect the rights of property in others, to fulfil the obligations correlative to those rights, is one thing; to make a good use of property, to be justly generous and generously just in giving and receiving, is another, and that may properly be treated as a special kind of virtue which appears in the duly blended prudence, equity, and generosity of the ideal man of business. Another special kind will be that which appears in family relations; where indeed that merely negative observance of right, which in other relations can be distinguished from the positive fulfilment of moral duties, becomes unmeaning. As we have seen, there are certain aggravations and perpetuations of wrong from which husband or wife or children can be protected by law, but the fulfilment of the claims which arise out of the marriage-tie requires a virtuous will in the active and positive sense—a will governed by unselfish interests—on the part of those concerned.

250. What is called 'moral sentiment' is merely a weaker form of that interest in social well-being which, when wrought into a man's habits and strong enough to determine action, we call virtue. So far as this interest is brought into play on the mere survey of action, and serves merely to determine an approbation or disapprobation, it is called moral sentiment. The forms of moral sentiment accordingly should be classified on some principle as forms of virtue, i.e. with relation to the social functions to which they correspond.

251. For the convenience of analysis, we may treat the obligations correlative to rights, obligations which it is the proper office of law to enforce, apart from moral duties and from the virtues which are tendencies to fulfil those duties. I am properly *obliged* to those actions and forbearances which are necessary to the general freedom, necessary if each is not to interfere with the realisation of another's will. My *duty* is to be interested positively in my neighbour's well-being. And it is important to understand that, while the enforcement of obligations is possible, that of moral duties is impossible. But the establishment of obligations by law or authoritative custom, and the gradual recognition of moral duties, have not been separate processes.

They have gone on together in the history of man. The growth of the institutions by which more complete equality of rights is gradually secured to a wider range of persons, and of those interests in various forms of social well-being by which the will is moralised, have been related to each other as the outer and inner side of the same spiritual development, though at a certain stage of reflection it comes to be discovered that the agency of force, by which the rights are maintained, is ineffectual for eliciting the moral interests. The result of the twofold process has been the creation of the actual content of morality; the articulation of the indefinite consciousness that there is something that should be—a true well-being to be aimed at other than any pleasure or succession of pleasures—into the sentiments and interests which form an 'enlightened conscience.' It is thus that when the highest stage of reflective morality is reached, and upon interests in this or that mode of social good there supervenes an interest in an ideal of goodness, that ideal has already a definite filling; and the man who pursues duty for duty's sake, who does good for the sake of being good or in order to realise an idea of perfection, is at no loss to say what in particular his duty is, or by what particular methods the perfection of character is to be approached.

SUPPLEMENT

———◦◦———

Some Quotations rendered into English. (*See p.* 49 *ff.*)

FROM Sect. 32.—*Tractatus Politici,* II. 4 ('Per jus itaque'). 'By right of nature (natural right) I understand . . . the actual power of nature.' 'Whatever an individual man does by the laws of his nature, that he does with the highest natural right, and his right towards nature goes just as far as his power holds out.'

'Jus naturæ' = 'natural right.' 'Potentia' = 'power.' 'Jus' = 'right.' 'Jus humanum' = 'right of man,' or 'right *qua* human.'

Ib. II. 5 ('Homines magis'). 'Human beings are led more by blind desire than by reason; and hence their natural power or right should be marked out not by reason but by any inclination by which they are determined to act, and by which they endeavour after their own preservation.'

'Jus civile' = 'civic right or law.'

Ib. II. 14 ('Quatenus homines'). 'In as far as human beings are troubled by anger, jealousy, or any emotion of hate, so far they are drawn in different directions and are antagonistic to one another, and therefore they are more to be feared in so far as they are more powerful, and more shrewd and astute, than the other animals; and because human beings are in the highest degree liable by nature to these emotions, therefore they are natural enemies (to one another).'

Ib. 15 ('Atque adeo'). 'And so we conclude that natural right can hardly be conceived unless where human beings have laws in common, (human beings) who have power at once to assert possession of the lands which they are able to inhabit and to till, and to defend themselves, and to repel all violence, and to live in accordance with the common sentiment of all. For (by art. 13 of this chapter) the more that thus come together into one, the more right they all together possess.'

Ib. 16 ('Ubi homines'). 'Where human beings have laws in common and all together are guided as by one mind, it is certain (by art. 13 of this chapter) that each of them has so much the less right as the rest are together more powerful than he; that is, that he in fact has no right over nature beyond that which the common (social) law concedes him. But whatever is enjoined upon him by common consent, he is bound to perform, or (by art. 4 of this chapter) he is compelled to it by law.'

Ib. 17 ('Hoc jus'). 'This law (or right), which is coextensive with the power of the plurality, is usually called "imperium"' ('authority,' 'government').

Ib. III. 2 ('Multitudinis quæ'). 'Of a number or plurality, which is guided as if by a single mind.'

'Status civilis' = 'civic, or social, condition.'

Ib. III. 3 ('Homo ex legibus'). [In the civic condition as well as in the state of nature] 'man acts from the laws of his own nature and consults his own interest.'

'Sui juris' = 'in its own right,' 'autonomous.'

Sect. 33 (1).—*Ib.* III. 7 ('Civitatis jus'). 'The right of the state is coextensive with the power of the plurality which is guided as if by one mind. But this oneness of minds is inconceivable, unless the state has for its main intention what sound reason shows to be for the interest of all men.'

(2). *Ib.* III. 8 ('Subditi eatenus'). 'Subjects are not in their own right, but under the right (or law) of the state, so far as they fear its power or threats, or so far as they love the social condition (by art. 10 of preceding chapter). From which it follows, that all those acts to which no one can be impelled by rewards or threats lie outside the right (or law) of the state.'

(3). *Ib.* III. 9 ('Ad civitatis jus'). 'That belongs to the right of the state in a less degree, which causes indignation in a greater number.' ('Sicut'). 'Like the individual citizen, or the man in a state of nature, the state is less in its own right in proportion as it has greater cause for fear.'

Sect. 34.—*Ib.* III. 11 ('Nam quandoquidem'). 'For seeing that (by art. 2 of this chapter) the right of the supreme power is nothing but the actual right of nature, it follows that two governments are to one another as two men in the state of nature, except that the state can defend itself against external aggression in a way impossible for man in a state of nature, inasmuch as he is overcome daily by sleep, often by disease or distress, and in the end by old age, and besides this is exposed to other inconveniences, against which the state can protect itself.'

Ib. III. 13 (' Duæ civitates'). 'Two states are natural enemies. For men in the state of nature are enemies. Those, therefore, who retain the right of nature, as not being in the same state, are enemies.'

Ib. III. 14 (' Nec dici potest'). 'Nor can it be said to act with craft or perfidy in that it dissolves its promise as soon as the cause of fear or hope is removed; because this condition was the same for both contracting parties, that whichsoever is first enabled to be free from fear should be in its own right, and should use its right according to the sentiment of its mind ; and, moreover, because no one contracts for the future except on supposition of the circumstances under which he contracts.'

Sect. 35.—*Ib.* II. 18 (' In statu'). 'In a state of nature there can be no transgression, or if one transgresses, he does so against himself, not against another; . . . nothing is absolutely forbidden by the law of nature, except what no one has power to do.'

' Commune decretum ' = ' the common (or social) behest.'

Ib. V. 1 (' Non id omne '). 'Not everything which we say is done rightfully, do we affirm to be the best to be done. It is one thing to till a field within your right, and another thing to till it in the best way ; it is one thing, I say, to defend yourself, preserve yourself, give judgment &c. within your right, and another thing to do all these acts in the best way; and accordingly it is one thing to govern and manage a state within its rights, and another thing to do this in the best way. Thus, now that we have treated in general of the right of every state, it is time to treat of the best condition of every state.'

' Finis status civilis ' = ' the end or aim of the civic or social condition.'

1b. V. 2 (' Homines enim '). 'Men are not born of civic temper, but become so. Moreover, the natural dispositions of men are everywhere the same.'

Ib. V. 4 ('Pax enim'). 'Peace is not absence of war, but a virtue which arises from fortitude of mind; for obedience is a constant will to perform that which the common behest of the state requires to be done.'

Ethics, III. 59, Schol. (in footnote on preceding passage) ('Omnes actiones'). 'All the actions which follow from the affects which are related to the mind, in so far as it thinks, I ascribe to *fortitude*, which I divide into *strength of mind* and *generosity*. By *strength of mind* I mean the desire by which each person endeavours, from the dictates of reason alone, to preserve his own being. By *generosity* I mean the desire by which, from the dictates of reason alone, each person endeavours to help other people and to join them to him in friendship.'

('Quæ maxime'). 'Which is mainly coextensive with reason, the true virtue and life of the mind.'

('Quod multitudo libera'). [An authority which] 'a free plurality institutes, not one which is acquired against the plurality by the right of war.'

Sect. 36.—'Suum esse conservare' = 'to preserve his own being.'

'Homini nihil' = 'nothing is more useful to man, than man.'

'Homo namque.' See on sect. 32.

'Constans voluntas.' See on sect. 35.

'Vitam concorditer transigere' = 'to live in harmony.'

Footnote on 'Libera multitudo,' II. 11 ('Hominem eatenus'). 'The sense in which at all I call a man *free* is in so far as he is guided by reason; because thus far he is determined to action by causes which can be adequately understood out of his nature alone, although by them he be necessarily determined to action. For freedom of action does not deny but affirms necessity.'

On Sect. 37.—II. 15 ('Jus naturæ'). See on sect. 32.

On Sect. 39.—πόλις = state, including much that we mean by 'society.'

τέλος = end, aim, final cause.

πολίτης = citizen.

φύσει πολιτικός = social, or civic, by nature.

πολίτης μετέχει. 'The citizen takes his share both in governing and in being governed.'

On Sect. 40.—Footnote, *Eth.* IV. *Appendix*, xxxii ('Ea

quæ'). 'We shall bear with equanimity those things which happen to us contrary to what a consideration of our own profit demands, if we are conscious that we have performed our duty, that the power we have could not reach so far as to enable us to avoid those things, and that we are a part of the whole of nature, whose order we follow. If we clearly and distinctly understand this, the part of us which is determined by intelligence—that is to say, the better part of us—will be entirely satisfied therewith, and in that satisfaction will endeavour to persevere; for, in so far as we understand, we cannot desire anything excepting what is necessary, nor absolutely can we be satisfied with anything but the truth. Therefore, in so far as we understand these things properly will the efforts of the better part of us agree with the whole order of nature.' *Eih.* IV. *Preface* ('Per bonum'). 'By good, therefore, I understand in the following pages everything which we are certain is a means by which we may approach nearer and nearer to the model of human nature we set before us. . . . Again, I shall call men more or less perfect or imperfect in so far as they approach nearer and nearer to the model of human nature we set before us.'

On Sect. 41.—'Nihil positivum in rebus in se consideratis' = 'nothing positive in things considered in themselves.'

In all the quotations from Spinoza's *Ethics* Mr. Hale White's translation has been followed.